D0105039

WAR CULTURE

Social Change and Changing Experience in World War Two

Edited by

PAT KIRKHAM

and

DAVID THOMS

WAR CULTURE:
Social Change and Changing Experience in World War Two Britain

WAR CULTURE:
Social Change and Changing Experience in World War Two Britain

EDITED BY
Pat Kirkham and David Thoms

LAWRENCE & WISHART
LONDON

Lawrence & Wishart Limited
144a Old South Lambeth Road
London SW8 1XX

First published 1995 by Lawrence & Wishart

ISBN 0 85315 824 X

British Library Cataloguing in Publication Data

A catalogue record for this book is available from
the British Library.

Cover design by Jan Brown Designs
Photoset in North Wales by
Derek Doyle & Associates, Mold, Clwyd.
Printed and bound in Great Britain by
Biddles Ltd, Guildford, Surrey.

Contents

v

CONTENTS

SECTION 3:
PICTURES AND THE PUBLIC

SECTION 4:
POPULAR PASTIMES

SECTION 5:
BEYOND THE PALE: ETHNIC MINORITIES
AND THE WAR

CONTENTS

SECTION 6:
PERSONAL TESTIMONIES

For Kate, Alex and Sarah
and
Rachel, Hugo and Kate

Introduction

Each of the different wars of the twentieth century has its own particular characteristics but within Europe the events of 1939 to 1945 have generated more interest than any of the other international conflagrations of this period. For Britain, as for the other belligerents, the Second World War was an event of enormous immediate and long-term significance. The scale and nature of change gave this period a unique character in terms of the involvement of the civilian as well as the military population, a fact which was well recognised by government. As one official of the Ministry of Information commented, 'If the Home Front breaks, everything breaks.' Studies of the Home Front have tended to focus upon the social disruption caused by mobilisation, both military and industrial, material shortages, evacuation and the aftermath of the blitz, but broader cultural matters, including cinema, painting and literature, have not been neglected. Although many of the essays in this wide ranging anthology address issues and topics hitherto largely unexplored, the volume as a whole falls within an established tradition of Home Front scholarship to which we are all greatly indebted. *War Culture: Social Change and Changing Experience in World War Two Britain* is also offered as a contribution to the commemoration of the fiftieth anniversary of the end of the war.

Although the sub-title of the book emphasises change and we acknowledge the enormity of the disruptions emanating from the war, we are aware that it has been all too easy for historians to neglect the many continuities with the pre-war period which informed and made more bearable everyday life in Britain between 1939 and 1945. This stated, it is important to note that the processes of change resulting from the interaction between pre-war and wartime forces impacted differentially. For example, women's wartime fashions owed a great deal to pre-war precedents while, by contrast, the war offered many women greater sexual freedom than they had enjoyed in the 1930s. Many of the wartime developments in the arts and popular entertainment were rooted in pre-war practices yet even within one medium, such as film or popular music, there were many and varied responses to the unique pressures of a long and arduous war. Furthermore, while the bombing raids exacerbated the demand for hospital beds for civilians (and undoubtedly contributed towards the creation of the National Health Service), dissatisfaction with the nation's rudimentary provision for health and other forms of social care had been growing in the 1930s and may well have resulted in reforms without the catalyst of war. However, despite the many continuities, the disruptions associated with, for example, armed combat, conscription (including women), rationing and mass bombing (all on a scale hitherto unknown), ensured that British society and culture were fundamentally altered by the experience of war.

This volume of essays emerged from a staff seminar programme in the School of Arts and Humanities at De Montfort University and reflects the interests of current and former members of that School who teach and research in History, Literature, Cultural Studies, Film and Media Studies and Art and Design History. Although the essays grew out of the multifarious interests of staff, they focus upon morale and propaganda and aspects of culture and leisure as well as national, racial, community and personal identities. There is also a strong emphasis on the experiences of ordinary people, including the testimonies of men, women, teenagers and children who lived through the war.

In the first section, *Maintaining the Home Front: Morale and Patriotism*, David Thoms explores some of the pressures which served to undermine civilian morale during the blitz, while Pat Kirkham considers the emphasis on beauty as womanly duty in order to maintain not only the morale of women and the Home Front but also of the men fighting in the armed forces. The essay on Orwell by John Newsinger raises the issue of patriotism, not in the context of fashion or mass bombing, but in terms of the competing claims of nationalism and socialism.

Film: Propaganda and Pleasure opens with Michael O'Shaughnessy's essay on *A Canterbury Tale* (1944), 'a film about what Britain was fighting for', which also deals with issues of nationalism and patriotism – here within the context of rural England and 'traditional' values. Following this essay, which invokes the spirit of Chaucer's England, Imelda Whelehan and Deborah Cartmell examine the resonances of the Shakespearean heritage for British cinema audiences in Laurence Olivier's *Henry V*. These mainstream movies combined entertainment with propaganda, as did the Disneyesque animated films of Halas and Batchelor discussed by Paul Wells. More overtly propagandist were short documentaries, including the output of The Workers' Film Association, discussed in Alan Burton's essay. *Pictures and the Public* opens with Robert Richardson's story of the protection of part of the 'national heritage' by means of the removal of 'key' works of art to safe places and moves on to two studies of official war art – John Rimmer's study of Paul Nash's battle paintings and Adrian Lewis's examination of the shelter drawings of Henry Moore.

There is an emphasis on leisure and pleasure in the fourth section entitled *Popular Pastimes* – which ranges from reading Agatha Christie to watching Stanley Matthews. Steve Chibnall examines the growth of a paperback book culture just before and during the war and reveals a whole world of American-influenced pulp fiction; of sin, sex, violence and romance well outside the cosy world of the more respectable Penguin books. While questions of 'female' genres and reading habits are discussed in a broad way by Chibnall, Kathleen Bell examines a single example of the most popular of 'female' genres, the historical romance, written by leading author, Georgette Heyer, in which the heroine cross dresses. Stephen Knight also takes up a genre touched upon in Chibnall, namely crime fiction, which he dicusses with particular reference to Agatha Christie and Peter Cheyney. The emphasis of the section then shifts from individualistic leisure pursuits to the more collective ones of radio listening and of watching football. Tim O'Sullivan considers the response of the BBC to war-time conditions and suggests important areas for further research. The closing essay in this group, by Pierre Lanfranchi and Matt Taylor, tells not only the story of how and in what ways football survived during the war but also what happened to the league, players and the grounds at different times during the years 1939 to 1945.

The section *Beyond the Pale: Ethnic Minorities and the War* shifts the emphasis away from 'culture' towards the experiences of particular ethnic groups in Britain during a period of social flux and intense nationalism. Panikos Panayi discusses the size and composition of the main minority groups and considers the different forms of hostility towards both 'enemy' and non-enemy minorities. By contrast, Ian Spencer focuses upon migrants from the Indian sub-continent and the West Indies and the changing nature of the views of government officials in relation to immigration during and immediately after the war. Using the testimonies of the victims themselves, Rinella Cere offers a feminist perspective on a particular example of hostility towards 'enemy' aliens, namely the internment of women, and on subsequent interpretations of their experience. Personal testimony forms the final section of this anthology, with essays by Alan Sillitoe and Peter Davison about their teenage years and their early manhood.

Collectively, these essays are linked by a number of related themes which cut across the inevitably somewhat arbitrary sections into which we have grouped them. We hope, however, that readers will find our arrangement helpful but not so prescriptive that they are precluded from drawing their own connections between essays and across sections. We greatly enjoyed working together on this project, and with our colleagues – all of whom we thank most warmly. Our thanks also to the School and to the University for research funding which helped make this project possible.

Pat Kirkham and David Thoms
September 1995.

Section 1: Maintaining the Home Front: Morale and Patriotism

The Blitz, Civilian Morale and Regionalism, 1940-1942

David Thoms

The blitz is one of the dominant themes of Britain's wartime experience. The attack from the air began in the spring of 1940, though it was not until the autumn that the raids occurred on such a scale and with such intensity as to pose a serious threat to civilian morale. By that time, too, the German pilots were flying during the day as well as at night and were also moving inland from their original targets on the coast. The blitz was associated with the prolonged bombing of London from 7 September until 26 November, though the term soon came to be applied to any major air raid. The final three months of 1940 saw major attacks on Liverpool, Manchester, Birmingham and Coventry. The raids continued into the New Year and, although concentrated at first on Britain's coastal ports, soon became dispersed around the country as a whole with many towns and cities being visited by the German bomber squadrons on several occasions. In June 1941 the Luftwaffe's attention switched elsewhere, most notably Russia, and it was not until April of the following year that attacks on Britain were resumed. Although involving considerable destruction and loss of life, these raids were not of the same severity as the earlier sorties and were effectively Germany's last concerted attempt to crush Britain from the air using conventional aircraft.[1]

According to Addison, 'morale was the woolliest and most muddled concept of the war.'[2] It was a term often discussed by central

3

government but rarely defined with any clarity. This is partly explained by the Home Office's failure to establish criteria against which public sentiment or opinion could be measured. It was also, however, a reflection of the inconsistencies of approach adopted by the authors of the many different reports on the bombing raids which reached the Home Office. Under these circumstances it was easier for ministers and their officials to catalogue the factors which influenced civilian morale than to establish precisely the nature of the phenomenon which they were investigating. Yet, although six-monthly cycles in public morale were first identified in 1941, a credible explanation was still being sought some two years later. The significance of astrological predictions was among the more bizarre explanations of peaks and troughs in public morale to be discussed by Home Office officials. A Ministry of Information Home Intelligence report of August 1941 noted that 'A large number of people, and especially women, not only show a high degree of interest in press predictions, but they also place considerable reliance on them. From the evidence we have accumulated during the past few weeks there is reason to assume that this interest is growing, and may in time have a very serious impact on morale.'[3] The information base which the Government accumulated was used by the head of Home Intelligence to produce a detailed and measured report on civilian morale in October 1941. This distinguished between material and mental factors, with the former deemed to be of greatest significance and including security, rest, food and leisure. Psychological considerations did not embrace astrological predictions but focused instead upon public perceptions of the justice of war, the likelihood of victory and equality of sacrifice.[4]

In the absence of a social scientific definition of morale and its ingredients perhaps this was as far as the Ministry could go at that time. Yet it did not allow for reasoned consideration of, and policy initiatives towards, apparent manifestations of decline in public fortitude, such as the unplanned evacuation which occurred in many provincial areas known as trekking. One of the Home Office's most interesting and significant documents on the problem of measuring the public mood was prepared in February 1943 and noted that:

> Air-raid morale may be defined as a factor which influences the response of towns to air attack, apart from the direct physical damage they suffer. This definition does not imply that physical damage has no effect on

morale, but it stresses the difference in response to equivalent degree of damage which may be dependent on existing differences in air-raid morale.[5]

Somewhat belatedly, the Home Office had come to recognise that the interaction between the blitz and civilian morale must necessarily be approached within a local or regional context. As early as September 1941 the Home Planning Committee questioned 'whether it was really thought necessary to have a specific campaign to improve morale in general.'[6] These sentiments perhaps assumed that the civilian population was now able to withstand air attack, but they may too reflect an appreciation that national propaganda did not necessarily address morale at the local level.

The blitz produced a variety of experiences which were shared in varying degrees by the bulk of the population. The approach of enemy aircraft signalled danger, though uncertainty might remain concerning the exact location of the target. One resident of Birmingham described the attack on Coventry of November 1940 in the following terms:

> It seemed like an aerial Armada was assembling, circling like racehorses waiting for the 'off'. The noise of aircraft engines grew louder and louder until the flying squadrons suddenly streamed off towards Coventry. In a matter of minutes numerous flashes from the direction of that city lit up the horizon and the sources of explosions mingled with the scream and rumble of aerial engines.

He continued:

> Two days later I went through the town and the only building of any size standing was the Police Station. Street after street which a few days earlier had been a busy town centre was now piles of rubble. It was terrible.[7]

Death, injury and physical destruction inevitably accompanied a major raid. Their particular impact was highly personalised but did create a background of hardship and suffering which were universally recognisable in those parts of the country which had experienced the blitz. That recognition transcended city boundaries to encompass a broader parameter. Mrs Clara Milburn, who lived near the village of Berkswell, some ten miles from Coventry, recorded in her diary how

'One still feels the pain of Coventry's raid. I cannot really imagine what it looks like there, nor do I want to see it, but the loss of life must be much greater than at first thought. One hears of streets that have no houses left in them.'[8]

Morale was influenced by the intensity of a raid and the scale and nature of the damage sustained. However, it seems clear that people's ability to withstand attack declined as the raids increased in frequency, or threatened to do so. This was sometimes related to specific circumstances. For example, one of the targets of the blitz on Birmingham of 19 November 1940 was the British Small Arms (BSA) factory, which suffered very heavy casualties. The local authority attempted to contain news of the incident in order to limit public alarm, with exactly the opposite result. Rumours circulated that the disaster was so great that rescue workers had to be brought in from areas well beyond the Birmingham area in order to remove the large number of victims buried under mountains of rubble. With the threat of further attack, workers at the BSA plant remained in a state of nervous anticipation. This culminated in near chaos when several thousand employees demonstrated their concern to management on the safety issue by taking over the main gates and thereby effectively assuming control of the works.[9]

Repetitive large-scale bombing undoubtedly proved one of the Luftwaffe's most potent weapons in undermining the resolve of the civilian population. The raids on Plymouth from November 1940 to April 1941 appear to have brought the city close to breaking point. During this period Plymouth was attacked with unprecedented consistency, culminating in five successive nights of ferocious bombardment in April 1941. According to McLaine, these attacks induced Home Intelligence to come 'as close as it ever dared to say that morale had gone.'[10] From its experience of Plymouth and similar medium-sized towns, Mass-Observation believed that repetitive bombing was 'much the hardest type of attack to get used to', adding that 'it is very doubtful if people can condition themselves to more than three nights of intensive attack in a week.'[11]

Evidence assembled by Mass-Observation and similar organisations demonstrates that the blitz generated many concerns associated with the progress of the war which were shared nationally. Perhaps paramount among these was a belief that the Prime Minister should moderate the tone of his public speeches since it was felt that threats and challenges to the enemy increased the possibility of further attack.

6

This was typified by a report from the Hull and East Riding Information Committee in July 1941 concerning Churchill's invitation to the Germans to 'Do their worst.' The Committee noted that 'Whilst there appears to be no lack of courage on the part of the people, some seem to be under the impression that such speeches are an incitement, the consequences of which are borne by the civilian population.'[12] Perhaps this was as close as the Committee felt able to go in condemning the Prime Minister's words as reckless. However, the coded message seems clear. The German bombers should not be given any incentive to attack when the country's civil defence arrangements were so limited and when the military appeared unable to strike back effectively at the enemy. A further popular irritant concerned exaggerated government claims on the progress of the war, particularly when juxtaposed with the severity of German attacks on the home front. More generally, during the intensive period of the blitz in 1940 and 1941 the national mood was for news, but not of the censored variety allowed by the government authorities.

The concerns shared by the broad mass of the population are fundamentally important to an understanding of the ebb and flow of civilian morale. Yet observations from a national perspective obscure regional and local variations that are essential to an appreciation of this aspect of the culture of war. Although the social observers of the period were usually far from scientific in the way they defined their criteria or collected their information, they were often sufficiently experienced to allow the historian to attribute some credence to their conclusions. Important and interesting questions are raised when one report is contrasted with another. Was it really the case, for example, that by the end of 1941 a 'blitzed town atmosphere' had become characteristic of the south of England and that this compared unfavourably with parts of the country further north? Similarly, was Mass-Observation correct in its claim that 'going from Liverpool to Manchester was like going from an atmosphere of reasonable cheerfulness into an atmosphere of barely restrained depression'?[13]

These location specific reports are also valuable because the information they contain is sometimes sufficiently detailed to open further avenues of enquiry or to suggest fruitful ways of approaching particular issues. One of the interesting features of the Mass-Observation report on Liverpool which followed a visit lasting from 24 December 1940 to 3 January 1941 is its attention to specific social groups. It was said, for example, that young people under twenty years of age were distinctly more cheerful than their seniors, a phenomenon which was parallelled in London. The upper and middle classes of Liverpool were reported to display noticeably 'less good morale than the working classes.' One of the sources of evidence for this was the dislocation of voluntary services dependent on women from the higher social classes which, it was suggested, sometimes created very serious problems. One of Liverpool's most characteristic social features was its high proportion of Irish workers, a group which received special attention from Mass-Observation. However, although many of the city's Irish inhabitants were without local ties, 'little was found to differentiate their morale from that of other groups.'

The Mass-Observation report on Liverpool yields a number of interesting insights into the kind of specifically local factors which its volunteers claimed influenced the public mood. The report was at pains to stress that 'morale in Liverpool is appreciably higher than in any other blitzed town observed so far.' Eleven indicators were introduced to prove the case, mostly concerned with the general temper of the local population. Thus it was claimed that there was 'good humour and laughter' and a 'large amount of singing and whistling' in the streets. It was also noted that 'The centre of Liverpool after dark is a mixture between a bump supper night at Cambridge (when Pembroke is head of the river), and a Bank Holiday at Blackpool. Nowhere have we seen more drunkenness, more singing and shouting and cat-calling, more picking up, or more people being sick'.

The buoyant state of Liverpool's morale was attributed in part to its position as a major seafaring city. It was argued that the 'sailors brought an atmosphere of revelry and holiday' but that, more fundamentally, the city's seafaring tradition, combined with the economic problems which it suffered during the interwar period, created an emotional resilience which was transferable to the conditions of war. Moreover, it was suggested that sailors' wives were used to living alone for extended periods of time and that 'This stands them in good stead as compared with the wives of Coventry munition workers or Cockney bus conductors.' Perhaps of greater significance, however, was the nature of the December attack. This followed a series of relatively minor raids, fifteen alone in September, which may have helped to prepare the public for the more serious onslaught which was to follow. In addition, the principal attack left the city centre relatively unscathed. This was considered important by Mass-Observation since

'There is a subtle psychological tie-up between the citizens, however apathetic, and the centre, the heart of their city.'[14]

Tom Harrisson noted of the situation in Liverpool that 'Merseyside responded almost joyously to the pre-Christmas blitzing; as if it had won.'[15] Yet the suspicion remains that the Mass-Observation volunteers may have been unduly optimistic in their conclusions, a natural reaction perhaps to the signs of distress which they identified elsewhere. The Liverpool report itself makes reference to low morale among dock workers, though this was attributed to conditions of employment rather than the impact of the air raids. Indeed, industrial unrest does appear to have been an important drag on morale throughout the traditional industries of northern England. Nevertheless, at least at the specific point in time of late December 1940 the bulk of Liverpool's population appears to have retained a high degree of morale during a major period of blitz.

Mass-Observation volunteers visited Coventry in the two days immediately following the raid on the city of 14 November 1940. Their report caused considerable government alarm since it suggested that civilian moral had disintegrated in the wake of the raid. People were said to be extremely pessimistic, with ' "Coventry is finished" ' and ' "Coventry is dead" ' being typical responses to the attack. It was also claimed that extreme behavioural abnormalities became manifest.

> There were more open signs of hysteria, terror, neurosis observed in one evening than during the whole of the past two months, together, in all areas. Women were seen to cry, to scream, to tremble all over, to faint in the street, to attack a fireman and so on.[16]

It is evident that a very short visit immediately following such a devastating air raid was not the most appropriate basis upon which to construct such damaging conclusions. In addition, the report itself failed to reconcile its impression of general panic and depression with such statements as there were 'very few grumbles', no signs of 'anti-war feeling' and 'admiration for the ARP and AFS services'.[17] Moreover, intercepted telephone calls for the week ending 25 November demonstrated that morale 'is of the highest order, notwithstanding the town's ordeal.'[18] Yet an investigation some twelve months later by A. Hope-Jones, an official at the Ministry of Food, suggested that emotions in the city were at an extremely low point with a level of introspection close to paranoia.[19]

The economic situation in Coventry in the 1930s contrasted sharply with that in Liverpool, with a high level of employment in the light engineering industries and nationally favourable wage rates, trends which were reinforced by the growth of the munitions sector locally. With the onset of war, however, Coventry provided few opportunities for this income to be translated into consumption. The air raids removed many of the city's social facilities, including the Empire Theatre, the municipal swimming baths and a large number of its public houses. Social reconstruction was painfully slow in the months following the November attack so that even a year later cinema performances were restricted to certain hours, while many pubs remained closed, and those that were open suffered from a shortage of beer. According to Hope-Jones, Coventry's morale could only be lifted by a 'brightening up of life'. Even the absence of a military presence, he argued, served to depress spirits and weaken resolve.[20]

The scale of the Coventry blitz, its significance as the first major raid upon a provincial city and the symbolic importance of the destruction of the cathedral attracted national attention. In contrast to Liverpool, much of the city's central area was reduced to rubble demolishing most of the familiar landmarks. The fourteenth-century cathedral suffered terrible damage from fire retaining only its tower, spire and burnt-out shell. Many of the city's principal civic buildings were also ruined, together with over 75 per cent of shops in the central precinct. Some 46,000 houses within the city boundaries were damaged, with more than 2000 rendered uninhabitable. One of the major reasons for the high degree of physical and human destruction was Coventry's relatively compact nature which reflected its medieval origins. This particular spatial feature was said to have generated a high level of personal acquaintanceships so that 'nearly everybody knew somebody who had been killed or was missing.' This was probably one of the chief reasons why in the aftermath of the attack Coventry was said to be dominated by 'talk of disaster and destruction'.[21] The narrow streets impeded the rescue services and also rendered it difficult for the communications network to be restored. Once again this contrasted with the situation in Liverpool where because of its physical characteristics, the damage 'was not so concentrated as in other towns'. As the Mass-Observation team noted, Liverpool 'has not yet had to stand the test of one concentrated blitz on one area of the town.'[22]

Wartime reports indicate that civilian morale in the post-blitz period was influenced by a broad range of local factors with the quality of the defence and rescue services, and arrangements for feeding and accommodating the homeless being matters of particular and common concern. More generally, national concerns were also important in moulding public attitudes, both before and after specific raids. However, the particular issues discussed in relation to Coventry and Liverpool do illustrate how local studies may provide valuable insights into the generation and dissolution of morale. Coventry also provides an example of how the psychological damage to the community inflicted by a raid could linger long after its immediate physical impact had been alleviated. Government officials were clearly perplexed by the relatively poor state of morale revealed by the Ministry of Food report of November 1941. Hope-Jones himself suggested that the attention Coventry's plight had received from royalty, politicians and the media following the blitz a year earlier may have been self-destructive since when 'the excitement died down, important visitors became fewer, and Coventry began to feel neglected.' In response, Sir Frank Tribe, Deputy Secretary at the Ministry of Labour, conceded that 'it is a pity that it (Coventry) was so much "fussed" over when it was first blitzed.'[23]

This essay has not attempted to define or to chart the relationship between the blitz and civilian morale but has worked within the parameters defined by the social observers of the period. Nor has it attempted to be exhaustive in its consideration of the dynamics of interaction. Rather, it has drawn attention to the value of Mass-Observation and other reports in providing the basis for a comparative study of the bombing raids and suggested that the significance of these attacks can only properly be understood within a local and regional context. Generalisations around the 'Dunkirk spirit' reveal little about the public mood and its response to the blitz of 1940-1942.

NOTES

[1] For a discussion of the timing of the air raids and their impact, see T.H. O'Brien, *Civil Defence*, HMSO, London, 1955, chapter X.
[2] P. Addison, *The Road to 1945*, Cape, London, 1975, p121.
[3] Public Record Office (PRO), HO 199/454, Ministry of Information Home Intelligence Report, 47, 20-27 August 1941.
[4] Addison, *op.cit.*, p185.
[5] PRO, HO 199/456, *A note on the meaning and measurement of the morale of towns in relation to air raids*, 2 February 1943.

[6] Quoted in M. Yass, *This is Your War*, HMSO, London, 1983, p29.

[7] Imperial War Museum, Papers of C.J. Rice, undated.

[8] P. Donnelly (ed), *Mrs Milburn's Diaries*, Harrap, London, 1977, p71.

[9] D.W. Thoms, *War, Industry and Society*, Routledge, London, 1989, p118.

[10] I. McLaine, *Ministry of Morale*, Allen and Unwin, London, 1979, p134.

[11] T. Harrisson, *Living Through the Blitz*, Collins, London, 1976, p212.

[12] PRO, HO 199/45, *Effects of enemy air raids upon Hull on 18 July 1941*, report by Hull and East Riding Information Committee.

[13] PRO, HO 199/442, *Report on Selected Blitz Towns*, p8.

[14] *Ibid*, pp2-8.

[15] Harrisson, *op.cit.*, p239.

[16] PRO, HO 199/442, Mass Observation, *Report on Coventry*, p1.

[17] *Ibid*.

[18] PRO, INF 1/292, *Weekly reports*, 25 November 1940.

[19] PRO, HO 207/1069, Ministry of Food, *Report on the shopping difficulties of women war workers in Coventry*, 3 November 1941.

[20] *Ibid*.

[21] PRO, HO 199/442, Mass Observation, *Report on Coventry*, 18 November 1940, p1.

[22] PRO, HO 199/442, *Reports on Selected Blitz Towns*, p7.

[23] PRO, HO 207/1069, Sir Frank Tribe to Sir Henry French, 3 December 1941.

Beauty and Duty: Keeping Up the (Home) Front

Pat Kirkham

It is your duty to make yourself look your best. *Woman's Own*, 1940.

It is axiomatic that the good spirits of the fighting men depend on the civilian and more particularly the female of the species. And what do hers depend on? Well largely on her clothes ... this business of looking beautiful is largely a duty. *Vogue*, 1941.

Figure Precautions. It's bad for morale to let figures go – and it's bad for efficiency too. Advertisement, Berlei, 1941.

Morale was a central issue for the British wartime government which took extremely seriously issues related to the well-being of women. In a period of national austerity the British state called upon its women to make enormous material sacrifices *vis-à-vis* their appearance, but to look as if they had not. Women were exhorted to beautify themselves to keep up morale – not only the morale of the home front but also that of the men fighting abroad. Because it could not be sure that women's concerns with something that was considered ephemeral and non-functional could or would survive either drastic shortages or the tremendous drain on energies that a sustained war demanded, morally worthy overtones inflected discussions of beauty and dress in wartime Britain.

In the concern to boost morale and create a common outlook and *national* identity amongst all women, emphasis was placed on features of women's culture which closely related to the shaping of their

WAR CULTURE

individual identities. The personal parallelled the collective. Furthermore, the majority of women related to an interest in their appearance
– from those just entering womanhood to women of more mature
years who had given up bearing children but had not given up wearing
make-up. But the national collective in this instance was unlike that
invoked by references to Britain's great and glorious past or great and
glorious landscape. This was gender specific and could have
encouraged views of women as narcissistic and concerned with
inconsequential matters at a time of national crisis. Some women
themselves felt that way but, by and large, the national and patriotic
overtones of the 'beauty as duty' discourse, particularly as articulated
in the women's magazines, were sufficiently strong to over-ride such
considerations. In the drive to uphold morale, what had previously
been matters of individual pleasure and pride now became patriotic
issues central to the war effort. What had previously been regarded as
trivial by men became represented as a mainstay of the home front –
quite literally so in the case of stays or corsets. The Government was so
worried about female morale that the Board of Trade set aside scarce
materials, particularly rubber and steel, for corsets[1] and the well
known fashion contour firm of Berlei was commissioned by the
Ministry of Defence to produce a regulation issue corset for women in
the armed forces.[2]

In 1940 the Government established a committee comprised of the
editors of women's magazines and others whom it considered
represented the interests of British women[3] in order to take advice and
ensure that official 'lines' on matters related to women, including dress
and appearance, were conveyed to those concerned as effectively as
possible. Beauty as duty became a recurrent theme in features and
advertisements in the main women's magazines, such as *Woman*,
Woman's Own, *Woman and Home Journal* and *Vogue*, as well as in
magazines of more general interest, such as *Illustrated* and *Picture
Post*.[4] Some manufacturers made the connections between beauty and
duty before the governmental committee. In December 1939, for
example, an advertisement for Evan Williams Shampoo showed the
head and shoulders of an attractive woman air raid warden and those of
a civilian. The caption read 'Hair Beauty – is a duty, too!' and the text
urged women to beautify their hair 'for the Christmas re-unions ... the
men of the services on leave will expect and deserve it.'[5] 'Beauty Is
Your Duty' captioned an Icilma beauty aids advertisement of January
1940 which featured a nurse at work and also looking glamorous

14

dressed in an evening gown and dancing with a dashing army officer. The same firm plugged a similar line in its February advertisement – this time with a pretty factory worker whose class origins ensured that she was represented with a sergeant.[6] Vinolia soap advertisements also stressed that it was a woman's 'duty to stay beautiful' and Tangee lipsticks promised 'beauty on duty', as did Conlowe rayon underwear.[7]

The national call was for a *united* front of *individual* female 'fronts' to keep up appearances and maintain the illusion of normality in the face of extraordinary odds, a masquerade seen to be in direct contrast to Germany where visible signs of sacrifice and hardship seemed to denote the ideal female supporter of the war effort.[8] It was certainly in contrast to the Australian experience where the government's 'austerity campaign', launched in September 1942 to promote material sacrifice in the 'national interest', was endorsed by women's magazines which proclaimed that it was 'smart to be without make-up' and urged women to forgo their face powders and creams as well as stockings.[9]

Many women dreaded the thought of being without their corsets or 'a bit of face powder or lipstick'.[10] The British government understood the centrality of such aids used in the construction of femininity to the everyday lives of women and grasped something of the anxieties of facing quite daunting situations without one's familiar 'face' or body shape – without one's 'front'. In 1942 the Board of Trade weighed the pros and cons of prohibiting cosmetics. The pros were savings of labour, plant and materials, the con was that cosmetics were 'essential to female morale'[11]; the result was that production continued, albeit further restricted. One of the clearest acknowledgments of the importance of women munitions workers to the war effort and of make-up to their morale is the decision by the government to grant them special allowances of high-grade face make-up. These were issued by the Ministry of Supply from August 1942, together with a booklet entitled *R.O.F. Beauty Hints. Look to Your Looks'.*[12] In 1942 Ernest Bevin made it easier for hairdressers to keep 'their key operators out of factories ... since a neat head is held to be an invaluable booster of feminine morale'[13] and, in late 1943, there was such 'acute feminine consternation everywhere, including ... machine shops and mess rooms' at the suggestion that lipstick and nail varnish would be taken off the market that the Board of Trade was forced to placate 'the female half of the population somewhat by announcing that there would be a small increase in the amount of cosmetics released for consumption'.[14]

Some cosmetic powders and creams were designated as medical supplies or sold as separate unmixed ingredients in order to by-pass elaborate government restrictions and the heavy purchase tax imposed upon cosmetics.[15] Demand remained high despite the cost and many women still remember the excitement when supplies of well known brands such as Coty came into the shops.[16] One described at the time her delight at finding a range of cosmetics on sale in the streets of Blackpool in 1942 and, a year later, looking like a miser at her 'little cherished hoard of perfumes, lipsticks and powder'.[17] Many women who regarded it as immoral to obtain other items illegally had few scruples when it came to 'grey market' (under the counter) or 'black market' cosmetics or stockings for which they paid quite high prices.

Women were supposed to find common cause – and many did – in conjuring up extra time and energy to pin curl their hair at night, remember to use Pond's face cream, make fashionable hats out of odd scraps of material or dressing-gowns from blankets or old coats. All this at the end of a day of exhausting war work and, for many, looking after a home too. One woman told me recently that she became so used to scraping out the last bits of lipstick from the container and applying the colour with her finger tip that she continued to do so for the next fifty years.[18] Some women took more care with their dress and appearance than others, but one should not dismiss the importance of such matters which formed an important part of women's everyday conversations and culture at the time, particularly, but not exclusively, that of younger women. The slogans for national survival and beauty care became interchangeable; the ideal woman became the one who, in the words of the Yardley advertisements, *No Surrender*, honoured 'the subtle bond between good looks and good morale'.[19]

But state and media proclamations about beauty or duty did not necessarily succeed in recruiting women to patriotic ends, particularly young working-class women. It was defiance of *anyone* who wanted them to change their ways more than patriotism which sustained the determination of many young working-class women to keep up appearances at all costs. Tom Harrisson, Director of Mass Observation, noted in his introduction to Celia Fremlin's 1942 observational study of women factory workers that the aimlessness, apathy and boredom she found amongst the young were confirmed by other studies. He wrote of '*the dangerous decline in positive citizenship*', especially amongst the young, and this was precisely what the Government needed to guard against if it was to harness all forces in a national united effort to win the war.[20] Fremlin herself noted that the 'patriotic posters ("It all depends on me", "We want your help", etc, etc) which plaster the walls of every room in the factory might as well be so much ornamental scroll work for all the notice that is taken of them, by the machine shop girls at least'.[21] Ironically, it was those suffering from what Harrisson called 'cultural passivity', dislike of bosses and working hours which left little time for leisure or sleep who took most care to make themselves look attractive. For some a 'bolshi' attitude towards authority was extended to a generalised 'they', usually meaning their bosses but also official bodies. Peggy, a lively, good-looking, twenty year old factory worker in Wiltshire who went out dancing most evenings, for example, was noted as a slapstick worker who 'always wears nice dresses and stockings to work, regardless of the fact that among the dirt and oil of the machine shop they are going to be ruined very quickly'.[22] She stated that she was not going to work in 'slops' for anyone; she had always worn nice things for work and 'they' weren't going to stop her.[23] There is no doubt that she and her fellow workers took their appearance seriously. In one week in 1942 an unskilled companion spent over £1 (nearly half of her weekly wages of £2-14s-0d, overtime included) on beautifying herself: 12/11d went on dance shoes, 2/6d on an ornamental flower for her dance dress, 4/6d on a shampoo and set and 1/9d on nail polish remover.[24] Another spent over half her wages on wool and knitting needles for a jumper (7/11d), a pair of stockings (3/6d), a jar of cold cream (2/6d), a jar of vanishing cream (1/6d), ribbon (5d) and shoe repairs (5/11d).[25]

The skills of 'putting on a front' in terms of appearance were acquired by most girls, as part of learning to be a woman, but keeping up a respectable appearance and good grooming were more entrenched in British middle-class culture than in that of the working class. Furthermore, beauty as duty discourses were inflected with something of the stiff upper lip associated with the British upper classes. In the case of corsets, the wearing of which by women was widespread before the war, there was a transposition to the stiff upright back – a metaphor for moral rectitude and fortitude – associated with middle and upper class modes of comportment as well as the military. In other words, for many women, elements of gender and class training coincided and combined in curious and compound ways during the war years.

During the crisis of war, appearance, and certain related objects,

Figure One: Beryl Lewis in turquoise high-necked dress illustrating the use of overstitching to create pattern and texture, circa 1940.

Figure Two: Phyllis Davis (Wren), Lieutenant Bollingbroke (Royal Marines) and Beryl Lewis, 1941: Phyllis wears a Utility suit in mauve and Beryl a brown woollen mix coat.

Figure Three: Cover of *Woman*, 1943. Courtesy *Woman*, IPC.

Figure Four: Harella advertisement for a Utility suit, 1945.

took on new symbolic meanings and the 'front' erected by women not only functioned as a morale booster for the boys overseas and the home front but also gave a degree of psychological protection to individual women. The corset, for example, protected the psyche as well as the spine. Bright lipstick was a symbol of defiance against Hitler as well as against those who regarded it as morally suspect; it was a declaration of patriotism as well as of identity and sexuality. One Warwickshire woman recalls, ' ... my lipstick and my engagement ring were two protections against Hitler. I'd never go out without those'[26] – a theme captured in the cover illustration of *Woman*, 19 June 1943, (Fig 3). Wartime beauty might have been posed as a duty to boost national morale but it also lifted spirits at an individual level, the familiar functioning as a fount of confidence and comfort.

In wartime fiction and in 'real life', hats, dress and make-up were consciously used by women to boost their morale. Middle-class women such as Ernestine Carter could afford to buy new hats (exempt from coupons) to cheer themselves up 'when the news was extra bad'.[27] Less well-to-do women had to make do with knitting one, making one from scraps of materials or altering an existing hat. Nella Last, a respectable middle-aged working-class housewife from Barrow-in-Furness, whose war diaries are a constant and poignant reminder of the small and daily heroisms of women, made herself a fashionable beret from an old astrakhan cap and managed to find her 'dream hat' (a new one of wine-coloured straw) when on a day trip to Blackpool in 1942 for only 16/11d when it was not unusual for attractive hats to cost £2 and upwards.[28] Far from 'flighty' and one of the town's most dedicated voluntary workers, her very respectability, age and broader social and political interests (she was a dedicated 'Mass Observer') underlines the fact that their appearance remained important for most women, not just the young or those lacking other interests. Last consciously used dress and make-up to bolster her spirits when they were flagging. The day before her youngest son went off to war in mid-September 1939, for example, she noted 'Tonight I looked a bit washed out, so after tea I changed into my gayest frock and made up rather heavily'. When depressed after the fall of France, she put on rouge, lipstick and 'a gay flowered dress' to cheer herself up and, in May 1941, after a night of bombing and a day sick with fear, very deliberately applied powder and lipstick to help her 'face' the possibility of another terrifying night of bombing.[29] She wrote with remarkable honesty and self-awareness of her shift from a pre-war 'retiring' woman to one who 'uses too bright lipstick and on dim days makes the corners turn up when lips will not keep smiling'.

Despite the 'beauty is duty' discourse, the wearing of make-up remained a problematic activity for some women, particularly older women and those who had led a relatively sheltered life. At the age of fifty, Nella Last had to endure the vocal disapproval of a co-voluntary worker who made 'sick-making noises' about her make-up – although she was later rewarded when that very woman commented, 'It would not be a bad idea if we all bought a lipstick and got little Last to show us how to paint a smile'.[30] Although older moral strictures about vanity and slack morals in relation to make-up had been breaking down in the inter-war years, nevertheless there were those women who felt that the national mood of austerity should be reflected in female appearance. One accused her sister-in-law of the unpatriotic act of 'dolling' herself up and reported, in a letter to *Home Chat* in March 1942, that when she remonstrated with her all she received was the response that it cheered people up to see well-dressed women about. The magazine reply was sympathetic to the sister-in-law.

Nella Last and thousands of others stand testimony to the immense efforts made to maintain individual and national morale as well as the creativity involved in so doing. 'Make do and mend' was more than just the name of an official campaign. I never tire of hearing women's stories about making 'something out of nothing'[31]; skirts and dresses out of curtains or tablecloths, wedding dresses out of lace bedspreads and net curtains, camiknickers out of parachute silk, blouses out of men's pyjama jackets. Almost any garment you can think of was knitted, from swim suits to lacy stockings, and seams were drawn up legs browned by sand, gravy salt or a patent lotion. Necessity was frequently the mother of invention and 'tips' were willingly passed on in an extension of the supportive collective culture enjoyed by many women before the war.

Dress was a major factor in maintaining female morale. The Civilian Clothing scheme of 1941 (CC41, or Utility as it was better known) not only rationalised the production and distribution of materials and clothes in order to free manufacturing resources for war work but also aimed to create attractive items that could be mass produced at prices most people could afford.[32] Scarcity, soaring prices and discontent because it seemed that the well-to-do were faring better than others in what was supposed to be a national common effort, persuaded the government to introduce regulated and rationed dress. It took care, however, to ensure that the products would meet with the approval of those who had to wear them and brought in top designers, including Hardy Amies, Digby Morton, Victor Stieber, and Worth, to ensure that the women's garments in particular were up-to-date in terms of fashion. That they were is witnessed by the welcome they were given in *Vogue* (which exaggerated the extent to which they would democratise dress) and other women's magazines. Another indicator of their acceptability is the fact that the Utility styles were copied and adapted in the non-regulated section of the trade (15 per cent of total production).

Maintaining the morale of women in the armed services was also important to the Government. Women did not suddenly lose interest in fashion when they joined the services, indeed they continued to wear make-up and take an interest in civilian clothes which they wore when on leave. Many were glad of the Government issue Berlei corset which proved a scarce commodity in civilian life, but others complained that you were lucky to get one that fitted you – or a brassiere for that matter.[33] The tension between women feeling comfortably smart, attractive and 'feminine' and being part of a well-disciplined military machine was resolved, by and large, by an emphasis on good grooming and smartness which was both fashionable and appropriate to military conventions. Uniformed dress, like its Utility counterpart the tailored suit, incorporated the longer jacket and slim but slightly flared skirt raised to knee length featured in the haute couture collections of London and Paris just before the war.[34] But not every uniform looked or made a woman feel as good as a couture suit – although those tailored for officers by firms such as Austin Reed or Moss Bros were remarkably smart.[35] Class differences were reflected in service life and the quality and cut of the uniforms of the 'other ranks' were much inferior to those of the officers. Some uniforms were considered more attractive than others and many women based their choice of military or quasi-military service on the uniform. WRNS and WAAF uniforms were generally more popular than that of the ATS, though it had its devotees (particularly the 'jaunty' or 'perky' walking out cap and the trim peaked cap for duty-wear). For some women, the appeal lay in the overall style of a uniform, some the colour (which usually related to their own colouring and what they looked best in) and for others it was the hats.

Women's magazines featured advice for women in uniform on how to look good and in the fictional short stories therein the woman in uniform *always* got her man. Women in uniform took beauty and duty just as seriously as their civilian sisters. However, certain officers felt that some women went too far in their concern with beauty *on* duty. Some turned a blind eye to nail polish that was less than pale and discreet, hair that was 'too long' and make-up they considered too thick or too bright. In other instances women were regularly disciplined over such matters and many risked punishment to assert their more glamorous versions of femininity over those approved by their superior officers – providing yet another example of discord at a time when the nation was supposed to be 'pulling together'.[36] In order to maintain their morale and reinforce their individual identities in the face of the threats of uniformity and individual anonymity, some uniformed women went as far as unpicking uniforms seam by seam to re-sew so as to better fit the figure, padding the already severe shoulders of jackets with government issue sanitary pads or stockings to obtain a more fashionable silhouette, substituting more delicate knickers for the fleecy-lined government issue 'passion killers' or 'blackouts', surreptitiously rolling up their skirts (which in 1939-40 were the same length as the civilian fashionable skirt but by 1942-3 were an inch longer)[37] or by wearing just that little bit too much make-up. This was the first war in which British women were conscripted. Each in their own way tried to negotiate the complexities of being a woman and a member of the armed forces and maintain morale both on and off duty.

Some civilian women maintained their morale and, at the same time, signalled their patriotism by wearing objects that directly referenced the war effort and fused the beautiful with the dutiful. 'Sweetheart' brooches in the form of the regimental insignia of a loved one were popular. Selfridges bag department offered 'your name in his handwriting in gilt letters' (8/9d for a brooch or 7/- for a bag ornament) and, for the well-to-do, Ciro of Old Bond Street offered the emblem of the royal Tank Regiment in diamonds and enamel for four guineas.[38] V for Victory brooches came in transparent perspex, and women's magazines recommended making patriotic lapel adornments in red, white and blue from ribbons, felt or flowers. In March 1942 Jacqmar, the fabric manufacturers, produced a series of propaganda prints using themes from wartime Britain which were made into dresses, blouses, aprons and scarves. Titles included *Happy Landing, The Navy's Here, Fall in the Firebomb Fighters, Dig For Victory* and *Home Guard*.[39] The same firm also produced the Fougasse *Careless*

25

Talk posters as silk squares, while cheaper, and possibly more uplifting, was their artificial silk head-scarf in the *Shoulder to Shoulder* print. The printed cotton *Victory* came with its selvedges decorated with the morse-code signal for victory while another depicted happy evacuees. For those women who wished to be reminded of loved ones far away or simply display their patriotism, there were 'male style' pyjamas patterned with miniature aeroplanes or bars of music from popular military tunes or with military emblems on the breast pocket. It is easy to smile at some of these today but, in their time, they had wit, charm and symbolic meanings not always easy to comprehend fifty years later.

In this short essay I have not been able to do justice to the wealth of wonderful tales relayed to me by women in the recent past or to those written down by women at the time, and since. However, I hope to have given a glimpse of the home front campaign to keep Britain's women looking smart and attractive, and of some of the ways that some of the women managed to do just that – at least some of the time.

NOTES

I would like to thank all those women who have spoken to me about World War Two. Each occasion was a pleasure and a privilege. I would also like to thank Philip Warren, Assistant Keeper of Costume and Textiles, Leicestershire Museums, Art Gallery and Records Service, the Leicester Living History Unit (for organising a *Leicester Women in Wartime* 'oral history' day complete with video box in December 1993), Margaret Maynard, University of Queensland and all those friends, colleagues and students who have either commented on this article or simply shared my enthusiasm for the topic.

[1] Angus Calder, *The People's War: Britain 1939-45*, Panther, London, 1971, p438.
[2] *Picture Post*, 2 March 1940.
[3] Jo Spence, 'What Did You Do In The War Mummy? Class and Gender in Images of Women', in *Photography/Politics One*, Photography Workshop, London, 1977, p33.
[4] Spence, *op.cit.*, p33. *Picture Post* appointed a Woman's Editor in February 1941 with a brief which emphasised fashion, beauty and comfort.
[5] *Picture Post*, 16 December 1939, p66.
[6] Caroline Lang, *Keep Smiling Through: Women in the Second World War*, Cambridge University Press, Cambridge, 1989, p100.
[7] See Jane Waller and Michael Vaughan-Rees, *Women in Wartime: The Role of*

Women's Magazines 1939-1945, Macdonald and Co. Ltd, London, 1987, pp99-100 and *Woman*, 9 August 1941.

[8] See Lou Taylor and Elizabeth Wilson, *Through the Looking Glass*, BBC Books, London, 1989, pp107-108. *NB.* Privately shot film (home movies) of the wives and other women of high-ranking German staff suggest that, despite the head of the Nazi Women's Bureau urging German women to deny themselves luxury and pleasure, these women wore and took pleasure in luxurious and fashionable clothes. After the war it was said that the extravagance of Parisian fashion was deliberately aimed at taunting the dowdy German women who resided there (christened *les souris gris* – 'the grey mice') but the question of the collaboration of the fashion houses makes this an exceedingly complex and (still) touchy issue. See Lou Taylor, 'Paris Couture, 1940-1944', in Juliet Ash and Elizabeth Wilson, *Chic Thrills*, Pandora, London, 1993, p130, and *The Lady*, 6 June 1944, quoted in Caroline Lang *op.cit.*, p92.

[9] Sandi Clarke, Introduction to catalogue, *Dressed to Kill, 1935 to 1950*, Brisbane Gallery, Queensland, Australia, 1985, p3.

[10] Nearly all the women to whom I have spoken made comments such as this.

[11] Calder, *op.cit.*, p321.

[12] *CC41. Utility Furniture And Fashion 1941-1951*, Catalogue, Geffrye Museum, London, 1974, p33. *NB.* In 1942 the labour shortage was acute and every effort was made to get women into factories.

[13] Mollie Panter-Downes, *London War Notes 1939-45*, (ed. William Shawn), Longman, New York, 1972, p257.

[14] *Ibid.*, p310.

[15] Calder, *op.cit.*, pp436-437.

[16] Beryl Brooshooft, interview, June 1994.

[17] Richard Broad and Suzie Fleming (eds), *Nella Last's War: A Mother's Diary 1939-45*, Sphere Books, London, 1981, pp200-266.

[18] Beryl Brooshooft, interview, June 1994.

[19] Yardley advertisement, July 1942, cited in Waller and Vaughan-Rees, *op.cit.*, p102.

[20] Tom Harrisson, 'Industrial Survey', in Celia Fremlin, *War Factory: Mass-Observation*, The Cresset Library, London, 1987, p9.

[21] Fremlin, *op.cit.*, p48.

[22] *Ibid.*, p34.

[23] *Ibid.*, p34.

[24] *Ibid.*, p93.

[25] *Ibid.*, pp93-94.

[26] Maggie Wood, *'We wore what we'd got': Women's Clothes in World War II*, Warwickshire Books, Warwickshire County Council, 1989, p62.

[27] Joan Heath, *'Fashion by Government Order': Fact or Fiction?*, unpublished undergraduate thesis, History of Art and Design and Complementary Studies, North Staffordshire Polytechnic, 1988, p29.

[28] Heath, *ibid.*

[29] Heath, *ibid.*
Studies), North Staffordshire Polytechnic, 1988, p29.

[30] *Ibid.*, p58. *NB.* Last too had her prejudices – against those who used the war

as an excuse for what she saw as sloppiness and laziness about their appearance.

[31] Elsie Lyall, interview, June 1994. No novelty to working-class women, 'making do' with what materials, clothes and accessories were available (new and second hand) drew out creative skills that some women had not realised they possessed or that previously had lain dormant or been expressed in other ways.

[32] For Utility clothing see Taylor and Wilson, *op.cit.*, esp. chapter 4; Elizabeth Wilson, *Adorned in Dreams: Fashion and Modernity*, Virago Press, London, 1985, pp80-82, 219; Elizabeth Ewing, *History of Twentieth Century Fashion*, Batsford, London, 1986, esp. chapter 7; and Peter McNeil, ' "Put Your Best Face Forward": The Impact of the Second World War on British Dress', *Journal of Design History*, Volume 6, Number 4, 1993, pp283-299.

[33] Peggy Burbage, interview, December 1993.

[34] See *Vogue*, 6 September 1939.

[35] Taylor and Wilson, *op.cit.*, p111.

[36] Woods, *op.cit.* pp42, 433.

[37] *Vogue*, 6 September 1939.

[38] *Woman and Home*, December 1940.

[39] *CC41. Utility Furniture And Fashion 1941-51*, p34.

My Country, Right or Left: Patriotism, Socialism and George Orwell, 1939–1941

John Newsinger

> We cannot win the war without introducing Socialism, nor establish Socialism without winning the war. At such a time it is possible, as it was not in the peaceful years, to be both revolutionary and realistic. A Socialist movement which can swing the mass of the people behind it, drive the pro-Fascists out of positions of control, wipe out the grosser injustices and let the working class see that they have something to fight for, win over the middle classes instead of antagonizing them, produce a workable imperial policy instead of a mixture of humbug and Utopianism, bring patriotism and intelligence into partnership – for the first time, a movement of such a kind becomes possible.[1]

George Orwell regarded the approach of war between the European powers in the late 1930s with grim trepidation. He considered the coming conflict as a clash of rival capitalist-imperialisms in the course of which Britain, or rather England, as he habitually referred to his country, would inevitably proceed down the road towards totalitarianism. His attitude was very much informed by his experiences with the POUM militia in Spain. There an anarchist revolution had been forcibly suppressed by the Communists and their allies, and a Communist regime, which Orwell viewed as totalitarian, had taken power behind the Republican lines before Franco's final victory. In the event of a European war, this experience would, he

29

believed, be replicated on a larger scale. In early March 1939 he wrote to the anarchist and art critic Herbert Read that over the next few years war or the preparations for war would result in 'a fascizing process leading to an authoritarian regime i.e. some kind of Austro-fascism'. The greater part of the left would associate itself with this fascizing process 'which will ultimately mean associating themselves with wage reductions, suppression of free speech, brutalities in the colonies etc.' There was, he concluded, 'not much hope of saving England from fascism of one kind or another.' Nevertheless, 'one must put up a fight' and take a stand against war and its consequences. He attempted to enlist Read's support for preparations for underground propaganda activity in the event of a crackdown against the anti-war left. Orwell himself was to publicly oppose the coming conflict and wrote an anti-war pamphlet, no copies of which seem to have survived.[2]

This stance was, of course, to be dramatically abandoned. Orwell's own account of his shift to a pro-war position appears in his celebrated article, 'My Country Right or Left', in *Folios of New Writing* published in the autumn of 1940. Here he revealed that the night before the Russo-German Pact was announced, he had a dream that revealed two important things about himself that he had either forgotten or suppressed: 'first that I should be simply relieved when the long-dreaded war started, secondly, that I was patriotic at heart, would not sabotage or act against my own side, would support the war, would fight in it if possible.' While Orwell was prepared to concede that there was something in the argument about supporting the British war effort as a lesser evil than acquiescing in a Nazi victory, he made it clear that he had been swept along by feelings of patriotism. In his own words, 'the long drilling in patriotism which the middle classes go through had done its work ... once England was in a jam it would be impossible for me to sabotage.'[3] He was to emphasise the importance of patriotism on a number of other occasions. In a review of Malcolm Muggeridge's *The Thirties*, a polemical indictment of British politics and society, Orwell made clear his sympathy with and understanding of 'the emotion of the middle class man, brought up in the military tradition, who finds in the moment of crisis that he is a patriot after all.' The time comes 'when the sand of the desert is sodden red and what have I done for thee, England, my England.' He does not, it has to be said, embrace this sentiment himself, but makes it absolutely clear that he can sympathise with it; even at its most stupid and most sentimental, this emotional response 'is a comelier thing than the shallow self-righteousness of the leftwing intelligentsia.' The discovery of his own bedrock patriotism was to lead him to undertake his own explorations of England and Englishness.[4]

One important factor that eased Orwell's transformation was, without doubt, the Russo-German Pact of August 1939. His almost certainly apocryphal story of a dream changing his views the night before this diplomatic revolution was announced points in this direction. One immediate consequence of the Pact was that Communist Party policy in Britain changed, almost overnight, from advocacy of an alliance between Britain, France and the Soviet Union to opposition to the aggressive war preparations being carried out by British and French imperialists. This was not, it has to be insisted, a case of the Communists taking up an identical stance to that which Orwell was in the process of abandoning. He regarded the Russo-German Pact as the coming together of the two totalitarian powers and would never have acted as an apologist for such an unholy alliance. Moreover, his hostility towards Communists and towards the Soviet Union after his Spanish experiences was such in 1939 that he would have found it considerably more difficult to support a war being conducted in alliance with Russia. Once the Communists had adopted an anti-war position themselves, his own change of heart became all the easier.[5]

While patriotism was the most important motivation for Orwell's decision to support the war against Nazi Germany, this did not involve any weakening of his commitment to the cause of socialism. He emphasised in 'My Country Right or Left' that patriotism had, in his opinion, nothing to do with conservatism and was perfectly compatible with revolutionary politics. Indeed, he argued that it was those people 'whose hearts have never leapt at the sight of a Union Jack who will flinch from revolution when the moment comes.' He goes on:

> Let anyone compare the poem John Cornford wrote not long before he was killed ('Before the Storming of Huesca') with Sir Henry Newbolt's 'There's a breathless hush in the Close tonight'. Put aside the technical differences, which are merely a matter of period, and it will be seen that the emotional content of the two poems is almost exactly the same. The young Communist who died heroically in the International Brigade was public school to the core. He had changed his allegiance but not his emotions. What does that prove? Merely the possibility of building a

> Socialist on the bones of a Blimp, the power of one kind of loyalty to
> transmute itself into another, the spiritual need for patriotism and the
> military virtues for which, however little the boiled rabbits of the Left
> may like them, no substitute has yet been found.

It seems he recognised himself as another example of a socialist built on
the bones of a Blimp.

He proceeded to adapt the politics of the Spanish POUM to the
British wartime situation. Whereas the POUM had argued that the
completion of the socialist revolution in Republican Spain was the only
way to defeat Franco, Orwell argued that socialist revolution was the
only way that Britain would emerge victorious from the war with
Hitler. Moreover, this revolution was already underway. It was quite
likely that 'the London gutters will have to run with blood' but 'when
the red militias are billeted in the Ritz I shall still feel that the England I
was taught to love so long ago and for such different reasons is
somehow persisting.'[6]

As far as Orwell was concerned the series of disasters that
overwhelmed Britain, leaving the country facing the Nazis alone,
under air bombardment and in imminent danger of invasion had, by
the summer of 1940, created 'what amounted to a revolutionary
situation.' After twenty years of 'being fed on sugar and water the
nation had suddenly realized what its rulers were like.' This had
created a 'widespread readiness for sweeping economic and social
changes.' An unprecedented opportunity existed 'to isolate the
moneyed class and swing the mass of the nation behind a policy in
which resistance to Hitler and the destruction of class privilege were
combined.' The two were inextricably linked: the country's perilous
situation had convinced a growing number of people that only a
socialist revolution that swept away the old discredited ruling class
would make it possible to defeat the Nazis. This was true not just of
the working class, but of the middle class; indeed Orwell believed that
if anything the middle class was the more reliable. It would have been
possible, he argued, for the left to make use of the 'patriotism of the
middle class'. There was every likelihood that the 'people who stand to
attention during "God Save the King" would readily transfer their
loyalty to a Socialist regime if they were handled with tact.' Writing in
January 1941, he recognised that the opportunity had been missed, that
the 'quasi-revolutionary mood (had) ebbed away', at least for the time
being, largely because 'there was no one to take advantage of it? The

Labour Party leadership, in particular, had allowed themselves to be made tame cats of the Government.' Nevertheless, he continued to believe that victory without a socialist transformation was impossible.[7]

What was Orwell's contribution to the revolutionary situation that he believed had developed in 1940? His involvement in the Home Guard was an important part of his political activity in this period. He somewhat optimistically believed that the Home Guard could become a potential revolutionary army, a sort of people's militia, comparable to the POUM militia that he had fought with in Spain. He was also involved in editing a series of short books, the *Searchlight* series, together with Tosco Fyvel and the publisher Frederic Warburg. The series was intended as a political intervention arguing the case for a socialist transformation at home and for the adoption of socialist war aims. It was very much an intervention on the non-Communist left at a time when the Soviet Union was still allied with Nazi Germany and British Communists were anti-war.[8]

Ten *Searchlight* volumes were published in 1941 and 1942. Orwell's own *The Lion and the Unicorn* appeared in February 1941 (an extract entitled 'The Ruling Class' appeared in *Horizon* in December 1940). It was followed by Sebastian Haffner's *Offensive Against Germany*, Ritchie Calder's *The Lesson of London*, William Connor's *The English at War*, T.C. Worsley's *The End of 'The Old School Tie'*, Arturo Barea's *The Struggle for the Spanish Soul*, Joyce Carey's *The Case for African Freedom*, Bernard Causton's *The Moral Blitz*, Olaf Stapledon's *Beyond the 'Isms* and Stephen Spender's *Life and the Poet*. There was an eleventh volume, Richard and Kathleen Titmuss' *Parents Revolt*, that had been commissioned as part of the series but appeared in identical format after the series had been abandoned. The whole series is of interest but this essay focuses on Orwell's contribution, *The Lion and the Unicorn*.[9]

It is there that Orwell makes the most comprehensive and coherent statement of his politics, attempting to marry socialism with Englishness. He develops a sympathetic analysis of English culture and of the continued vitality of patriotism, an indictment of capitalism and of the English ruling class, and a critique of the left. While some commentators have subsequently seen the volume as helping to prepare the way for the Labour Party's 1945 General Election victory, it was written with other purposes in mind. Orwell saw himself as intervening in a potentially revolutionary situation in wartime, a situation in which the Labour Party was part of the problem.[10] It has also been argued that the politics of *The Lion and the Unicorn* were compromised by the embrace of Englishness and celebration of patriotism.[11] This arguably mistakes Orwell's strategy of attempting to make acceptable to the new middle class a socialist revolution, something far more radical than Labour was to attempt in 1945-51. There are, of course, problems with Orwell's argument, not least that the hoped for revolution never took place, but it is still important to recognise both the nature of its extremism and the character of the political context that he believed he was addressing.

A crucial part of his argument is of the need to recognise 'the overwhelming strength of patriotism' in the modern world. Compared to 'national loyalty', Christianity and International Socialism are 'as weak as straw'. Patriotism is not just an illusion conjured up by unscrupulous nationalist politicians intent on exploiting prejudice and superstition, but, according to Orwell, is actually a material phenomenon; national cultures, he insists, actually exist and are recognisably different. His enthusiasm for English national culture, for the 'English genius', is well known although frequently misunderstood:

> When you come back to England from any foreign country, you have immediately the sensation of breathing a different air. Even in the first few minutes dozens of small things conspire to give you this feeling. The beer is bitterer, the coins are heavier, the grass is greener, the advertisements are more blatant. The crowds in the big towns, with their mild knobby faces, their bad teeth and gentle manners, are different from a European crowd.

There is, he insists,

> something distinctive and recognizable in English civilization. It is a culture as individual as that of Spain. It is somehow bound up with solid breakfasts and gloomy Sundays, smoky towns and winding roads, green fields and red pillar-boxes. It has a flavour of its own. Morever it is continuous, it stretches into the future and the past, there is something in it that persists, as in a living creature.

It is necessary, he argues 'to try and determine what England is, before guessing what part England can play in the huge events that are happening.'

What Orwell meant by culture was not the official culture taught in the schools and universities, enjoyed by the ruling class and sanctioned by the state. Instead, he celebrated the 'genuinely popular culture … that goes on beneath the surface, unofficially and more or less frowned on by the authorities.' It was this popular culture of the common people that had produced a civilization characterised by its gentleness. England was 'a land where bus conductors are good-tempered and the policemen carry no revolvers.' There was an 'English hatred of war and militarism' such that 'no Hymn of Hate has ever made any appeal to them.' He briefly considers the paradox of this gentle, anti-militarist nation somehow conquering and ruling over a great Empire, 'a quarter of the earth', but this is quickly put aside. Militarism has not contaminated England, despite the Empire.

But surely this England bitterly divided by class conflict, is, in fact, two nations – the rich and the rest. Certainly there is great inequality of wealth: 'It is grosser than in any European country, and you have only to look down the nearest street to see it.' But while economically there is more than one nation, 'at the same time the vast majority of the people feel themselves to be a single nation.' 'Patriotism', he insists, 'is usually stronger than class hatred,' and goes on to characterise England as 'a family', but 'a family with the wrong members in control.' This comfortable analogy masks, perhaps deliberately, the radicalism of the indictment that he goes on to make and of the proposed remedy.

England was controlled by a 'decayed' ruling class that had long since lost its dynamism and was incapable of effectively confronting Nazism and Fascism. It was not, however, just a case of replacing the people in control of the family. What the war had demonstrated was that 'private capitalism … does not work' and that a transition to socialism was necessary. Orwell's socialism, 'the common ownership of the means of production,' did not mean 'that people are stripped of private possessions such as clothes and furniture, but it [did] mean that all productive goods such as land, mines, ships and machinery, are the property of the State.' Socialism also required approximate equality of incomes, political democracy, and the abolition of all hereditary privilege, especially in education. It did *not* involve the introduction of social reforms and the modernisation of industry, after the manner of the 1945-51 Labour government, but was rather a revolution to shift power from the ruling class to the people. Whether or not it would involve bloodshed 'is largely an accident of time and place', but he certainly did not shrink from it.

Who or what was to bring about socialist transformation? He

rejected both the 'timid reformism' of a Labour Party that had never aimed at 'any fundamental change' and 'the nineteenth century doctrine of class war' advocated by the Communist Party. (Marxism was, as far as he was concerned, 'a German theory interpreted by Russians and unsuccessfully transplanted to England.') Neither addressed the central task: how to win over the new indeterminate middle class 'of skilled workers, technical experts, airmen, scientists, architects and journalists, the people who feel at home in the radio and ferro-concrete age'. What was needed was a new movement, native to England' to carry out a socialist revolution and turn the war into 'a revolutionary war.' *The Lion and the Unicorn* was written and the *Searchlight* books were published in an effort to help bring about such a movement.[12]

Of course, Orwell's hopes of revolution were not to be realised and the war was eventually won (by the Soviet Union and the United States) without Britain ever becoming a socialist society. Nevertheless, his attempt to reconcile patriotism and socialism remains of considerable interest. According to John Rodden, 'Orwell's rebellious fury ... was successfully draped in the conventional pieties' and thereby contributed to the Labour Party's victory in 1945, while for Gregory Claeys the book had a long term significance because of the way it outlined 'the possibility of a new form of socialism based upon the democratic and liberal heritage of Great Britain.'[13] More important, however, was Orwell's perception of the circumstances in which he came to write the book: that a socialist revolution was both possible and necessary if the war was to be won and Nazi Germany defeated. Once his hopes for this particular outcome had passed, he somewhat symbolically went to work for the BBC.[14]

NOTES

[1] George Orwell, *The Lion and the Unicorn*, Penguin Books, Harmondsworth, 1982, pp100-101.
[2] CEJL 1, pp425-426. All references to George Orwell's *Collected Essays, Journalism and Letters* (CEJL) are to the Penguin four volumes of 1971. For a discussion of the development of Orwell's thinking in the period before the war see Malcolm Smith, 'George Orwell, War and Politics in the 1930s', *Literature and History* Volume 4, Number 2, Autumn 1980.
[3] *Ibid.*, pp590-591.
[4] *Ibid.*, p586.
[5] For sympathetic accounts of Communist Party policy in this period see Noreen Branson, *History of the Communist Party of Great Britain 1927-1941*,

Lawrence & Wishart, London, 1985 and Kevin Morgan, *Against Fascism and War*, Manchester University Press, Manchester, 1989.

[6] *CEJL* 1, pp592-593.

[7] *CEJL* 2, pp67-68.

[8] There is a growing literature on popular attitudes and politics during the war. Of particular interest are Angus Calder, *The People's War*, Cape, London, 1969; Arthur Marwick, 'People's War and Top People's Peace' in Alan Sked and Chris Cook (eds). *Crisis and Controversy*, Macmillan, London, 1976; Cultural History Group, 'Out of the People: The Politics of Containment 1935-1945', *Cultural Studies*, 9, Spring 1976; Clive Ponting, *1940: Myth and Reality*, Cardinal, London, 1990, Tony Mason and Peter Thompson, ' "Reflections on a revolution"? The political mood in wartime Britain' in Nick Tiratsoo, *The Attlee Years*, Pinter, London, 1991; and David Morgan and Mary Evans, *The Battle for Britain: Citizenship and Ideology in the Second World War*, Routledge, London, 1993.

[9] The *Searchlight* series as a whole has been seriously neglected in Orwell studies, but see David Costello, '*Searchlight* Books and the Quest for a People's War', *Journal of Contemporary History* Volume 24, Number 2, April, 1989 and my own unpublished paper 'George Orwell and *Searchlight*: A Radical Initiative on the Home Front'.

[10] Orwell wrote to the American journal *Partisan Review* on 15 April 1941 that 'the Labour Party, as such, has now no policy genuinely independent of the Government. Some people even think that the Left Conservatives (Eden and possibly Churchill) are more likely to adopt a Socialist policy than the Labour men': from George Orwell, *CEJL* 2, p146. Orwell's attitude towards and relationship with the Labour Party deserves further excavation.

[11] Raymond Williams, *Orwell*, Fontana, London, 1979, pp21-28.

[12] *The Lion and the Unicorn*, op.cit., pp37, 40, 41, 48, 53-54, 73, 74, 75, 112, 121.

[13] John Rodden, *The Politics of Literary Reputation*, Oxford University Press, Oxford, 1989, p180; Gregory Claeys, 'The Lion and the Unicorn: Patriotism and Orwell's Politics', *The Review of Politics*, Volume 47, Number 2, April, 1985, p193.

[14] For the later development of Orwell's ideas see in particular C. Fleay and M.L. Sanders, 'Looking into the Abyss: George Orwell at the BBC', *Journal of Contemporary History*, Volume 24, Number 3, July, 1989; Paul O'Flinn, 'Orwell and Tribune', *Literature and History*, Volume 6, Number 2, Autumn, 1982; and, of course, Bernard Crick, *George Orwell: A Life*, Penguin, Harmondsworth, 1992.

Section 2:
Film, Propaganda and Pleasure

'What wouldn't I give to grow old in a place like that': *A Canterbury Tale*

Michael O'Shaughnessy

A Canterbury Tale, written at a time when the first crisis of World War Two was over and the long term predictions were for an allied victory, was made during the summer and autumn of 1943 and released in Britain in 1944. It was produced by Michael Powell and Emeric Pressburger's Independent Pictures company, The Archers. This company had established an unusual position during the war. Like all other filmmakers Powell and Pressburger had to collaborate with and satisfy both the Ministry of Information – by producing films in support of the war effort – and their financial backers – in this case the Rank Organisation. However, they came up with their own script ideas and, once these were approved by the Ministry, they were given full support in terms of money, film-stock, facilities and personnel. Rank allowed them total freedom of control over the story and filming. This freedom was the result of their established commercial success – seven box office hits prior to *A Canterbury Tale* – and their refusal to make artistic compromises.[1]

They had had previous notable success with war effort pictures like *49th Parallel* (1941), and *The Life and Death of Colonel Blimp* (1943), and would have so again with *A Matter of Life and Death* (1946), made at the close of the war to consolidate Anglo-American relationships and chosen for the first Royal Command Film Performance at the high point of British cinema in 1946. *A Canterbury Tale*, by contrast, was a box-office failure. Only years later was it reassessed and seen as one of Powell and Pressburger's most interesting films.[2]

The film in Powell's words was about 'explaining to the Americans, and to our own people, the spiritual values and traditions we were fighting for.'[3] As such it was one of a whole host of films which aimed to define and map out the characteristics of Britishness and national identity, the cultural values of the nation, in order to unite and rally the country internally and win worldwide support for Britain's war efforts. As propaganda it has been described as a film concerned not with *how* we fight, or who we are fighting against, but what we are fighting *for*.[4] Such films reflected and contributed to the changing popular consciousness about national identity. These changes have been summarised well elsewhere.[5] In brief, it has been suggested that between 1939 and 1945 Britain went through a major shift towards popular democratic ideas which found their expression in the landslide victory of the new Labour government in 1945 and the vision of establishing a 'New Jerusalem' characterised by nationalised industries, sharing wealth and the Welfare State looking after everybody. This vision was triggered by the very experiences of war – mass mobilisation, evacuation, bombing, community living, working women – and was a reaction against the Tory policies of the 1930s which had maintained class and social inequalities.

The films offered a variety of critiques and ways of understanding British society, exploring some of the causes of social malaise and offering blueprints for future success. They looked both backwards to Britain's past and forwards to its future. Documentaries like *Dawn Guard* and the films of Humphrey Jennings exemplified this, but feature films also offered analyses of class relations – for example *Millions Like Us, Went The Day Well* – and explored what a future Britain might look like – for example *They Came To a City*.

Richards and Aldgate have pointed to two traditions for understanding British culture: the first, basically conservative, celebrates the myth of Britain as 'a timeless and mediaeval village and agricultural society', celebrating a rural and nostalgic view of the past; the second, more radical and closer to the real experiences of the majority of the population, sees Britain as an urban, industrial culture, building its future on invention and manufacture.[6] *A Canterbury Tale* clearly belongs to the first; Powell himself described it as a 'crusade against materialism.'[7] Yet even within this celebration of a rural past we can see the seeds of recognition of its outdatedness and eclipse in

42

the ambiguities and tragedy of its central character, Thomas Colpepper.

The film, in classic narrative style, sets up a series of oppositions between an old, traditional, rural, spiritual world and a new, modern, urban, materialist one. The clash of lifestyles and cultural values is presented through the four main characters. An American sergeant, Bob Johnson, an English sergeant, Peter Gibbs, and an English Land Army girl, Alison Smith, all arrive in the Kent village of Chillingbourne, like modern-day Canterbury pilgrims. They are the representatives of the new. Johnson is part of the American New World, his main interest is cinema and he is continually confronting and questioning British traditions; Peter Gibbs is a Londoner who rejects the traditional world of music in favour of a well-paid job as a cinema organist and spends his spiritually bankrupt Sundays playing cards and waiting for the pubs to open; Alison Smith is a London department store assistant. Her Land Army status emphasises women's new-found strength and wartime independence but she is linked to the past through her boyfriend archaeologist who three years earlier took her to excavation sites on the old Pilgrims' Road. As a Land Army Girl she quickly fits in with the rural lifestyle and is most closely linked with Thomas Colpepper.

Colpepper is the representative of the old world; he is the local magistrate and a member of the landed gentry (though we see him at work in the fields almost like a peasant and are told he is no millionaire). It is he who voices the traditional values of the countryside delivering benevolently paternalist lectures on the history and beauty of England's rural past. (Though the film supports Britain's war effort, this is very much an English film, indeed a southern English one as the map close-ups at the beginning of the film showing the road from Winchester to Canterbury signify.) The film is beautifully filmed in Kent locations which dwell on the lush summer vegetation and traditional architecture, shot for the most part in a luminous summerlight haze.

However, there is a dark side to this community. This is shown in the first 20 minutes of the film, shot at night in film noirish style, where we learn that the village 'girls' are threatened by 'the glueman' who attacks women at night by pouring glue on their hair. The three newcomers, showing democratic initiative, resolve to help each other uncover the mystery. Early on in the film it is made clear that Colpepper is the glueman and it seems that his traditional values are discounted by his role as sinister glueman. Yet, while the narrative trajectory is towards change and the future through the unmasking of Colpepper, each character is enriched and develops positively by what they learn from Colpepper and the old ways. Bob Johnson, linking with the traditional rural craftsmen, remembers his own ancestors' timber-building past; he is finally more concerned with understanding and appreciating the old traditions of England than seeing the latest show in London. Peter Gibbs' organ skills link him back to classical music and Christian traditions which are then articulated to the war effort as he plays the organ in Canterbury Cathedral for the latest group of embarking troops. Alison Smith recognises the beauty of the country life: 'What wouldn't I give to grow old in a place like that.' But in addition to this all three find miracle endings linked to Colpepper's spiritual beliefs, a religious English mysticism which seems positively mediaeval.

In all of this the war is identified as a key instrument of social change. In an important interchange filmed on an idyllic hillside location, Gibbs remarks: 'I'd hardly realized there was a countryside before the war,' to which Johnson replies, 'Funny that, how the war can open your eyes to a lot of things.' Canterbury Cathedral itself can now be seen clearly as bomb damage has opened up new vistas. Alison remarks: ' "Good family", "shop-girl" – rather dilapidated phrases for wartime.' She sees war as an 'earthquake', but an earthquake which throws up new exciting possibilities, displacing the old. It is also the war which gives Colpepper the chance to share his knowledge and educate the young men who are passing through Chillingbourne as part of their war-training. It is important to note that the war facilitated the development of adult education and intellectual discussion in a more open and egalitarian way than before, and one which contributed significantly to the new democratic awareness. However Colpepper's lectures in *A Canterbury Tale* articulate this towards an education of traditional values. The tensions of the film in trying to look forwards and backwards at the same time are seen in the role of a group of boys who carry out mock battles with initiative and energy symbolizing the future, while their childhood innocence reflects something of Powell's own childhood in pre-World War One Kent which he is consciously evoking in the film.[8]

Other scenes in the film provide discussion about the two worlds and their values. In all of these contrasts, the film endorses the superiority of country over city. It is during his lecture that Colpepper argues that past and present are linked in a universal and mystical democracy. This is one of the film's most cinematically exciting sequences. The use of lighting, sound and editing as we cut between Colpepper moving from dark to light, and Alison from reality to dream, prefigures the miracles that Colpepper can work. It is a magical and mystical moment realising the cinema's extra-realist possibilities. Yet Colpepper, the spokesperson for the old, is a very ambiguous character and this gives the film its complexity and edge. Identified as the villainous glueman, he is made suspicious to us by several shots of his silent reactions and also by the bachelor life he shares with his mother. It is here that the film introduces its bizarre undercurrent themes of deviant sexuality.

The glueman's activities – putting glue in women's hair to stop them going out at night and distracting the men – carry Freudian sexual overtones. Colpepper has a solitary personal life and his acts of suppression, because the soldiers 'were always with girls or after girls', speak of his own repression. Consequently the old values he represents are linked to sexual repressions often argued to be found at the heart of English culture. This is not an uncommon perception today, but to have it so explicitly presented in the 1940s was unusual; indeed, there are links with Powell's later work *Peeping Tom*, which shocked the nation in 1960. While Powell and Pressburger's work often dealt with repression it carried quite extraordinary erotic charges, in marked contrast to the 'poverty of desire' syndrome which Charles Barr has suggested characterises so much British cinema.[9] Here the symbolism of the glueman's actions and the erotic charge between Colpepper and Alison give a further dimension to the clash between past and present, old and young, aristocracy and working class.

The resolution provides romantic unions for both Alison and Bob, suggesting integration of old and new in a mystical future. But though Colpepper has partly been the instrument of this integration, he himself, the source of misogynist repression and eroticism, is left alone and isolated. Furthermore in the struggle between old and new the film recognises the passing of the old. Before Colpepper's lecture we hear Johnson read out the following lines:

> Not heaven itself upon the past has power;
> What has been has been and I have had my hour.

This is a subtle contradiction to all that Colpepper argues, and stands as an epitaph for him. While he offers all three pilgrims new life – blessings – he does penance in the shadows, unconnected to the people around him, and in particular to Alison to whom he cannot even be a surrogate father.

The film thus offers a complex and ambiguous view of the relationship between old and new – a tragic-romantic view rather than a simple celebration of the past. The box-office failure of the film at the time may be linked to a number of factors: its implied political conservatism which did not connect with popular sentiments of the time which focused on the New Jerusalem; its bizarre and unusual storyline; its so-called 'unpleasantness'.[10] Looked at now, we can see it as a *tour de force* of stylistic film-making which explores many of the tensions and complexities of English culture.

It sought to reconcile past and present, the worlds of war and peace, as shown in the opening shots of the falcon which becomes a spitfire. Like so many films of the period it espoused a strong sense of community and unity through diversity. This is made explit in the links Colpepper finds between men (*sic*) from all walks of life, both in the past and the present. The film delights in showing a number of eccentric and humorous English types who all blend together; the war unites cockneys and country lads as the young boys together help uncover the glueman mystery. However, the humour around these types is close to literary traditions which have always shown the working class and peasants as figures of amusement.

Colpepper's hierarchical position is that 'There are higher courts than the local bench of the magistrate' and the film's lighting – haloes around Gibbs, sudden burst of sunlight on Colpepper – and its soundtrack – choirs of heavenly angels – support this. Powell and Pressburger's individualistic romanticism is at odds with the coming bureaucracies of an egalitarian society, implicitly critiqued in their view of heaven as a black and white world of order and conformity in *A Matter of Life and Death*. *A Canterbury Tale's* conservatism is found in its greater interest in looking back rather than forward. Yet while its ultimate political position displaces serious questions of democracy and social change and avoids examining the world of industry and the city, as so much British culture has done, it offers us a lushness, a mystical tradition, an eroticism and a move beyond cinematic realism which expand some of the more traditional film versions of Englishness into new and exciting areas, and which link with the cinematic/TV dreams of later British film-makers like Derek

A CANTERBURY TALE

Jarman, Peter Greenaway and Dennis Potter.

NOTES

[1] Powell comments: '*A Canterbury Tale* looked on the surface conventional, but it was filled with subversive material. Emeric's story, worthy of Maupassant, was too continental for Rank and Davis. But we were so sublimely confident, so sure of ourselves, that nobody dared to say out loud what they were thinking, and they obediently put the money up for it. We had never had a failure.' Michael Powell, *A Life In Movies*, Heinemann, London, 1986, p438.

[2] 'It was not until thirty three years later, at the retrospective of our films organized by the British Film Institute in 1977, that it was recognised as one of our most orginal, iconoclastic and entertaining films.' *ibid.*, pp451-452.

[3] *Ibid.*, p437.

[4] '*A Canterbury Tale* is a new story about Britain, her unchangng beauty and traditions, and of the Old Pilgrims and the New. As the last scene of the picture fades away, to those who see it and are British there will come a feeling – just for a moment – of wishing to be silent, as the thoughts flash through one's mind: "These things I have just seen and heard are all my parents taught me. That is Britain, that is me." ' *A Canterbury Tale* press book, BFI microfiche.

[5] See for example Charles Barr, *Ealing Studios*, Cameron & Tayleur, London, 1977; Angus Calder, *The People's War*, 1971, Granada, London, 1971; Geoff Hurd (ed), *National Fictions: World War II in British Films and Television*, London, 1984.

[6] Jeffrey Richards and Anthony Aldgate, '*A Canterbury Tale*' in *British Cinema and Society 1930-1970*, Basil Blackwell, Oxford, 1983.

[7] Michael Powell interview with Gavin Millar on BBC 2's *Arena*, 1981.

[8] 'I had never made a film in the orchards and chestnut woods of East Kent, where I was born, and I couldn't resist it ... Wasn't every lane around Canterbury and every stone in Canterbury itself familiar to me?' Powell, *op.cit.*, p437.

[9] ' "Poverty of desire" comes to form an inevitable accompaniment to ... the notions of social responsibility and community which the British cinema, in the war years and after, so assiduously reflects and promotes.' Barr, *op.cit.*, p17. See in contrast Powell and Pressburger's *Black Narcissus*: 'It is the most erotic film that I have ever made. It is all done by suggestion, but eroticism is in every frame and image from the beginning to the end.' Powell, *op.cit.*, p584.

[10] Contemporary critics for example remarked that 'The story is silly beyond belief', *Daily Telegraph* 18 April 1944; and on the theme of the film: 'Nothing will make it either a sensible or pleasant one. This fellow may be a mystagogue with the love of England in his blood, but he is plainly a crackpot of a rather unpleasant type ... only a psychiatrist, I imagine, would be deeply interested in his behaviour.' C.A. Lejeune, *Chestnuts In Her Lap*, London, 1947.

Through a Painted Curtain: Laurence Olivier's *Henry V*

Imelda Whelehan and Deborah Cartmell

It is now a commonplace to regard Laurence Olivier's film *Henry V* as a consummate piece of wartime propaganda: filmed from June 1943 to July 1944 and premièred in London on 22 November 1944, it appropriates Shakespeare for ideological purposes. Olivier's view of the Shakespeare play coincides with dominant contemporary Shakespeare criticism, which can be seen to reflect a society fearful of change, taking refuge in a desire for an idealised hierarchical order. Graham Holderness has illustrated how in the 1940s Wilson Knight's book *The Olive and the Sword* and E.M. Tillyard's *Shakespeare's History Plays* paid timely homage to what they regard as Shakespeare's vision of national unity: 'their real ideological commitment ... was only indirectly to the order of a vanished historical state, and directly to the political and ideological problems of Britain in the late 1930s and 1940s'.[1] Wilson Knight regards Henry V, without irony, as a 'Christian warrior' and, writing in 1943, asserts that 'we need expect no Messiah, but we might at this hour turn to Shakespeare, a national prophet if ever there was one, concerned deeply with the royal soul of England.'[2]

During the war years and immediately after, criticism of the play tends to be guarded. Tillyard is critical in his overall view of the play, confidently remarking that it is flawed because it lacks the 'cosmic lore that marks the other History Plays'[3] – in short, the play does not sustain the political order which Tillyard finds so appealing in Shakespeare. Mark Van Doren, writing in America in 1939, argues that '*Henry IV* both was and is a successful play; it answers the questions it raises ... it is remembered as fabulously rich and at the same time simply ordered. *Henry V* is no such play. It has its splendours and its secondary attractions, but the forces in it are not unified'.[4] He maintains that the heroic idea is splintered and that Shakespeare himself, aware of his own artistic failure, accordingly begins the play with an apology. Derek Traversi writing for *Scrutiny* (a quarterly literary review, edited by F.R. Leavis, L.C. Knights and D.W. Harding, among others) in 1941 sees the necessity of defending the play as an English epic which 'demands in the monarch an impersonality almost tragic'.[5] The *Scrutiny* establishment take issue with Tillyard's notion of an Elizabethan world order, arguing that order is found in what Traversi later defines as Shakespeare's 'concern for permanent human values'.[6]

What becomes clear from the tenor of these criticisms is that Shakespeare's *Henry V* is generally considered within the context of his entire History cycle, and that in all cases the central concern should be with the figure of the king, whom Ellis-Fermor believes is 'a composite figure – that of the statesman-king, the leader and public man, which Shakespeare builds up gradually through the series of the political plays from *Henry VI* to *Henry V*.'[7] Similarly, when Wilson Knight says of Henry that 'this king is to be different from all predecessors, at once humble, religious, and assured in action'[8], he is not referring to historical chronology, but the chronology of Shakespeare's work. Wilson Knight implies that the Bard's vision of kingship was in a constant process of refinement, and that the qualities of good leadership are something that Shakespeare, the critics of the 1930s and 1940s and their readers then and now can fundamentally agree upon as if they are innocent of historical, cultural or political processes.

In the light of this and other observations of the play's discontinuity,[9] particularly about the role of the 'statesman king', Laurence Olivier eliminated approximately 1700 lines of the play to produce the unity which critics had found missing. The result was that Olivier's *Henry V* 'supported the mythical idea of a wholly integrated British literary culture in which Shakespeare was as meaningful to the masses as the songs of Vera Lynn'.[10] To both Olivier and critics alike the idea of Henry V as statesman king, a figurehead who can be appropriated to represent historical continuity, lineage and tradition is isolated from the play's deeper contradictions in order to represent inherent 'truths' about the English nation and its people's character –

the 'permanent human values' of Traversi's reading of the play. Just as Shakespeare presents the Earl of Essex as Henry's spiritual son, and, via the French king, reminds us that Henry is of the same stock as Edward the Black Prince,[11] Olivier gives us a picture of Henry as man of the people with a Churchillian resonance – and the cycle of British history is presented as reassuringly unbroken.

The cuts that Olivier made for his screenplay represent possible sites of discontinuity and obscurity; he omits the treatment of the traitors prior to Henry's departure for France, the threats of rape and pillage made to the people of Harfleur, Henry's exchange of gloves with Williams, the acknowledgement in prayer before battle of his father's guilt as usurper of the throne, the hanging of Bardolph, the order to slay French prisoners in reprisal for the slaughter of the English boys, Henry's bawdy exchanges with Burgundy and Catherine, and the final remarks of the Chorus which remind us that Henry's heir 'lost France and made his England bleed'.[12] The dubiousness of Henry's claim to the French throne is conveniently elided through the process of rendering the first act comic and 'stagey' and two of the more tedious scenes watchable, but at the cost of trivializing the tension between church and state which is evident in the play. Olivier's deft excision of images of conflict, usurpation and historical discontinuity creates a patriotic celebration of Henry's heroism and victory (with perhaps a faint qualification, in the interpolated scene depicting Falstaff's death at the beginning of the film; as the hostess reminds us Falstaff's lineage is even older and more fundamentally English than Henry's, residing in 'Arthur's bosom').

Until Olivier's *Henry V*, Shakespeare scholarship tended to dismiss Shakespeare on film as popularising through reduction and trivialisation.[13] In many ways it appeared that Olivier's view of the proper uses and meanings of Shakespeare was directly in accord with the literary critics of the time; his film might be regarded as a 'serious' appropriation of a text for a different medium because of its perceived dual function – as both state propaganda and as an answer to the literary critics who had both outlined major flaws with the play, and had signalled the enduring contemporary relevance of Shakespeare's history plays. Olivier seems to anticipate the major reservations of Shakespeare academics about the seemingly contradictory notion of filming Shakespeare by asserting in his Preface to the screenplay that

Shakespeare in a way 'wrote for the films'. His splitting up of the action

51

into a multitude of small scenes is almost an anticipation of film technique, and more than one of his plays seems to chafe against the cramping restrictions of the stage.[14]

This absurd statement has a curious logic when related to the writings of academics such as Wilson Knight who view the study and understanding of Shakespeare as nothing short of essential to national survival, 'since in a vital understanding of Shakespeare's work lie the seed and germ of a greater Britain';[15] perhaps such critics were prepared to stomach a 'sensitive' cinematic interpretation in order to disperse such seeds on fertile ground at a time of national emergency. Later, Olivier was to defend his editorial decisions in tones of evangelical urgency: 'I had a mission ... My country was at war; I felt Shakespeare within me, I felt the cinema within him'.[16] Indeed, one of the most powerful effects of this film is its fusion of the past into the present, coupled with its heady mixture of 'realism' and visual pyrotechnics – although herein lie certain attendant risks. Olivier most assuredly succeeds in bringing a heroic literary/historical figure 'to life', and perhaps rejuvenates a sense that the essential core of 'Englishness' is untainted by the passing of time; yet a possible obverse effect is that his audience will recognise in this ultimately sanitised vision of war that the chroniclers of great events in history are inclined, in their celebrations of the doings of the great, to omit the sufferings of the many.

The figure of the Chorus is crucial to the propagandist effects of the film, and with its opening dedication 'To the Commandos and Airborne Troops of Great Britain, the spirit of our Ancestors', it is hard not to view the fragmentation of the Chorus's speeches to voice-over as evocative of a wartime correspondent describing, through newsreel coverage and in uplifting tones, the events leading up to the victory of D-Day. Yet the figure of the Chorus should theoretically be the most dispensable in the translation from theatre to film; one function of the Chorus being to apologise for the deficiencies of the theatre in portraying the epic qualities of the story of Henry V – in particular the Battle of Agincourt itself. Another function of the Chorus appears to be to mark the disparity between the reports which comprise the annals of history versus the experiences of participants.[17] In the play, the Chorus's gloss on events is ironically counterpoised with the ensuing scenes – this is particularly clear in the prologue to Act Two where we are told that 'the youth of England are on fire' (line

1), but this is immediately followed by a scene featuring the jaundiced Eastcheap crowd (the companions of Henry V, then Prince Hal, in *Henry IV*, Parts One & Two) who seem far from expectant and are certainly not young, and serve to remind us of Henry's rejection of the now-dying Falstaff. The eulogies of the Chorus are never quite realised in the ensuing scenes. Whilst Olivier attempts to elevate the drama to match the epic tones of the Chorus, removing the most discordant episodes, his retention of this figure as voice-over in the 'filmic' section of the film suggests a latent anxiety on his part. Olivier, as we have seen, was by no means loathe to cut large sections of the play to serve his wider purpose; yet the nature of his translation of the Choric figure suggests an investment in its role as an aspect of 'authentic' Shakespeare.

The initial appearance of the Chorus as actor in the 'Globe' scenes emphasises the limitations of Elizabethan stage in comparison to the spectacle which we, the audience, are about to witness, particularly with the inclusion of the apologetic prologue in full. But Olivier's chief intention appears to be to accomplish a sense of closeness between film audience and the theatre audience we watch taking their seats for the performance. In a sense the opening scenes are subordinated to the responses they engender in the 'Elizabethan' audience – and these responses serve as object lessons in theatre history for the film's audience. One message is that such plays constituted the mass entertainment of the day, and therefore the film audience is encouraged to identify with the theatre audience. Parallels between the two are stressed when, as each actor appears on stage, the audience signals their recognition and admiration of favourite actors behind the characters, just as the film's audience is treated to a roll call of some of the most distinguished actors of the time, culminating in the entrance of Olivier himself.

After the initial scene, the Chorus directs our attention to a painted curtain depicting the coast of Southampton, and guides us from what Jorgens calls the theatrical mode to the realistic mode[18] and to full technicolor combined with William Walton's triumphal music. The passage through the painted curtain, transporting us from 1600 to 1415 (and the stylised painted scenery of Lindegaard based on Pol de Limbourg's illuminations in *Les Tres Riches Heures*[19]) recalls the movement of Dorothy from Kansas to Oz in 1939 (from black and white to colour, accompanied by George Stoll's similarly phantasmagoric music). The comparison to *The Wizard of Oz* is pertinent, because the audience, like the evacuees of war in C.S. Lewis' novel *The Lion, the Witch and the Wardrobe*, are transported to another world, a world of colour and excitement, in which the wooden acting of Olivier's Henry V is metamorphosed into the statesman king whose inspirational rhetoric paid tribute to Churchill's speeches during the blitz. Olivier has consolidated Henry into an ideological force – an historical figure who attains transhistorical relevance very much in the spirit of Wilson Knight's and Tillyard's criticism which regards Shakespeare as the spokesman of national unity.[20] James Agee's tribute to the film in 1946 testifies to the fact that Olivier's production worked as both political propaganda and legitimisation for the filming of Shakespeare.

> I was persuaded, and in part still am, that every time and place has since been in decline save one, in which one Englishman used language better than anyone has before or since, or ever shall; and ... that some of us are still capable of paying homage to the fact.[21]

Agee endorses the film as 'authentic' Shakespeare, significantly without reference to Olivier's omissions and interpolation. Agee, as representative of Shakespeare critic and film spectator, has himself been transported through the painted curtain, from the staid world of theatre to the active and more colourful world of film, and contributes to the myth that Shakespearean language 'speaks for itself' innocent of any interpretative overlay offered by director, actors or dominant cultural meanings.

While Olivier made many deletions there is one significant *addition* – that of the Battle of Agincourt itself. The play, for obvious reasons, eschews any attempt to stage the battle; rather the pivotal scenes focus on events preceding and following the battle, and there appears to be a certain irony in one of the battle vignettes – that of Pistol's cowardly ransoming of a French soldier (IV.4). Olivier chooses to delete this scene, but reproduces Act IV, Scene 1 (where Henry walks through his camp on the eve of battle) almost in its entirety. This latter scene is visualised in such a way as to remind us that Harry of England has the common touch as he debates with soldiers Bates and Williams about the king's responsibility for his soldiers' lives if his war is deemed unjust. Williams' fear that they may be cannon fodder in a war for a king who may ransom himself over their corpses hangs like a question mark over a later war for the cinema audience, despite Olivier's efforts at reassurance. When Henry (disguised) claims that his cause is 'just and his quarrel honourable', Williams replies 'That's more than we know' (Act IV, Scene 1, lines 122-4) – a response which perhaps echoed the feelings of some of Olivier's contemporaries.

Since most of the battle takes place 'offstage' in the play, Olivier has the luxury of creating a scene which is sheer visual pageant with its multitude of extras who fill the screen as the camera pans a substantial location (ironically, Enniskerry in Eire). Arguably, it is in this portion of the play that Olivier consolidates his portrait of Henry V as a hero for all times. From the scene prior to battle where Henry is portrayed as a true Christian king who cares for the lives of his men as much as for his own, we move towards an image of Henry as swashbuckler – from the St Crispin's Day speech when any reluctant soldier is offered free passage home (another possible ironic touch, one feels, for audiences of 1944) to the moment when victory is clear.

The long, uncut, shot of the French charge into battle remains breathtaking (Olivier achieved it by putting a camera on rails); once they meet the hail of arrows fired in unison by the British footsoldiers the audience enters a spectacular twilight zone where Olivier's interpretation of Shakespeare and medieval history meets the swashbuckling heroes of 1920s and 1930s Hollywood – most notably Douglas Fairbanks and Errol Flynn. Henry, in common with such screen heroes, is faced by overwhelming odds against him, and he will eventually be called upon to prove his physical prowess in hand-to-hand combat. This moment is realised when Henry, on hearing of the murder of the boys in the camp, rides alone into battle and engages in a sword fight with a French horseman;[22] after both fighters lose their swords Henry swiftly dispatches his opponent with a single blow of his fist. In another scene a group of English soldiers are seen to ambush French soldiers by dropping out of trees in the fashion of a Robin Hood film. This overt reference to a major folk hero and mythic 'merrie England', reinforces the film's sense of an essential and timeless English character with a nascent sense of justice and fairplay.[23]

With the aid of numerous intertextual references, Olivier manufactures a Henry who is the democratic statesman king (necessarily an oxymoron); he echoes Churchill ('Never in the field of human conflict was so much owed by so many to so few'), but most definitely Churchill as movie star – slim, handsome and devastatingly athletic.[24] This image of Henry is prefigured in the 'theatrical' section of the play when 'actor'-Henry, angered by the Dauphin's 'gift' of tennis balls, communicates his determination to revenge himself; on leaving the stage he tosses his crown behind him and it neatly circles the back of his throne. Even Catherine conforms in some degree to the 'damsel in distress' of the swashbuckling movies, in that she is consistently portrayed as confined; on her first appearance her lady-in-waiting unlocks a gate to admit her to a garden; when they re-enter the door is locked firmly behind her: in a sense Henry 'liberates' her from a monarchy portrayed as effete. Just as Olivier's interpretation of the play would be generally accorded by contemporary critics as the 'natural' one, so his adoption of some of the most successful formulae of popular film genres renders *Henry V* a palatable action film which subscribes to Hollywood's illusion that war is quick, bloodless and apolitical, and sustains this illusion through a contradictory admixture of realism, historical 'authenticity' and spectacle.

One of the most significant deletions is the ending in which the Chorus relates the short-lived nature of Henry's triumph. Instead we are spirited back to the Elizabethan theatre with the image of Catherine and Henry, hands clasped in betrothal (an image which links the 'realistic' to 'theatrical' mode, to the point where it is difficult for the viewer to decide whether the Catherine in the final frames remains Renée Asherson – although consistent with the narrative we return to the boy actor seen at the film's opening[25]). It is as if the couple, in the tradition of the romance, will persevere happily into the future. This at once symbolises a marriage of past and present, of film and theatre, although it is a distortion of Shakespeare's jaundiced portrait of Henry in which the sexual conquest (or rape) of Catherine is compared to his conquest of France. By naturalising contingency into 'love' and empire-building into a righteous crusade, Olivier's version is in accordance with the dominant Shakespeare critics of the period; he offers the audience an England with which they are supposed to be proud to identify, where the English fighting spirit and the immortal lines of Shakespeare make the country a force to be reckoned with. Such a reworking can be seen as analogous to the dominant view of Shakespeare's place within the National Curriculum today. In a pamphlet produced for the Government's 'think-tank', the Centre for Policy Studies, John Marenbon insists upon the teaching of Shakespeare in terms which are peculiarly close to those of Agee, Wilson Knight and Tillyard. Marenbon calls for the need for students to read Shakespeare (along with other pre-twentieth century canonical writers) in order to preserve our national heritage – as if the seeds of nationhood lie transparently in the words of the Bard. In his final evangelical words Marenbon recommends that politicians and committees must keep English literature away from the control of teachers. They must be 'distrustful of experts and chaste towards fashion. May God grant them sharpness of mind and firmness of resolve, for in the future of its language there lies the future of a nation!'[26]

But although Olivier's production contributed largely to the myth of 'authentic' Shakespeare and succeeded, as did contemporary critics, in creating another moment in the Shakespearean national heritage, there are, as we have suggested, points of fissure in the film that facilitate the possibility of dissident (or at least contradictory) readings. An important example is Burgundy's speech during the final scene of the play – a speech curiously left virtually intact. The speech is a plea for peace, not a celebration of the achievement of peace as is argued by Wilson Knight when he concludes that 'the play ends in concord'... 'Burgundy's pastoral lines crown, as with the chaplet of flowers, Shakespeare's historic sequence'.[27] Burgundy's nostalgia for the past in his meditation on the cost of war is visually accompanied by his view out of the window. Olivier presents here, as he does elsewhere in the film, a play within the play.[28] Burgundy, visually recalling the Chorus' transportation through the painted curtain, glances through the Pol de Limbourg landscape which is metamorphosed into a landscape hitherto unfamiliar in the film. Almost imperceptibly we move forward in time – the rural scenes are close to a Constable landscape, and all of a sudden the audience is confronted with two children standing before a gate. The children provide illustration for Burgundy's lines:

> Even so our houses and ourselves and children
> Have lost, or do not learn for want of time,
> The sciences that should become our country.
> But grow like savages (Act V, Scene Two, lines 56-9).

This image of the boy and girl by the gate (visually recalling the gates of Harfleur, the gates Catherine sees opening in the garden, as well as the passageways through the painted curtain and painted window) lasts only fleetingly. The children, a boy and a girl, belong to 1944 rather than 1415 – the image is photographic, the children, barefoot and poor, are superimposed on a still landscape, evocative of wartime evacuees engaged in a game of make-believe. Close inspection of this sequence reveals that they are filmed rather than photographed: the boy actually blinks. The audience's point of view has shifted: no longer are we looking *through* the painted window, but *at* it. The camera pans away from the boy and girl to reveal the painted Louvre where Burgundy was a few minutes before. Burgundy's voice-over – although mourning the passing of the old world – is blatantly reassuring and slightly patronising in tone. This is one place in the film where the morale-boosting tone of the voice-over, the contents of the speech, and the visuals are strangely at odds. A rare note of censure appears in Harry Geduld's full-length celebration of Olivier's film when he glosses over this sequence:

> Here the visuals supply a superfluous and rather too picturesque objectification of Burgundy's images of neglect, ruin and devastation; they culminate ineffectively in a glimpse of two attractive children leaning over a fence – supposedly representing the savage state to which war reduces children.[29]

Kenneth Branagh's response to this speech in his film version is to accompany it with flashbacks of his film, illustrating the casualties of Henry's victory; Olivier's image, however it may direct us to a similar response, is strangely out of keeping with the overall thrust of the film and its effect is unsettling rather than reassuring and morale-boosting.

Although the film is clearly wartime propaganda, the escapist elements which glamorise and sanitise war also at times display the limits of their own fictionality. The film is concerned with transportations from one state to another – from theatre to film and from one moment in history to another, supposedly united in a timeless location by the language of Shakespeare; but there are seams which announce the dubiousness of such an enterprise, and we are left in the final sequence back on the Elizabethan stage at the close of the performance, separated by both history and medium. The means by which such transportations have been achieved are visualised in the image of the Chorus looking through the painted curtain and Burgundy looking through the painted window, intermediaries for the spectator watching the film. It is possible that embedded in the text is a slight note of caution and a potential critique of the escapism offered by the film as a whole. If we go too far beyond the curtain or if we look too closely at the film, we may, like Dorothy when she finally comes face to face with the Wizard of Oz, find ourselves, alarmingly, very much in our own time.

NOTES

[1] G. Holderness, *Shakespeare Recycled: The Making of Historical Drama*, Harvester, Hemel Hempstead, 1992, p22.
[2] W. Knight, *The Olive and the Sword*, Oxford University Press, Oxford, 1944, pp3 and 29.
[3] E.M. Tillyard, *Shakespeare's History Plays*, Chatto, London, 1944.
[4] M. Van Doren, *Shakespeare*, Holt, New York, 1953, p144.
[5] D. Traversi, 'Henry the Fifth', *Scrutiny*, 1941, Volume IX, p364. Traversi's article represents the only account of *Henry V* in *Scrutiny* during the war years.
[6] 'Henry IV Part 1', *Scrutiny*, Volume XV, 1947.
[7] U. Ellis-Fermor, *The Frontiers of Drama*, Methuen, London, 1945, p36.
[8] Knight, *op.cit.*, p28.
[9] U. Ellis-Fermor, for example, remarks that the picture of the 'statesman king' is not carefully sustained, *op. cit.*
[10] J. Collick, *Shakespeare, Cinema and Society*, Manchester University Press, Manchester, 1989, pp48-9.
[11] The Chorus refers to 'the General of our gracious Empress' (line 30) in the Prologue to Act V; the French King refers to the Black Prince in Act II, Scene 4, line 56. All quotations from *Henry V* are taken from Gary Taylor (ed), Oxford University Press, Oxford, 1994.
[12] Epilogue, line 12.
[13] See Anthony Davies, 'Shakespeare and the Media of Film, Radio and Television: A Retrospect', *Shakespeare Survey*, 1986, pp1-11.
[14] 'The Making of *Henry V*', *Laurence Olivier's Henry V*, Lorrimer Publishing Ltd, New York, 1984.
[15] Knight, *op.cit.*, p88.
[16] Laurence Olivier, *On Acting*, Simon and Schuster, New York, 1986, p275.
[17] For further discussion of the ideological function of the Chorus, see Günter Walch, '*Henry V* as Working-House of Ideology', *Shakespeare Survey* 40, Cambridge University Press, Cambridge, 1988.
[18] Jorgens, in *Shakespeare on Film*, Indiana University Press, Bloomington, Indiana, 1977, considers three types of cinematic modes: the theatrical mode (which uses film as a transparent medium), the realistic mode (which shifts the emphasis from actors to actors in a setting) and the filmic mode (a poetic rendering). In his study of the Olivier film, Anthony Davies in *Filming Shakespeare's Plays*, Cambridge University Press, Cambridge, 1988, examines three levels of time in the film: renaissance time, medieval time and universal time. He suggests that the shift from 'narrative congruency to narrative co-operation between chorus and camera' achieves a spatial concentration which reveals 'universal time' (p29). Lorne Buchman in *Still in Movement*,

59

Oxford University Press, Oxford, 1991 (Chapter 5), considers the dialectics of filmic and theatrical spaces and discusses the manipulation of three types of space in Olivier's film: theatre space (the Globe Theatre section), the self-consciously illusionistic space (from Southampton to Agincourt) and the expansive space of cinematic movement (in the Battle of Agincourt).

[19] The careful reconstruction of the fifteenth-century illuminations is discussed by Dale Silvera, *Laurence Olivier and the Art of Film Making*, Fairleigh Dickinson University Press, N.J., 1985.

[20] A sleight of hand which Terence Hawkes succinctly describes as the 'Shakespeare Effect': 'The Shakespeare Effect is silent but deadly. It creates a barrier between the works of the Bard and the political dimensions of concrete experience. It guarantees that whatever the extent to which the play offers comment on the events surrounding its production, the audience will see and hear only something called Shakespeare,' 'Battle of the Bard', *Guardian*, 11 February 1989.

[21] In G. Mast and M. Cohen (eds), *Film Theory and Criticism*, Oxford University Press, Oxford 1974, p334.

[22] During this scene a crowd of English footsoldiers look on, and this reminds us that for the most part the English army is portrayed on foot, whereas the French are mostly on horseback. It is as if Olivier is trying to convey the impression that all the English soldiers are swashbucklers in their own right – an impression strengthened by the pre-battle portrayal of the quite literally unwieldy French. They have to be winched onto horseback by a series of ropes and pulleys.

[23] *The Adventures of Robin Hood*, directed by Michael Curtiz and starring Errol Flynn had been released in 1938, and it is likely that many filmgoers would be familiar with it.

[24] This of course *is* the picture of Olivier during the 1940s. After his marriage to Vivien Leigh in 1940 they seemed to become the Hollywood equivalent of royalty. *Olivier*, a three-part documentary televised by the BBC in February and March 1985, which contains the reminiscences of numerous fellow actors from this period, confirms this view. One might well conclude that Olivier's portrayal of Olivier is as crucial as his portrayal of Henry V.

[25] Just as Olivier's hairstyle changes back to its 'actorly' form.

[26] *English Our English: The New Orthodoxy Examined*, Centre for Policy Studies, 1987.

[27] Knight, *op.cit.*, pp39-40.

[28] Jorgens, in *Shakespeare on Film*, examines the visual motif of gates in his analysis of Olivier's *Henry V*.

[29] Harry Geduld, *Filmguide to Henry V*, Indiana University Press, Bloomington, Indiana, 1973, p46.

Dustbins, Democ and Defence: Halas and Batchelor and the Animated Film in Britain 1940–1947

Paul Wells

Despite the attention given to the achievements of British Cinema in the 1930s and 1940s, particularly in the field of documentary and propaganda, the British animated film of this period has been consistently neglected. The recent Oscar-winning success of Nick Park (*Creature Comforts* 1991, and *The Wrong Trousers* 1993) and Daniel Greaves (*Manipulation* 1992), are also seen as isolated achievements, rather than as part of a rich and varied tradition of animation in Britain. This is largely the result of prevailing interest in the 'realist' tradition which informs most dominant filmmaking practices in Britain. It is a tradition generally resisted by the animated film, but ironically, intrinsic to aspects of animation made by the Halas and Batchelor studio during the war period. Partly influenced by the documentary ethos and the Hollywood drives for a particular kind of 'realism' defined by the Disney studios, the wartime films of John Halas and Joy Batchelor are a significant, and unsung, contribution both to British filmmaking and the animated form in general.

During the late 1930s and early 1940s, the animated film flowered into a recognised art form, mainly because of the technical and aesthetic innovations of the Disney studios. If the animated film had previously been understood as 'a cartoon', lasting up to six or seven minutes, composed of a mixture of sight-gags and musical performance with some limited characterisation, Walt Disney was to ensure this perception would change. In producing *Snow White and the Seven Dwarfs* (1937), Disney had created the first full length, fully synchronised, animated film in technicolor, deploying important devices like the 'multi-plane' camera to heighten the 'naturalism' of the situations and character. Disney's heightened naturalism harnessed to fairytale narratives was readily used to ideological purpose. As early as 1933, with the 'Silly symphony', *Three Little Pigs*, the animated film demonstrated its capacity to reach and affect audiences with its resonant optimism and energy in the face of the Depression. Even in its ditty, 'Who's Afraid of the Big Bad Wolf?', the film was clearly coded as a defiant resistance to difficult times. The film proved that popular entertainment could simultaneously raise morale and provide pleasure while transmitting important political messages.

As a young man in Hungary, John Halas saw the film, and was inspired to make his own animated film. This was a simple stop-frame animation lasting one minute which became an advertisement for a local chain of butchers! Halas then worked as an apprentice graphic designer with George Pal,[1] learning much from Pal before training in design under Alexander Bortnyik and Lazslo Moholy-Nagy in Paris. He finally came to London in 1936. Three years later, he met Joy Batchelor, a London Art School graduate, with whom he formed a graphic design partnership, before they married. At the beginning of the war, Halas and Batchelor immediately became involved in advertising campaigns and making films for the Ministry of Information.

Halas recently recalled that he and Joy 'discovered early on that flexibility and adaptability were essential in order to survive' and suggested that it was 'far more difficult here to create a popular character along the lines of Mickey, Donald or Popeye as well as maintaining the momentum of the studio'.[2] Although the kind of Disney 'personality' animation Halas cites was extremely popular, it also had its drawbacks. It located animation as a form predominantly associated with children, and consequently a form that remained innocent, innocuous and lacking in artistic seriousness.

Ironically, within the context of its use as propaganda these very qualities have proved invaluable; animation can carry important messages in an accessible form which meets little resistance or suspicion in audiences. In not being defined as 'propaganda' or 'documentary', the 'cartoon' can support important ideas and information without *apparently* carrying an overt ideological or political position. There were complexities in this scenario for the British audiences during the war, however, which created difficulties for Halas and Batchelor. Though Disney made 73 films specifically for the armed services and created overt propaganda in Donald Duck vehicles like *Der Fuerher's Face* (1943), their feature length films remained free of politics. British audiences mainly saw the feature films, and perceived Disney, and by definition, 'animation' as unchallenging entertainment. Halas and Batchelor wanted to deploy animation in a different way, for more specific purposes, and therefore needed to overcome certain assumptions made by audiences.

Mass Observation issued a questionnaire to cinema-goers in Bolton at the beginning of the war to determine the frequency of visits to the cinema, the affects of certain films, and the preferences of the audience in regard to types of film watched.[3] 'Cartoons' formed the least preferred of the genres cited, but it is clear that audiences did value the animated film. One interviewee, one of the 167 men interviewed in the survey, suggests 'Cartoons are well liked by everyone, old and young',[4] and there was a genuine appreciation of the quality of Disney productions:

> I am waiting patiently for the time when I shall see Walt Disney's *Snow White and the Seven Dwarfs* which I think will be first rate entertainment. There is no doubt that this film will begin a new era in the colour cartoon industry which I think will be welcomed by the public in general.[5]

Such was the popularity of Disney films that a climate of expectation emerged in relation to the animated form which necessitated that if animation was to be used in the service of propaganda, it must exhibit both technical and aesthetic excellence, but also accord specifically with the Disney aesthetic as opposed to the more surreal or anarchic offerings of the Warner Brothers or Fleischer studios. Disney films, while having their fair share of sight-gags, rely a great deal on character comedy – for example, the amusement derived from the failings of Goofy or the frustrations of Donald Duck – and in particular, the *empathy* created for these characters. In attempting to create animation which sought to provoke pathos as well as humour, Disney introduced a model ideally suited to entertain audiences and also, crucially, in the terms of its use in wartime, to engage their sympathies. John Halas felt that it was necessary to emulate the standards of Disney, particularly in regard to design and characterisation. He knew that films made by Halas and Batchelor had to have immediately recognisable figures, like Donald or Mickey, to sustain the customary warmth and appeal associated with Disney's creations.

Although neglected since by film historians, the animated film was not neglected at the time by the Ministry of Information (MOI) in Britain, who had a clear policy with regard to propaganda, and produced a range of films 'to cover every aspect of life on the Home Front'.[6] The MOI requested that cinema exhibitors show the animated films as part of their regular programmes, sometimes offering financial incentives, as well as providing the films free of charge. They helped to fulfil the quota obligations of each cinema to show a particular number of films determined by the government in any one year. They were also shown in local halls, schools and by mobile film units. Unfortunately, the MOI films were not particularly popular. According to Geoff Brown (writing in 1976),

> ... when the words 'Ministry of Information' loomed up in the darkness, audiences often groaned audibly and cinema audiences devised various ways of reducing their pain. The films were shown with the houselights up while the audience was leaving, coming in or filling up with a double-feature supply of food; the trailer length variety, which came attached to the end of the newsreels, were projected with the screen tabs closed; some weren't shown at all.[7]

The clear antipathy demonstrated by British audiences towards MOI propaganda films made Halas and Batchelor's task even harder. Audiences preferred escapist entertainment to earnest educational films. Halas and Batchelor recognised that they needed to make entertaining films that provided information in an accessible way, and in the first instance deployed some of the strategies they used in the advertising films they made for the J. Walter Thompson agency, with whom they worked when first starting out.

The first assignment undertaken for the agency, *Carnival in the Clothes Cupboard* (for Lux Soapflakes), was a five minute animated advertisement, made in 1940. This was followed by a second commission for Unilever, once again for Lux, entitled *Fable of the*

Fabrics, and an eight minute film advertising Kellogg's Cornflakes entitled *Train Trouble*. Perhaps the most significant aspect of these advertisements, however, is the fact that they were written by maverick British filmmaker, Alexander Mackendrick, who later directed *Whiskey Galore* (1949), *The Man in the White Suit* (1951) and *The Ladykillers* (1955). This is particularly important in that Mackendrick was 'a brilliant draughtsman'[8] who brought considerable skill to the story-boarding process preceding the creation of a fully animated film. He contributed a great deal to the 'Disneyesque' feel of these early pieces because he had a strong sense of narrative continuity and character development, both key elements in Disney film (though not necessarily in other animated films). Mackendrick's sketches of a bear and a squirrel for *Train Trouble* had a round-eyed, squash'n'stretch configuration, heightening the characters' cuteness. As Halas recalls, 'It was quite near Disney'. This engaging style in turn informed Halas and Batchelor's efforts for the Ministry of Information.

The partners had been introduced to the Ministry by John Grierson, the central figure in the development of the British documentary film movement in the 1930s, who recognised that animation could become an important educational tool precisely because it seemed ideologically innocent and was also instantly accessible. Two important examples of Halas and Batchelor's wartime output for the Ministry of Information were *Dustbin Parade* (1941) and *Filling the Gap* (1941), both delightful examples of persuasive propaganda. The films demonstrate a tension between the influence of Disney and Halas' Eastern European artistic background. The sentimentality of Disney combined with an Eastern European graphic boldness and darkness created a tone of whimsical pragmatism in the films, readily understood by British audiences, and, ironically, seemed to many to be intrinsically 'British' in its character.

The opening shots in *Dustbin Parade* part-echo the European expressionist tradition while foregrounding Disneyesque characters. The doom-laden image of twilight gloom in a back alley, full of oppressive shadows and distorted buildings and railings, is lightened by the dialogue between a spinning top, an empty tube of toothpaste, a bone and a tin-can, discussing how they can be useful in the war effort. The standard Disneyesque code of anthropomorphic characterisation is extended to the railings, who tell these bewildered items that because they are metal railings, they are already signed up for the Royal Navy, adding that the government is 'looking for fellas like you'. The idea of 'recruitment' was extremely familiar to audiences, so the suggestion that these household items 'sign up' endorsed already existing notions of commitment, purpose and consensus. It also implicitly suggested that even the most apparently worthless item (person) was potentially useful and might play a worthwhile part in the cause. The household items decide to join up and visit a recruitment office composed of old boxes. A queue of items including old teapots and domestic refuse efficiently 'parade' past the registration point, where they are stamped and directed to their next destination, the factory, where they willingly volunteer to be part of a new shell. Optimism is allied with efficiency as 'Disney' meets 'Documentary'. The factory mechanism sorts through bones, metal, rags, rubber and paper, and transforms them – the rags, for example, are pressed into new uniforms, the bones become mixed with explosive in the new shells while the metal constitutes the shell itself. Despite overt displays of co-operation and understanding, the factory grinds to a halt because there is not sufficient salvage to keep production going. Using the Disney model of necessary narrative crisis, the film has disrupted the demonstrable potential for success with the possibility of failure in order to better mobilise support from the viewing public.

A propaganda film like this is essentially a consciousness-raising exercise because it posits a solution to a problem which the public can immediately recognise as something which they can actually do. Indeed, the film continues with an extra search for salvage which involves searching domestic cupboards and bins. The newspaper headline informs the viewer that Britain is 'All out for Victory' and with the collection of new materials, faster production begins, and the new shells are tested by bombing a Nazi swastika – a safely distanced, symbolic representation of the enemy. The audience are encouraged to 'Mobilise your scrap'. Animation thus remains innocent in the face of necessarily pragmatic and destructive concerns. The film is politicised by the ambiguity of the phrase 'enjoying the drop' which conjoins the notion of collecting salvage with (the direct consequence of) dropping a bomb on the enemy.

Formally, the Expressionist-style black and white graphics combine effectively with the jaunty kineticism of the Disneyesque characters, epitomised perhaps by the Mickey Mouse-like white-gloved tin-cans diving selflessly into a cauldron of hot metal, ready to be poured into new shell cases. At one level, this may be read as a painful self-sacrifice, but it has no horrors for the audience because the cartoon softens the effect that a necessary 'transformation' might have. The film highlights the transformation of one object into another – a metamorphosis from one state to another. By transposing this sacrifice onto the cans, the sacrifice is one of 'change' and not potential endangerment or death.

One of the most interesting aspects of the film is its use of natural sound and music by Ernest Mayer, which like much of the music employed in Halas and Batchelor films is 'experimental'. Sound is employed to reflect the mood and atmosphere of the context, sometimes bringing emotional insight or pessimistic overtones to a situation. This approach attempts to resist the 'happy tune' sensibility of much of the Disney output. The most dominant aspect of *Dustbin Parade* however, is its graphic design and compositional innovation. Using unusual angles and perspectives, *Dustbin Parade* draws attention to small details and taken-for-granted elements of objects and environments. Halas and Batchelor were also aided on the project by the formidably talented Len Lye and Norman McClaren,[9] who were introduced to the couple by John Grierson. Lye and McClaren made some suggestions about design and narrative, and Lye actually funded the completion of the film after the MOI funding was exhausted. Running for ten minutes, the film was eventually shown in all cinemas and deployed in many educational contexts.[10]

Filling the Gap, Halas and Batchelor's next MOI film, distances itself further from the Disney model by employing a more graphic, diagrammatic style to enhance an approach more specifically passing information than creating a cartoon-like narrative. This anticipates Disney's *Victory Through Air Power* (1943) by two years and uses many of the same techniques. Halas particularly enjoys this approach:

> I like instructional films because you can simplify shapes, make clear shapes and forms and explain it in such a way that no other technique could penetrate.[11]

Graphic symbols of a bottle (representing milk), a box (representing vegetables), and a bag (representing grain), are used throughout the film to demonstrate which 'gap' in provisions requires filling. The film attempts to explain why more prudent efforts are needed in the management and use of land in order to provide more food. A figure of a man and a cow, not explicitly 'characters', but humorous representational shapes, are employed to convey to an ordinary person the part she could play in the war effort by cultivating land. It is stressed that 6 million tons of food is consumed by farm animals alone, generating a strong competition between the need to use the land for grazing or to use it for other purposes, such as vegetable production or arable farming. Amusingly, the bag (representing grain), and the bottle (representing milk), do battle over this and ultimately establish that additional space is required which can be used as farmland. Encouraging audiences to believe that gardens can become allotments, and providing the statistic that in 1941 there were one and a half million allotments, each feeding on average five people for a year, the film then uses further diagrammatic forms to illustrate how land may be reclaimed. 'Every bit of land must play its part' is the slogan as cows graze and new vegetables dance and play, in the film's most explicit Disneyesque moment. These vegetables are so appealing to the viewer that they operate not only as potential foodstuffs but as friends and allies.

Animation helped audiences to believe that their commitment to an everyday task like growing vegetables could make a difference to the cause. The graphic symbols and comic caricatures, exemplified in the dancing vegetables, draw attention to materials, objects and processes which audiences have taken for granted in their everyday existence. Halas and Batchelor's spare diagrammatic style coupled with statistical evidence provides both insight into the problem and necessary solutions possible to achieve. The later deployment of full character animation in the film provides amusement, optimism and reassurance in the face of the problem, and implicitly suggests that it may be solved if the message is heeded.

As the war progressed, there proved to be more opportunities for experimentation in relation to the animated propaganda film, and this resulted in further distancing from the established American models. Halas and Batchelor, for example, made a series of propaganda films for distribution in the Middle East, predominantly to local communities. Scripted by Alexander Mackendrick, the 'Abu' series became a collaborative effort, both in the aesthetic and political sense, illustrating Halas' desire to work with as many people from other backgrounds and experiences as possible. Halas explained the process thus:

> I tried to work with all nationalities involved in the war. For example, the Middle East was subject to German espionage and frontal attacks. I purposely decided to meet Arab design colleagues. From Cairo, a

caricaturist visited me named Nuri, and helped me develop the character of Abu, a little Arabic boy. I think that I have a special sense for caricature. Hitler and Mussolini were my targets ... in these anti-fascist films with Abu, this little Arab boy. He was to watch out and be careful because Hitler was represented as a snake and Mussolini as a frog.

He also noted the seriousness with which the Government took the issue of animated film:

> The Ministry of Defence as well as the Foreign Office knew very well that we were capable of constructing an instrument against spying and they involved us in details about what our attitude should be. They helped us design the Arabic caricatures and write the script so it was a joint effort. Stafford Cripps [Chancellor of the Exchequer] and other ministers, they all had a chance to suggest ideas and if they were good they were utilised. It was a highly intellectual and creative period for animation.[12]

This type of collaborative effort resulted in films like *Abu's Poisoned Well* (1942), which used animation for more abstract and metaphoric purposes. Representation of real people such as Hitler and Mussolini were manipulated and distorted to reveal their ideological imperatives to an audience, thus making Nazi and Fascist objectives more explicit and consequently more repugnant. The metaphoric associations of a snake and a frog determined an identity for Hitler and Mussolini which communicated a view about them much more quickly and detrimentally than any documentary merely showing footage of them or explaining their policies. Strategies were illustrated which showed how to prevent the enemy becoming effective. These events were played out against the innocence and naivety of a little boy, who simultaneously invoked sympathy and the desire to protect, two fundamentals of effective propaganda. Such propaganda worked in the same way as fairytales, in the sense that fairytales involve children in peril, threatened by numerous unpleasant and oppressive forces, but able to survive in order to become a more experienced and effective individual. This kind of propaganda-as-fairytale illustrated the very tensions which the war itself brought into focus for many ordinary people.

In 1944, Halas and Batchelor made *Handling Ships*, the first British full length, full colour animated film. Lasting seventy minutes,

Handling Ships was an instructional film made in association with the Admiralty, to impress upon naval personnel the importance of correct procedures. The film is a combination of two dimensional collage and three dimensional model animation, and Halas explains:

> They were proper cut-out ships and wooden material ships which kept above water. The objective of that film was that millions of boats had been lost by young people driving a ship like it was a car. A naval commander called Alan Crick, a brilliant technician and sculptor working with me, had the naval knowledge. He was the one who took me to Shoreham, near Brighton, and said to me 'Here it is John, you drive this ship!' and left me alone with it. I was terrified but the ship as well as me survived.[13]

As a result of this experience Halas made an instructional film that used the graphic and diagrammatic mode of animation and created it in three dimensions. He provided detailed illustrations of the way ships and boats should operate in a variety of conditions and in relation to particular Admiralty codes, conventions and needs.

Successful projects of this kind led to further collaborations with the government in the post-war period of reconstruction. In the two years after the war, the Halas and Batchelor studio created the 'Charley' series of films, featuring Charley, an argumentative youth, always challenging government policy. Charley makes a useful comparison to Private Snafu, a character created by the Warner Brothers' studio for Frank Capra's Army-Navy Screen Magazine in 1943. The creation of Private Snafu by Theodor Geisel, later better known as 'Dr Seuss', was a direct attempt to juvenilise the approach of instructional films for young soldiers.[14] The 26 'Snafu' films were directed by some of Warner Brothers' finest animators, including Chuck Jones, Frank Tashlin and Bob Clampett, and aspired to the madcap humour of the standard Warner Brothers' cartoon. The lazy, incompetent Private Snafu complained and prevaricated and was essentially a model of how things should not be done. The 'Snafu' films carried the implicit warning that American soldiers should take care not to follow his example. This method is an anti-intellectual approach and looks to the 'form' of animation to affirm this through its association with children and modes of parental/authoritarian control.

Halas and Batchelor's Charley, however, operated differently and with exactly the opposite intention. The character of Charley was suggested by Stafford Cripps, and as Halas explains:

The idea with Charley was that he was an objector, a sourpuss, always protesting against legislation. That was his function. He asked questions so that the ministers and the parliament should have a chance to explain the actual legislation. We explained the whole socialist parliament and its new laws, and at that time, animation became popular.[15]

Charley actually featured in seven short films: *Charley in the New Towns, Charley in the New Schools, Charley in 'Your Very Good Health', Charley in the New Mines, Charley Junior's Schooldays, Charley's March of Time*, and *Robinson Charley*.[16] All sponsored by the Central Office of Information, they sought to educate by direct means, and to promote the idea of the Welfare State in a new and differently democratic Britain. Unlike Private Snafu, who was passive and disinterested, as well as being unintelligent, Charley was active, inquisitive and provocative. Though arguably less likeable, Charley facilitated an intellectualisation of the animated form as a vehicle for important contemporary topics and issues. The omnipresent Charley was an awkward 'Everyman' asking questions on behalf of those without a voice, and prefigured a model deployed in Eastern European animation made in countries suffering the oppressions of authoritarian government and Soviet intervention. Charley operated as an emblem of democracy and his character carried important symbolic overtones. He also showed that British animation was a mature form that could support significant meanings. Conversely, Private Snafu operated in the benign and innocent confines of the cartoon, a form which, ironically, had become a conservative form in the USA, used to reinforce consensus and conformity through its familiarity. The 'cartoon' was still understood as entertainment for children and young adults, and thus an 'immature' form, capable of supporting moral and behavioural strictures, but not sophisticated political questions.

The British animated film, as epitomised by the work of the Halas and Batchelor studios, flourished during a period of creative experimentation and intellectual purpose. It defined its 'Britishness' by resisting ideological 'Disnification' and the juvenilisation of the American cartoon. Halas and Batchelor politicised the animated aesthetic in more complex terms than animated films from the United States, and as a result created a unique kind of animated film that remains an important and distinctive contribution not merely to the war effort, but the art of animation.

71

I would like to thank John Halas for his kind co-operation in the preparation to this essay. I would also like to extend my thanks to Pat Kirkham and to David Thoms.

NOTES

[1] John Halas served an apprenticeship under George Pal for four years (1925-1929). In Budapest, Pal made short animated advertisements at a rate of one a day and closely monitored audience reaction to them in regard to his own technical development as an animator. Pal eventually left Budapest and established a puppet studio in Eindhoven in Holland, sponsored by Phillips Electronics Company. His promotional films led to more personal films and the establishment of the Dutch animation industry. Pal then went to Hollywood and became a major director of science fiction movies, including *The War of the Worlds* (1953).

[2] J. Halas, *Masters of Animation*, BBC Books, London, 1987, p82.

[3] Jeffrey Richards and Dorothy Sheridan (eds), *Mass Observation at the Movies*, Routledge and Kegan Paul, London, 1987, pp32-37.

[4] *Ibid.*, p90.

[5] *Ibid.*, p61.

[6] G. Brown, 'Richard Massingham: The Five Inch Film-maker' from *Sight & Sound*, Summer 1976, pp157-158.

[7] *Ibid.*, p158.

[8] Philip Kemp, *Lethal Innocence*, Methuen, London, 1991, p8.

[9] Norman McClaren and Len Lye had been associated with John Grierson and the documentary film movement in the 1930s, but came to particular prominence through their work under Grierson at the National Film Board of Canada, where they made important animated and experimental live-action films, essentially attempting to extend the vocabulary of film form. McClaren's major works include *Boogie Doodle* (1940), *Neighbours* (1952) and *Pas De Deux* (1967), while Lye's major achievements include *A Colour Box* (1935) and *Rainbow Dance* (1936).

[10] *Any Old Iron* and *Salvage with a Smile*, two live action MOI shorts, shared similar themes to *Dustbin Parade*.

[11] John Halas, interview with Paul Wells, 28 February 1994.

[12] John Halas/Paul Wells, 1994.

[13] John Halas/Paul Wells, 1994.

[14] Eric Snoodin, *Animating Culture*, Roundhouse Publishing Ltd, Oxford, 1993, p73.

[15] John Halas/Paul Wells, 1994.

[16] Roger Manvell, *Art and Animation*, Clive Farrow Ltd, Keynsham, 1980, Introduction.

Projecting the New Jerusalem: the Workers' Film Association, 1938–1946

Alan Burton

Looking back on the Labour landslide victory at the first post-war election in July 1945, influential film producer Michael Balcon declared it a 'mild revolution'.[1] As production chief at Ealing Studios he had been instrumental in forging that particular blend of documentary-realism associated with the studio during the war, and evident in such critically acclaimed features as *Nine Men* (dir. H. Watt, 1943) and *San Demetrio London* (dir. C. Frend, 1943).[2] It was widely felt at the time that British cinema had achieved its 'finest hour', to borrow a famous contemporary phrase, with films exhibiting a new maturity and 'honesty' in their representation of ordinary people doing extraordinary things. In their depictions of British society during 'The People's War', many films sought representations of what the British were fighting for; whereas the 'People's Peace' remained a far more unfocused proposition, most obviously framed in the notion that 'never again' must conditions return to the poverty and disillusionments of the 1930s.[3] Important in that respect, Nicholas Pronay has persuasively argued that documentary films, distributed by the Ministry of Information (MOI), forcefully projected peace aims at a time when Churchill's coalition government found it more expedient to get on with winning the war and remained vague on matters of post-war reconstruction. As Pronay concludes: 'by the close of World War Two, significant sections of the British people had been treated to visions of a grandiose post-war Utopia which exceeded anything promised during World War One'.[4]

A strong claim can be made for the cinema's contribution to the radicalisation of the British electorate during the Second World War. The nature and extent of that popular radicalism remains hotly contested, but the lack of attention paid to film evidence in the debate remains remarkable.[5] In general, contemporary political commentators placed little significance on the contribution of the mass media, beyond newspapers, to the 'lurch to the left'. Conservative Party Chairman, Ralph Assheton, commenting on the Labour victory immediately following the election, declared that 'throughout the war the Socialists have never ceased to preach their material gospel ... in the popular press, in yellow-backed books and pamphlets, on platforms and at street corners, and above all, by ardent disciples in guard rooms and warden's posts, on fire watches and at factory benches.'[6] As befitted a senior Conservative Party administrator, Assheton exhibited a sound grasp of the significance of socialist propaganda in determining the election victory. In contrast the wartime comments of Basil Wright are indicative of both the mood for social and political change and the faith in the role cinema could play. Writing in 1942 he commented:

> Today the realist film needs to achieve greater punch. It must be active. It must without fail and without pause devote itself to the urgencies of the moment with the same dynamic emphasis which marked the revolutionary period of the Soviet film ... I believe absolutely that the revolutionary technique is now the only technique. Whether you like it or not, we are undergoing a world social revolution here and now, and it is a revolution which must continue after the war, and continue with increasing strength. For that is the only thing the people of Britain are fighting for. It is today the job of documentary to integrate the immediate war-effort with the facts and implications of radical social and economic changes which are part and parcel of it.[7]

Other filmmakers, notably Paul Rotha and Ralph Bond, held even more progressive views, and were responsible for 53 and 17 MOI productions respectively.[8]

Looking back it seems remarkable that filmmakers holding such radical social and political sensibilities could have found such easy access to one of the dominant means of mass communication, especially when one recalls the contortions the film censors underwent during the inter-war period to keep 'controversial' images off the cinema screen. During the inter-war period the labour movement had struggled to erect a viable framework of film production, distribution and exhibition. A lack of support from crucial sections of the workers' movement, and the consequent shortage of funds, allied to effective harassment tactics from censorship boards, local government and police forces, ensured that audiences remained small and generally confined to activists.[9] Ironically, during wartime, when the censorship structures were further tightened, all filmmakers, but in particular those working on documentary shorts, either found it possible to explore social themes deemed undesirable in the 1930s, for example, *Love on the Dole*, (dir. J. Baxter, 1941), or took full advantage of an extensive government-sponsored distribution system, screening films in schools, village halls and workers' canteens, which expanded audiences for documentary films well beyond what had been achieved previously by the documentary film movement for all but the most exceptional productions. Wartime Britain offered undreamt of opportunities for progressive propaganda as far as the cinema was concerned, and constituted an important, perhaps crucial, site of influence.

It is within this general context of film, propaganda and public opinion that the activities of the labour movement's own film organisation, the Workers' Film Association (WFA) needs to be considered. It was formed 'for the purpose of providing workers' organisations associated with the Trades Union Congress (TUC), the Labour Party and the Co-operative Movement with films, projection equipment, cameras and apparatus needed for the production and the showing of films of all types.'[10] As the film organisation of the labour movement, its aims and activities were closely allied to the official position of the Parliamentary Labour Party and the TUC. After May 1940, of course, that meant the coalition government headed by Churchill, a somewhat curious position for an oppositional group.[11] However, as we shall see, its radical aims for a planned and egalitarian post-war world were not contained by that political framework. Indeed, it became clear to the electorate through the propaganda promoted by such organisations as the WFA that hopes for reconstruction lay with the Labour Party and its contribution to the wartime coalition, and that was reflected in the popular vote in 1945.

The Association's instigator and driving force was the imaginative Alderman Joseph Reeves, who as the Education Secretary of the Royal Arsenal Co-operative Society (RACS) between the wars had been innovative and influential in promoting the use of film for democratic purposes, a role he further pursued as secretary to the film section of the National Association of Co-operative Education Committees from 1936. Reeves' talents and energies were apparent to the Joint Film Committee of the TUC and Labour Party which had itself begun to explore the potential of film for propaganda purposes by the mid 1930s. His vision of a film organisation representative of the broad labour movement was realised in the summer of 1938 with the establishment of the WFA, of which he was appointed Secretary-Manager.[12] A primary aim of Reeves had always been the production of workers' films. He had supported filmmaking as part of the society activities and, more ambitiously, had been instrumental in developing the 'Five Year Film Plan' of the four Metropolitan Co-operative Societies – Royal Arsenal, London, South Suburban and Enfield Highway – which commenced with the Popular Front classic, *Advance Democracy* (dir. R. Bond, 1938), produced by Basil Wright's Realist Film Unit. He wished to extend such activities and no doubt perceived in the WFA a notable opportunity to do so. The purpose of labour movement films was explained in the first WFA catalogue: 'the workers are not justified in expecting organisations which depend on the functioning of Capitalist Society, to provide them with films which seek to expose the contradictions in a capitalistic economy'.[13] In offering to supply a script, recommend production units and to supervise the production of an agreed project, the WFA hoped to expand the production of films by democratic and progressive groups. Some success was attained in the first year with the production of nine films, which included commissions for the Royal Arsenal Co-operative Society, the Woodcraft Folk and the Amalgamated Union of Building Trade Workers. The latter film, *The Builders* (dir. unknown, 1939), was greeted by the Secretary of the Association of Cine Technicians as the first film by a British trade union, and he perceived it as an important weapon to 'be used to strengthen the Trade Union Movement so that, come what may, we shall more forcibly realise our real freedom'.[14]

Progress was seriously curtailed by the outbreak of war and its attendant confusions and restrictions. Operations were maintained by a small nucleus of staff, but such production that was possible scarcely achieved Reeves' pre-war aspirations. In the period up to May 1941 the experience and energy of Reeves were lost whilst he acted as an adviser to the MOI, but it seems that his particular skills (and ambitions) were not fully appreciated and he was allowed to return to the WFA.[15] Despite an internal reorganisation of film production in 1942, 35mm work being undertaken on behalf of the WFA by the Co-operative Wholesale Society (CWS) film unit, and 16mm work being the responsibility of Pioneer Films (the production unit of the London Co-operative Society), the Association was disappointed that production remained 'our weak section'.[16] Little was produced beyond a series of short films for co-operative societies.[17] Turnover for film production which had stood at over £578 in 1940, had declined to a little over £40 by 1942. A more significant, though ultimately disappointing, project was the Association's participation in the production of *The Two Good Fairies* (dir. G. Burger, 1943) sponsored by the Scottish Co-operative Wholesale Society (SCWS). The film promoted the Beveridge Plan (in addition to the SCWS) and illustrated film's role in widening discussion about reconstruction and welfare, two of the key components of the emerging wartime social consensus. A reviewer for *Documentary Newsletter*, the journal of the documentary film movement, although critical of this over-idealistic and ponderous film, congratulated the Co-op 'that such an important and progressive movement should play a leading part in *this field of propaganda for the post-war world*'[18] [emphasis added]. Labour activists were advised to 'provide their constituents with an opportunity of seeing films which give visual point to the great injustices which the Report sets out'.[19]

The WFA's principal activity was providing film shows, with films drawn from established libraries like Gaumont British and the General Post Office, and after the commencement of the war, the MOI, to supplement those directly obtained from the labour movement. Before the war there was widespread interest in film propaganda by labour groups, with specialised distribution of progressive material by such organisations as Kino (a communist-influenced organisation founded in 1935 and quickly becoming the most important distributor and exhibitor of working-class films) and the CWS. Reeves had sought to consolidate and expand that activity through the WFA, yet once again was thwarted by the onset of hostilities. It had to be admitted that 'film shows were few and far between and the black-out made even the most enthusiastic hesitate before arranging a film show'.[20] However, the Association made a remarkable advance between 1940 and 1942, both in terms of the provision of 'road shows' and film hire. The stimulus came from the entry of Soviet Russia into the war in 1941. The WFA secured 'the exclusive distribution rights to the great proportion of Russian films released for showing on sub-standard [16mm] stock'.[21] Within a year over two hundred Soviet films were offered by the library through an arrangement with the Soviet War News Film Agency. Kenneth Morgan reminds us of the significance of Russia's entry into the war and of 'the enthusiasm undeniably generated by the Red Army, especially during the period after the battle of Stalingrad with the resultant pressure for a 'second front' in western Europe in 1943', and how it represented 'an essential element of the radical (and, by implication, pro-Labour) tide of opinion'.[22] In 1942 the WFA also became distributors on behalf of the Polish, Czechoslovak and Chinese governments, followed by the Norwegian, Belgian and the Free French in 1943. Furthermore, through an arrangement in 1942 with Pioneer Films, by which that unit would act as producer of 16mm films for the WFA, further films came to be at the disposal of the Association. Judging from contemporary accounts given in *Co-operative News*, those films were amongst the most radical productions of the early war years.[23]

The WFA's contribution to the radicalisation of political opinion in wartime was achieved by its impressive film show and film hire activities. Income from film hire expanded three-fold between 1940 and 1942, whilst returns for road shows increased dramatically by almost twentyfold in the same period. For 1942 that meant 548 roadshows. To maintain the service, scarce equipment had to be borrowed from sympathetic co-operative societies and trade union branches. In 1943 a Wolseley car was purchased to facilitate the transportation of film and equipment, and annual road shows were increased to 890. Annual film hire for that year reached 15,984 reels. In 1942 a second library of films was established in Glasgow, with the SCWS acting as the Scottish distribution agents and offering a film service utilising its three mobile film units, with the result that the WFA Projection Service became available anywhere on the British mainland.

By 1944 the WFA film library boasted 1000 titles. Organisations desiring to use the film service were left in little doubt as to the purpose of the exercise. In that year the WFA catalogue offered 'to provide democratic bodies with film exhibitions to illustrate lectures on the Social Security proposals of the Beveridge Report' and recommended apposite titles. Further shows were grouped under the subjects of

Educational Advance, Housing and Town Planning and the Nation's Health, and prominently featured at the front of the catalogue. Such material clearly integrated with those debates on which reconstruction centred and the films offered were largely the progressive documentary shorts sponsored by wartime ministries and kindred bodies; films such as Rotha's *Land of Promise* (1945) for the Gas Council and *Home of the People* (dir. K. Mander, 1945) sponsored by the *Daily Herald*. The aim was educational and patrons of the film service were informed that 'The public needs enlightenment on all these subjects and that post-war plans cannot be made without knowledge'.[24] Furthermore, organisations were urged to 'study all reports dealing with social problems and proposed reports, and to use their special films as an effective method of illustration.'[25] As would be expected, the bulk of roadshows and film hirings were by labour movement organisations – co-operative education committees, Labour Party branches and local trades councils. However, opportunities were also found or created that put the WFA's propaganda before more general audiences. A regular user of the Association's services was the expanding film society movement, which screened artistic, educational and technical films to its members. A more interesting strategy adopted by the WFA was its provision of free filmshows to gatherings of the population displaced by wartime military or industrial demand. Typical of that activity were WFA film exhibitions in south London's deep shelters, to audiences fearful of flying bombs or whose homes had been shattered. The shows commenced in September 1944 and were presented twice nightly on six evenings a week. Organisers were keen that films provided 'not only entertainment, but a reasonable measure of education' and it was 'noted that the social and documentary film makes a great appeal'.[26]

Earlier in 1942 the Association had made an arrangement with the Workers' Travel Association and the Holiday Fellowship to supply weekly programmes of films for their hostels, the accommodation having been contracted to the Ministry of Supply for use by migrant workers. Here the WFA found fertile ground for their 'propaganda with entertainment'. It is difficult to establish the extent of such activities and audience size, yet it is safe to surmise that, on a regular basis, thousands of citizens were willingly subjected to progressive ideas, and, where possible, also provided with the opportunity of discussing the issues raised. And that in addition to the enormous numbers viewing non-theatrically released MOI documentaries, as well as the millions who attended the commercial cinema each week who were sometimes presented with an idealistic/optimistic image of post-war society through feature films.[27]

There remains one final WFA activity of some importance. It displays a clear faith in the value of the medium of film as a weapon of propaganda, as well as indicating the expansive wartime social consensus that could bring important studio chiefs like Michael Balcon shoulder to shoulder with lifelong labour movement activists. The first WFA catalogue of 1939 explained the Association's willingness 'to advise groups or organisations on how to promote summer or weekend schools for the purpose of training interested members in the use of film equipment [and] the selection of programmes'.[28] It eventually transpired that the WFA became actively engaged in organising and sponsoring educational gatherings. An annual summer school was inaugurated in October 1940, with a three-day event at St. Albans, held in collaboration with the Association of Cine Technicians. The school set a pattern, with its curriculum a mix of practical demonstration and the consideration of film as an educational and propaganda medium. It also offered an impressive roster of lecturers who provided sessions on 'The Use and Purpose of the 16mm Film by Democratic Bodies' (J. Reeves, WFA), 'Films and Propaganda' (G.H. Elvin, ACT, and Ellen Wilkinson MP), and 'The Function of the Standard and Sub-Standard Film' (Thorold Dickinson, Feature Film Maker).

The Second Workers' Film School was held at Oxford over a four-day period in July 1941, and aimed to serve two main purposes: 'Firstly, to give technical assistance to those who are responsible for the organisation of film exhibitions, and secondly, to assist those interested in the production of 16mm films for exhibition to working-class audiences'.[29] The school once again attracted influential filmmakers and Labour parliamentarians. An opening address was given by the Government Minister, Arthur Greenwood MP, and the school's chairman was George Ridley MP, the actual chairman of the WFA, and also, significantly, Private Parliamentary Secretary to the Minister of Post-War Economic Reconstruction. During his address to the 1942 WFA Summer School, at Oxford, Reeves emphasised the Association's belief in post-war planning and reconstruction, and advised the MOI 'that in our propaganda to neutral and allied countries, our war and peace aims should be presented, otherwise it would be thought that we still wished to return to the outmoded futilities of pre-war Britain'.[30] The film trade began to sit-up and take notice of such activities, concluding that 'the mere fact that the WFA can secure such responsible speakers in these days is a tribute to its significance'. *Kine Weekly* was forced to declare that 'the industry cannot be indifferent to the ideas of such enthusiasts, who are the articulate mouthpieces of considerable sections of opinion'.[31]

From 1942 onwards further weekend schools were organised, in addition to the main summer school, which was extended to a week. A weekend school in September 1942, held in London, offered a lecture on 'The Use of Films for Post-War Reconstruction' by Thomas Baird (Films Division, MOI), in addition to a session on 'Film and Reality' by Basil Wright. It is apparent that such gatherings, of up to eighty activists, focused considerable attention on the film's place in society, and framed discussion on issues such as the nature of the post-war world. That was the theme of a presentation by noted documentarist, Edgar Anstey, at the 1943 WFA Summer School at Brighton, who lectured on 'Making Films For Public Instruction', and who concluded that 'We must not forget that it [film] is available in time of peace to teach us to be better builders of democracy'[32], whilst the Fifth Annual Workers' Film School held at Edgbaston in 1944 included a national conference on the 'Use of Films in Post-War Planning', attended by 300 delegates.[33] Progressive documentary filmmaker, Paul Rotha, spoke on 'The Use of Films in Preparing Young People For Their Post-War Tasks'; Joseph Reeves dealt with 'The Use of Visual Aids to Advance the Social Aims of the Workers'; George Elvin examined 'The Future of the Film Industry in This Country'; actor Bernard Miles discussed 'Should an Actor Endeavour to Use His Art as a Contribution to Social Progress?'; and commercial filmmaker Roy Boulting commented on 'The Film and the Future of Man'. In the spirit of the time, the conference held a 'Brains Trust' to debate the issues, and in addition screened three films that dealt with the post-war situation: Paul Rotha's *World of Plenty* (1943); *When We Build Again* (unidentified, but possibly sponsored by the Bournville Trust, 1944); and *Life Begins Again* (unidentified), a film made with the co-operation of the TUC.

The Annual Workers' Film School continued to attract influential speakers representing the Government and/or Labour Party, in addition to representatives of the various sectors of the cinema industry. A selection of speakers at the final two WFA film schools included Harold Laski (Labour Party), Oliver Bell (British Film Institute), Dilys Powell (film critic), Donald Alexander (documentary), Basil Dearden (feature film director), Sidney Bernstein (cinema exhibitor), Mary Field (film-maker and educationalist) and numerous technical advisers. At those schools a notable topic of discussion was the issue of nationalisation in general, and the specific nationalisation of the film industry in particular. Rank's increasingly monopolistic position within the British film industry was noted and advocates for the state-planning of the industry found sympathetic audiences. Some discussion centred on the possibility of the financially powerful co-operative movement entering the film business, and for a period the film trade nervously waited on events. It proved to be a while after the election of the majority Labour Government before some sectors of the industry were convinced that they were not to be part of the nationalisation programme.

The participation of such eminent film producers, directors, technicians and educationalists offers one of the clearest indications of the integration of the film industry with the radical mood. The war years witnessed a notable 'lurch to the left' and historians have stressed the keen debates evinced by the Beveridge Report, the striking by-election victories gained by Commonwealth candidates and other independents, and the unprecedented growth in membership of the Labour Party, regardless of the difficulties imposed by widespread population shifts, in that respect. Despite the convictions of certain Cabinet members and civil servants, the conditions of peace were widely discussed, and a progressive democratic organisation like the WFA actively sought a central role in furthering that discussion. The 'workers' school' was a traditional method adopted by the labour movement for training a core of activists for the coming struggle. The WFA Film School obviously fitted that criteria, and regardless of the dislocations of the war, it was 'thought to be well worth while to keep the school going during the war years in preparation for the peace!'[34]

The election result when it came was a stunning victory for the Labour Party. The WFA's most direct contribution to that success was the sale of £10,000 worth of loudspeaker equipment to local Labour Parties 'which added considerably to the efficiency of their electioneering campaign!'[35] However, the Association's longer term propaganda, attained at the numerous film shows, schools and discussions that were sponsored throughout the war years were arguably of more ultimate significance. As is the wont of the left, response to those propaganda activities was critical. Paul Rotha in particular, since the mid-1930s, had bemoaned the film activities of the labour movement as feeble. Further, an article that appeared in the *Documentary Newsletter* in 1947 asked 'can it be claimed that the Labour organisations have exhibited the interest in this new educational and propaganda force that one would expect of the forward-looking movement?[36] Such comment seems fair when levelled against the WFA's insipid successor, the more patriotically and less oppositionally named, National Film Association (1946-53). The new organisation had to make do without the experience and drive of Joseph Reeves who was one of the numerous Labour parliamentary successes in 1945, taking his seat for Greenwich as a Co-op-sponsored candidate. His tenacity and energy at the helm of the WFA during the war years had made it an ideological force to be reckoned with. The particular circumstances of the war years meant that its aims and ideals, reflecting those of the official labour movement, accorded closely with substantial sectors of the mainstream film industry. Taken in conjunction, aspects of the feature film, the documentary film and the activities of the WFA articulated a vision of a post-war world that motivated a hard pressed population in their fight against Nazism, and gave them something worth fighting for.

NOTES

[1] John Ellis, 'Made in Ealing', Screen, Spring 1975, p119. Balcon made the observation during an interview with Ellis in 1974.
[2] The best historical and critical examination of Ealing remains Charles Barr, Ealing Studios, C and T/D and C, London, 1977.
[3] For a good collection of essays on British Cinema in World War Two, see Philip M. Taylor (ed), Britain and the Cinema in the Second World War, MacMillan, London, 1988. For an analysis of key films see Jeffrey Richards and Anthony Aldgate, Britain Can Take It, Blackwell, London, 1986.
[4] Nicholas Pronay ' "The Land of Promise": The Projection of Peace Aims in Britain' in K.R.M. Short (ed), Film and Radio Propaganda in World War II, Croom Helm, London, 1983.
[5] See Nick Tiratsoo (ed), The Attlee Years, Pinter, London, 1991, pp1-6, for a general historiography.
[6] Quoted in Tony Mason and Peter Thompson, 'Political Mood in Wartime Britain' in Nick Tiratsoo, op.cit., p67.
[7] Basil Wright, 'Film and Reality', Documentary News Letter (DNL), March 1942, pp41-42.
[8] For further information on MOI film production see Frances Thorpe and Nicholas Pronay, British Official Films in the Second World War, Clio Press, 1980.
[9] See B. Hogenkamp, Deadly Parallels, Lawrence and Wishart, London 1986; S.G. Jones, The British Labour Movement and Film, 1918-39, RKP, London, 1987; D MacPherson (ed), British Cinema, Traditions of Independence, BFI, London, 1980.
[10] WFA Catalogue, 1939, p1.

[11] At various times the WFA was chaired by influential members of the trade union and co-operative movements and the Labour Party, including Tom O'Brien (General Council Member of the TUC), William Hewitt (Director of the SCWS) and Barbara Gould, a former National Chairman of the Labour Party.

[12] For further information on Reeves and his film activities see Alan Burton, *The People's Cinema: Film and the Co-operative Movement*, NFT, 1994, chapter 3.

[13] WFA Catalogue, 1939, p4.

[14] *DNL*, June 1940, p8.

[15] For Reeves' views on the Films Division of the MOI see J. Reeves, 'The War and Film Propaganda', *DNL*, August 1941, pp150-1.

[16] Annual Report of the WFA, 1943, p1.

[17] A WFA Newsreel was commenced in May 1941. There is no evidence that this progressed beyond the first edition. See *Labour Organiser*, May 1941, p5, and October 1941, p15.

[18] *DNL*, Jan/Feb 1944, p5.

[19] *Labour Organiser*, March 1943, p10.

[20] WFA Catalogue, 1946, p1.

[21] Annual Report of the WFA, 1942, p2.

[22] Kenneth Morgan, *Labour in Power, 1945-1951*, OUP, Oxford, 1984, pp21-22.

[23] *Co-operative News*, 9 March 1940, p4; 1 June 1940, p16; 7 September 1940, p5; and 5 October 1940, p1.

[24] WFA Catalogue, 1944, p5.

[25] *Co-operative News*, 3 July 1943, p7.

[26] *Ibid.*, 21 October 1944, p1.

[27] I have been unable to uncover any contemporary estimates for audience numbers for WFA film shows, although the organisation appeared content with the annual figure attained for the distribution of film reels quoted earlier in the text. For MOI film activities it has been estimated that in the 12 months to August 1942 an audience of twelve million was reached for official films distributed non-theatrically. See *DNL*, Feb, 1943, pp177-178. For the commercial cinema the war years have long been considered the 'Golden Age' of British Cinema when weekly attendance rose from 19 million in 1939 to 30 million in 1945.

[28] WFA Catalogue, 1939, p5.

[29] Letter, unsigned, June 24, 1941, WFA file, National Museum of Labour History (NMLH).

[30] WFA press release, n.d., WFA file, NMLH.

[31] *Kine Weekly*, 23 July 1942, p12B.

[32] *The Cinema*, 15 September 1943, p8.

[33] *Co-operative News*, 6 May 1944, p1.

[34] Annual Report of the WFA, 1943, p3.

[35] WFA Catalogue, 1945, p1.

[36] *DNL*, Jan/Feb 1947, p68.

Section 3:
Pictures and the Public

Closings and Openings: Leading Public Art Galleries During the Second World War

Robert Richardson

CLOSINGS

In the first year of the Second World War, British newspapers asked: where are the war poets?[1] They might also have asked: where are all the paintings and sculptures? The difference was that most people through common sense would have realised that they had been removed from the major galleries in order to protect them from the threat, posed by bombing, of destruction or damage.

The anticipation of war led to quite detailed plans for the safety of important national collections. As early as 1933, the recently formed Standing Commission on Museums and Galleries addressed itself to the problems of air raid precautions. This was studied intensively in the spring of 1938 by a small committee of representatives of the directors of the national institutions, which concerned itself with the practicalities of implementing and supplementing the existing plans. According to the Third Report of the Standing Commission (published in 1948 and summing up much of the wartime experience of the national museums and galleries), the Munich emergency of autumn 1938 provided a valuable test, and highlighted to the directors' committee the deficiencies in the arrangements for packing, transport and accommodation. These were considered with some urgency by a special sub-committee of the Standing Commission, which in 1939 issued a report to the national institutions stressing the importance of each institution, in consultation with HM Office of Works, making an early review of its requirements if war was declared. This was to include: the evacuation and storage of collections using both country houses and the London tube system; plans for the transporting of material by road or rail, and its security in transit; and the keeping up-to-date of arrangements, allowing for flexibility.[2]

On the evening of 23 August 1939, with the Polish crisis developing and war imminent, the most urgent measures were put into effect. By the outbreak of war they were complete, and the Standing Commission's Third Report was later to state that these initial precautions were 'carried out with remarkable smoothness and with none of the hazards which were anticipated from the prospect of immediate air attack.'[3]

To begin with, plans concentrated on Category A (that is, the most valuable) material, and further evacuations were realised according to circumstances. In 1942, the Standing Commission extended its concerns to the safety of collections in private and semi-private ownership in London and elsewhere. Owners were informed of accommodation made available with assistance from the Ministry of Works and Buildings, and the same information was given to about thirty local museums. From November 1941, for a period of six months, Neil MacLaren was seconded from the National Gallery, where he was an Assistant Keeper, to co-ordinate this evacuation scheme. Arrangements were made which involved paintings and other works of art from some twenty-five important collections, although 'the response was not as great as had been anticipated.'[4] This may have been because the scheme was operated on condition that the Exchequer would not be responsible for its expense.

Given the value of its paintings, both monetary and cultural, it is not surprising that the plans involving the National Gallery were the most elaborate. The aim was to move almost every one of its 2000 pictures to places of safe storage. Those which had been assigned to locations in Wales – the National Library of Wales at Aberystwyth, the University College of North Wales, and Penrhyn Castle at Bangor – were moved there by 2 September 1939. Subsequently there was further dispersal of material to country houses elsewhere. However, the need for flexibility which had earlier been identified became necessary because the atmospheric conditions in some of the places housing the National Gallery's collections were inadequate and inspection was made difficult by the dispersal of the collections to various places. This led, in July 1940, to a search for underground storage, and a suitable location was found at the Manod Quarry near Blaenau Festiniog. This became the repository where in August and September 1941, after complex road movements, the whole collection of the National Gallery including the library was assembled, and where it remained until the end of the war.

The Manod Quarry was selected because of the favourable conditions it offered. Although remote it could still be reached by road, and both electric power and water were available. A thickness of 200-300 feet of slate and granite covered the vast chambers used for storage. More importantly, the low and fairly constant temperature (47°F) and the relative humidity of about 95 per cent were very suitable. However, after tests on worthless panels, on which mould appeared, the construction of six large sheds within the chambers was found necessary.[5] Each was a self-contained unit with a plant-room and plenum system of ventilation. It was decided to achieve a relative humidity of 58 per cent and a temperature of 63°F, and it is a cause for admiration that these were maintained continuously for four years, with a variation of not more than 2 per cent in humidity and 1° in temperature.[6] There was a constant low illumination, for the purposes of invigilation and also to reduce the yellowing of pictures caused by total absence of light.

The arrangements of other leading national institutions were not quite so complex, but still impressive.[7] By the end of the first weeks of war, most of the Tate Gallery's pictures, again following a well prepared plan, were in places of safety: either in deep storage provided by the London tube system or at country houses. Accommodation in the country was also secured for the Wallace Collection, London and the National Galleries of Scotland, Edinburgh. The most important items of the Victoria and Albert Museum were evacuated, also early on, to Montacute House in Somerset (perishable material, along with that from the British Museum, was kept in air-conditioned accommodation in a West Country quarry). The V&A also strengthened parts of the museum to protect less valuable works, and those valuable pieces which were immovable were enclosed in heavy wooden crates. The enormous Raphael Cartoons, for example, were put into a specially constructed and air-conditioned shelter within the museum building.

The need for all these precautions was proved to be well founded, particularly for the London-based national institutions. The western half of the National Gallery was severely damaged by a bomb which exploded in the foundations. One gallery was completely destroyed together with the floors beneath it, putting out of use the West Reference Section where, before the war, the greater number of pictures had been stored. Although no fundamental damage occurred to the eastern half, almost all the glass was destroyed and ceilings were ruined. The Third Report of the Standing Commission stated: 'nine bombs fell within the area of the building and shrapnel allowed no part of it to escape altogether.'[8]

Although no other leading London public gallery suffered serious structural damage, others did not escape unharmed.[9] The National Portrait Gallery was struck twice, resulting in much broken glass, and Hertford House, home of the Wallace Collection, was also slightly damaged on two occasions. The V&A was not subject to any direct hits, but superficial damage occurred in the early war years, and in July 1944 the explosion of a flying bomb close to the museum caused extensive damage to the glass roofing. The Tate Gallery was hit by high explosive bombs in September 1940, destroying offices and roofs and seriously damaging the east wall. In addition, a bomb in front of the gallery, in May 1941, buried Frank Dobson's sculpture *Truth* – it was, somewhat symbolically, dug up undamaged.

There were limited and significant re-openings of the national art institutions, but the removal of almost all the important works of art, necessary though it was, can be thought of as a rather emphatic 'closing'. It deprived people of the opportunity to see these works just as much as if the gallery doors were constantly bolted. It also emphasises the material reality of visual art – that it exists spatially and as unique and very much physical objects. The high monetary value which many works of art have is, of course, bound up with this, but there is as well an actual physical vulnerability, a potential for being damaged or destroyed. The temporal arts of music, theatre, dance, film[10] and literature do not have the definitive existence of the visual arts, they are not open to destruction in the same way, and even if literary or musical texts are regarded as definitive, they can survive in multiple formats which retain their essential meanings. Reproduction of works of art are not directly comparable, for although they may adequately represent iconography, form and colour, they cannot successfully transmit the experience of a particular physical presence which is as difficult to define as it is to deny.

It is ironic that the famous piano recitals given by Dame Myra Hess in the National Gallery during the war can be interpreted as a less vulnerable art form – music – occupying space left vacant by the vulnerability of another. Being a temporal art form gives music the possibility to escape destruction, all it needs is another segment of time to exist again. The triumph of Myra Hess (beautifully captured in Humphrey Jennings' 1942 film *Listen to Britain*) was the defiant statement that art and culture, regardless of different art forms, could assert themselves in the face of barbarism.

If the disappearance into safe storage of many of the nation's paintings and sculptures was one type of 'closing', another less tangible one can also be perceived to have occurred. The Second World War was a door closing on two preceding decades which were without doubt, as far as museums and galleries are concerned, one of the most intense periods of examination and development. After previously being involved with initiatives for public libraries, the Carnegie United Kingdom Trustees had, in 1926, turned their attention to museums and convened a conference on museums and education. The result of this was the commissioning of a report and survey from Sir Henry Miers, a member of the 1919 Ministry of Reconstruction's Adult Education Committee on Libraries and Museums, and formerly the Vice-Chancellor of Manchester University. Published in 1928, the Miers Report was a comprehensive survey primarily concerned with the more general type of provincial museum, but there was nevertheless a section reserved for 'Picture galleries'.[11] The report instigated action and the Carnegie Trust subsequently directed funds towards a number of areas of organisation and development – for example, funds were granted to the Museums Association, establishing a diploma scheme to raise and guarantee standards.

Miers had good reason to ignore national institutions, since he knew they were the subject of a Royal Commission (which reported in 1929 and 1930).[12] Like the Miers Report, the Royal Commission on National Museums and Galleries led to concrete and practical consequences. The Standing Commission on Museums and Galleries was constituted by Treasury Minute in November 1930 as an advisory body. Before the war it published two reports, and has continued with its work of reports, surveys and advising and lobbying on behalf of museums and galleries to the present day – changing its name to the Museums and Galleries Commission in 1981.

In 1938 a follow-up to the Miers Report was published. Researched and written by S.F. Markham,[13] Miers' assistant in 1927-28, it paid more attention than the 1928 Report to provincial art galleries, finding that unlike other types of museum they had made little progress towards the more coherent displays which Miers had advocated. The Second World War prevented Markham, unlike Miers, from being a spur towards initiatives. In particular, it prevented the realisation of Markham's recommendation for the overseeing of museums by a central government body – that is, a grants board similar to that of the universities. This was under consideration by the Ministry of Education when war broke out, and the Minister, Lord de la Warr, was sympathetic to the idea.

Perhaps more important than the interruption to any particular development was the more general 'closing' which the Second World War brought to art galleries and to museums. It ended the momentum of an extremely productive period, as if the gears of a vehicle moving from third into top were suddenly crashed into neutral. A leading authority on the development of museums and galleries in Britain quite rightly regards the two major wars of this century as one of the reasons why these institutions often failed to reach beyond mediocrity. The wars were critically to undermine staff recruitment and availability as well as the continuity of work.[14]

OPENINGS

As well as these 'closings' involving the removal of pictures and the ending of a significant period of development, the war can also be interpreted as bringing 'openings' to Britain's public art galleries. From the spring of 1940, on the recommendation of the Standing Commission, most of the national museums and galleries achieved limited re-openings, although large scale bombing checked this development.[15] The National Gallery began a series of special exhibitions, as did the V&A until flying bomb attacks forced closure again in 1944. Some of the National Portrait Gallery's rooms were re-opened in March 1942, for both its own and outside exhibitions. The Tate Gallery, due to bomb damage, was not able to open at all, but provided exhibitions at the National Gallery. In Edinburgh, a limited re-opening of the National Gallery of Scotland took place from December 1940, while in Cardiff the National Museum of Wales managed to remain open throughout the war (storing valuable material, and replacing it with duplicates or less important works from the reserve collection).

War often provides a vehicle for scientific progress (albeit for the wrong reasons), but it can also generate enthusiasm for the arts – probably because they are seen as repositories for meanings which help to make sense of a situation which brings both epic events and personal loss. The limited re-openings attracted many visitors. At the National Gallery of Scotland the temporary exhibitions, held on average every three weeks, met with attendance figures of three or four times those of the pre-war level. In Cardiff attendance also reached record heights.

These temporary exhibitions were organised by the galleries themselves or in collaboration with the British Council, Government departments or the Council for the Encouragement of Music and the Arts (CEMA), the wartime organisation from which in 1945 the Arts Council was to evolve. Many temporary exhibitions were directly influenced by the war. The iconography of war was represented in the work of the War Artists.[16] Their images included both military campaigns and the home front. This reflected the war itself, as the entire population was the front line for air raids and civilian workers provided the technology for striking back and achieving victory. The text for a 1942 War Artists' exhibition catalogue stated that artists should not be limited to the battlefield, but look for subject matter 'in the blast furnace, the shipyard or village street.'[17] From July 1940, the National Gallery placed a number of its rooms at the disposal of the War Artists' Advisory Committee. A constantly changing and frequently enlarged exhibition was held continuously until May 1945,[18] and amongst the works shown were Henry Moore's tube shelter drawings with their powerful images of endurance and Stanley Spencer's memorable paintings of workers in the Glasgow shipyards. By March 1942, there were also three separate exhibitions of work by War Artists available for showing in the provinces. These were selected by CEMA, and included work by Edward Bawden, Graham Sutherland and Paul Nash.

There were exhibitions in which iconography emphasised the land being defended. This was best exemplified by the *Recording Britain* project, organised by the Pilgrim Trust. Artists were chosen with the aim of recording in water colour, gouache, pen or pencil 'any landscape, coast-line, village or city street, or ceremony characteristic of a period and of a district, and in danger of destruction or injury at the present time.'[19] *Recording Britain* exhibitions were held at the

National Gallery in 1941, 1942 and 1943, and, as with the War Artists, these were put at CEMA's disposal for circulation throughout the country.

Recording Britain is the patriotism of firm and controlled resolve, rather than a strident nationalism, which in the temporary exhibitions as a whole was absent. Eliot's 'History is now and England'[20] also seems to apply, with more emphasis on the *history being made* than the *historical*. The sense of a 'people's war' was not only present in exhibitions being taken to factories, British restaurants,[21] and military camps, but also in the promotion of exhibitions by those waging the war, either in the armed forces or on the home front. There were exhibitions by staff at factories, who suggested the showing of their own work after the circulation of CEMA exhibitions.[22] The National Portrait Gallery began a limited re-opening, in March 1942, with an exhibition of art and handicraft by 'all ranks and nationalities'[23] of London Command, and this was followed by artists on balloon barrage sites. In 1943, as well as exhibitions by the 'official' Middle East War Artists, the NPG also showed separate exhibitions of arts and handicrafts by women serving in the WAAF and WRNS.

There were of course exhibitions which had no direct links with the war. Indeed, Hertford House, stripped of the Wallace Collection, became the venue for a British Council exhibition which but for the war would have been shown at the 1940 Venice Biennale. When individual artists were featured without reference to the war – there was for example a CEMA touring exhibition of 'Moore-Piper-Sutherland' – they were invariably British, creating a patriotic subtext, and in this sense there is an indirect reference to the war. When an internationalism existed, it usually related to Britain's political and military alliances. In 1941, the National Gallery of Scotland held an *Art of Our Allies* exhibition, arranged in conjunction with the British Council. This collaboration continued in the years which followed, with a series of temporary exhibitions specifically illustrating the life, art and culture of: Czechoslovakia, the Netherlands, Poland, Norway, Yugoslavia, Belgium, Greece, USSR, France, China and United States. Another recognition of the Allies was the fund-raising exhibitions at Hertford House. In the summer of 1942, there was an *Artists Aid Russia* exhibition, and an *Artists Aid China* exhibition followed in spring 1943. As their names suggest, these were exhibitions of work donated by British artists, and the exhibition listings show that few works were directly connected to the war; nevertheless the context is one in which the urgency of war is present.

The emphasis on temporary exhibitions brought benefits in the post-war years because it focused attention more clearly on the coherent choice and presentation of art or artefacts. This was, on the whole, lacking in the exhibition, during the pre-war years, of permanent collections, which in 1928 Miers had found suffered from congestion and stagnation. The combination of a tendency to exhibit everything and the indiscriminate acceptance of bequests created a visual and conceptual clutter. Markham was able to report in 1938 that provincial museums appeared to have followed the advice of Miers and become much more purposeful in their exhibition practice, but he found art and ethnological collections had not improved.

The number of temporary exhibitions held during the war was quite remarkable, for example, eighty were held in four and a half years at the National Gallery of Scotland. As well as keeping open its permanent collections, the National Museum of Wales sometimes ran concurrently two or three temporary exhibitions. The success of wartime temporary exhibitions must have helped to drive home to museum and gallery professionals the issue, raised by both Miers and Markham, of the desirability of greater focus when exhibiting art.

One specific innovation at the National Gallery which has a continuing influence was *The Picture of the Month* scheme. From January 1942, beginning with the newly acquired *Portrait of Margaretha de Geer* by Rembrandt, pictures were brought back from storage in Wales and exhibited for three weeks at a time.[24] The scheme was immediately popular and set an agenda for concentrating on a single work of art which many galleries have since followed. This extracting and abstracting from permanent collections of single exhibits is a recognition of the direct aesthetic engagement between viewer and painting, rather than the art historical contextualisation which usually structures collections and exhibitions. In terms of exhibition display it can also be thought of as the ultimate in specificity and coherence, and a reaction against the jumble criticised by Miers and Markham.

These temporary exhibitions, with their high attendance levels, prefigure the 'blockbuster' exhibitions which began in the wake of *Tutankhamun* in 1972. However, this type of post-war exhibition depended a great deal on marketing and publicity, which was not present so much in 1947 when at its Van Gogh exhibition the Tate, for the first time in its history, had queues forming along Millbank.[25] This seemed more a continuation of the enthusiasm for the wartime temporary exhibitions.

NOTES

I would like to thank the archivists and librarians of various national institutions for supplying me with copies of documents relevant to this chapter.

[1] B. Gardner, 'Introduction', in B. Gardner (ed), *The Terrible Rain: The War Poets 1939-1945*, Methuen, London, 1966, pxviii. 'Where are the War Poets' is also the title of a poem by C. Day Lewis. It is a riposte to this clamouring by newspapers for patriotic verse. C. Day Lewis, *Word Over All*, Cape, London, 1943, p30.

[2] As late as June 1939, correspondence between John Beresford, Secretary of the Standing Commission on Museums and Galleries, and the Office of Works, shows anxiety, on Beresford's part, that all details of transportation were not satisfactory. He was particularly concerned that the necessary road transport might be requisitioned by the War Office. However, E.N. de Normann, of HM Office of Works, was, in July, able to reassure Beresford that the lorries would be available, and also that the War Office would provide military protection for works of art in transit outside London, since New Scotland Yard had made it clear that they would only be responsible for protection within the capital. PRO, EB 3/18.

[3] Standing Commission on Museums and Galleries, *Third Report*, HMSO, London 1948, p5.

[4] *Ibid.*, p5.

[5] In 1942, a *Daily Telegraph* article stated: 'it was as though a little settlement had grown up in that place so far below the thin turf of the mountain top.' Stewart Sale, 'I visit the National Gallery in its Mountain Cave', *Daily Telegraph*, 21 March 1942.

[6] Standing Commission on Museums and Galleries, Third Report, *op.cit.*, p13.

[7] There were of course evacuations of material belonging to leading provincial collections, but these were inevitably on a more modest scale. This is well illustrated by the transferring of the contents of Leeds City Art Gallery to nearby Temple Newsam House – by tram!

[8] Standing Commission on Museums and Galleries, *Third Report*, *op.cit.*, p14.

[9] This does not include the British Museum where there was a serious level of destruction, but here it is not counted as an art gallery.

[10] Perhaps the vulnerability to chemical change of film stock should be acknowledged.

[11] Sir Henry Miers, *A Report on the Public Museums of the British Isles (other than the national museums)*, Carnegie United Kingdom Trustees, Edinburgh 1928.

[12] Royal Commission on National Museums and Galleries, *Final Report, Part 1: General Conclusions and Recommendations*, HMSO, London 1929; Royal

Commission on National Museums and Galleries, *Final Report, Part 2: Conclusions and Recommendations Relating to Individual Institutions,* HMSO, London, 1930.

[13] S.F. Markham, *A Report on the Museums and Art Galleries of the British Isles (other than the national museums),* Carnegie United Kingdom Trustees, Edinburgh 1938.

[14] E. Hooper-Greenhill, *Museum and Gallery Education,* Leicester University Press, Leicester, 1991, p61.

[15] Limited re-openings followed a request, in November 1939, from the Treasury (responsible for most of the national institutions) to the Standing Commission on Museums and Galleries, for advice on the re-opening of all or some of the national museums and galleries in London. The Commission met to discuss this on 7 December 1939. A report, dated 20 December 1939, was produced by the Commission; it recommended limited re-openings for special exhibitions. PRO, EB 3/17.

[16] The War Artists' Advisory Committee had a wide definition of 'War Artist'. It was inclusive of artists they employed, or commissioned, or from whom they purchased individual works.

[17] Eric Newton, *War Pictures at the National Gallery,* printed for the Trustees of the Gallery, 1942.

[18] The National Gallery was closed from 11 October 1940 until the end of that month, due to heavy air raids. It was also closed for a few days in 1941 for urgent roof repairs. Other than this, the exhibition of War Artists was continuous.

[19] The Pilgrim Trust's 'own words' quoted in *CEMA Bulletin* Number 28, p14, August 1942.

[20] T.S. Eliot, *Little Gidding,* Faber and Faber, London 1942.

[21] British restaurants were set up as communal eating places for civilians.

[22] *CEMA Bulletin Number 20,* December 1941 and *CEMA Bulletin* Number 22, February, 1942.

[23] From the National Portrait Gallery's *Maniments,* a document written by the Director, numbered: D 39921-1 30 D/d 43 12/43, dated: December 1943.

[24] Other examples of paintings which were a 'Picture of the Month' include: Velazquez's *The Rokeby Venus* (September, 1943), *Landscape: Sunset* by Rubens (November, 1944), and Renoir's *Les Parapluies* (April, 1945).

[25] M. Hall, *On Display,* Lund Humphries, London 1987, p20.

Two Battles:
The Panorama of War

John Rimmer

What did it look like? they will ask in 1981, and no amount of description or documentation will answer them...
War Pictures by British Artists, 1942[1]

Paul Nash, an official war artist in both world wars, painted one of the best pictures from each war; *We Are Making a New World* (1918) and *Totes Meer* (1940). Both of these were in tune with Nash's existing artistic preoccupations and also successfully addressed wartime issues. The satirically titled and nicely nonpartisan *New World* is a symbolic transformation of western Europe into a shattered and alien landscape. The more overtly propagandist *Totes Meer* deals with the shooting down of German planes attacking Britain; the transformation is now a partisan one – from *enemy* war machine to scrap metal. In the booklet which accompanied the 1942 exhibition of war pictures at the National Gallery, Eric Newton described *Totes Meer* as 'the most successful attempt so far made by any painter to depict the disaster that came to the Luftwaffe in 1940.'[2]

Newton was right to praise *Totes Meer*; his prompt recognition of its qualities anticipated many later critics. Nash was to produce many more war pictures, but they were all inferior to an image distilled from the oily scrap metal of Cowley dump. Nash's photographs of the same site exhibit a more prosaic reality, ripe for imaginative enhancement, as had been 'Monster Field', Swanage, Wittenham Clumps, and others of his 'places', similarly both photographed and painted. *Totes Meer* is closely related to his paintings of the 1930s; more so, significantly, than his less effective war paintings.

If Nash painted war pictures that did not achieve the seemingly effortless excellence of *We Are Making a New World* and *Totes Meer*, it

Figure One: Paul Nash, *Battle of Germany*, (1944)
Oil on Canvas
Imperial War Museum

Figure Two: Paul Nash, *Battle of Britain, August-October, 1940* (1941)
Oil on Canvas
Imperial War Museum

was not because he had lost interest. In *Battle of Britain* (1941) and *Battle of Germany* (1944), painted some years apart but clearly linked in their titles, large size and ambitious approach, Nash attempted to paint pictures which transcended the limits of the traditional grounded view of most of his work between the wars. As in the earlier war paintings, these pictures were intended to derive a single evocative and pertinent image from the complexity of particular campaigns.

In November 1917 Nash had written from the Western Front, in an often cited letter to his wife, Margaret, that he was:

> no longer an artist interested and curious, I am a messenger who will bring back word from the men who are fighting to those who want the war to go on for ever. Feeble, inarticulate, will be my message, but it will have a bitter truth, and may it burn their lousy souls.[3]

But just as the two wars themselves were greatly different, so were the circumstances in which Nash found himself as an artist in each of them, and the 'message' of 1917 should not be read as necessarily informing Nash's endeavours in the later war.

It can be argued, however, that his work in World War One was, almost without exception, far from 'feeble' or 'inarticulate', whereas much of his art from World War Two was, for an artist of his stature – albeit an ailing one – less powerful. This is in keeping with a conflict which produced very few painted images which dealt convincingly with the war in a visual language appropriate to the approaching mid-point of the twentieth century, and its most memorable images are photographic ones.

The two *Battle* pictures, fine and impressive paintings in their own terms, but not above criticism as depictions of war in the mid-twentieth century, need to be viewed from a number of positions. Key themes include their relation to Nash's other war paintings, from both wars, and to his transcendental landscape themes from the inter-war period. These were to mature in an impressive mid 1940s flowering, contemporary with *Battle of Germany* (Figure One). Was Nash addressing the same issues as other artists, writers and filmmakers in World War Two, and were there other painters of 'the panorama of war'?

Two final questions, and crucial ones, are whether the *Battle* paintings are good paintings – or good *war* paintings – and what the latter are considered to be, if it is acknowledged that they constitute a distinct sub-category with values that might not be applicable to the whole field of painting.

While they share many characteristics, the two *Battle* pictures are also very different. *Battle of Britain* (Figure Two) is an epic aerial panorama, in which most features are easily identifiable, while *Battle of Germany* is best described as a kind of referential abstract work, far less easily read, even with Nash's own account as a guide, but containing signs of explosions and conflict, again from an aerial viewpoint. Though Nash had played an important role in the development of modern art in Britain for more than two decades, as artist, proselytising agent, and organiser of artistic action, both these wartime works seem to suffer from his efforts to paint modern panoramas without a focal point. They lack the 'naturalness' of the earlier works and seem forced and flawed, lacking the foregrounded object which serves as principal performer in many of his pre-war paintings, and also in some of his wartime ones.

Newton, in the same wartime booklet, described *Battle of Britain* as 'a kind of prelude' to *Totes Meer* – preludial in reference to the action depicted, rather than to the dates of manufacture of the two pictures.[4] He goes on:

> ... As a picture it is not quite so satisfactory ... It is a dance of death in the upper air with the shores of Britain spread out like a map below. The arabesque of white streamers in the sky ... is all the more pregnant with meaning because of its contrast with the lazy curves of the meandering river below and the rigid formation of the oncoming aeroplanes on the right of the picture.

It is easier for later audiences to interpret the 'white streamers' that Newton saw as the 'aerial flowers' that Nash was to write of in an essay of that name published in 1945.[5] The picture, in this context, becomes a stablemate for *Flight of the Magnolia* (1944), the earlier *Chestnut Waters* (1923), and other paintings which magnify plant forms, and translate them into aerial phenomena. Although in *Battle of Britain* the source is not in plant forms, even before World War One Nash had been preoccupied with 'visions' and more specifically with the creation of imaginary aerial forms. If this strategy is weakened in *Battle of Britain* it is because the fascinating complex of vapour trails and clouds, which also appear in contemporary films and photographs, is only one part of a larger panorama which deals also with formations of planes, airfields, barrage balloons and other contemporary wartime matters, all presented in an illustrative vein, reminiscent of the informative tableaux in wartime magazines and boys' comics. There is also Nash's typical, almost amateurish, thinness of execution, in which oil paintings can look like a water colour.

The painting is generally acknowledged as representing (from a great height) the city of London, or as it might be, English civilisation in symbolic form, which is under attack from the German bombers and their escorting fighters seen at the top right. British fighters take off to intercept them. Not surprisingly, however, in a painting by Paul Nash, who was rarely troubled by notions of absolute fidelity to observed reality, the windings of the river which makes its way to the sea bear no relation to the anatomy of the Thames, beyond loosely suggesting its serpentine progress through the East End. Neither does the meeting point of river and sea refer to the real Thames estuary. The sea forms a horizontal band; from the far side of this symbolic divide the enemy comes, and above it, and over the English countryside, the battle takes place.

Nash's own characteristically inconsistent account of the picture stressed that 'Facts, here, both of science and nature are used "imaginatively" and repeated only in so far as they suggest symbols for the picture plan which itself is viewed as from the air ...'6 But whatever 'symbols for the picture plan' might be, the result of Nash's flirting with both small-scale realistic detail as well as his more usual metaphor and whimsy is a weakening of the image. If aeroplanes and smoke trails can be presented with an eagerness which is almost child-like in its honesty, then artistic integrity could also allow a more faithful account of Britain's south-eastern geography.

The landscape in *Battle of Britain* might be an uneasy panorama but much of the picture's power lies in its symbolism of a land defended against threat; unlike the landscape in *Battle of Germany* each part coheres with every other. In the later picture Nash had clearly decided to make a less illustrative work, and any coherence it possesses is a formal one of abstract forms in balance.

What do we see in *Battle of Germany* before consulting Nash's own account? Only the upper left-hand portion of the painting can be read without difficulty, though even here there is ambiguity. A large sun or moon, low in a blue-green sky, hangs over what appears to be a sheet of water. The squarish patch of sky is violently interrupted by an irregular column of smoke. To the right of the smoke, the sky, or the continuation of the area that was sky, is maroon. It is perhaps polluted by smoke and has a greenish band near horizon level. This two part sky is thus a companion to the day/night passages of *Landscape of the Vernal Equinox* (1943) and draws on earlier, similarly apocalyptic devices within his work. The lower half of the painting defies easy interpretation; it is formed largely of regularly sized brownish-grey shapes, with a central focal point of white circular forms – artillery blasts and/or parachutes below white clouds or smoke. All of these shapes are set against a mauve ground, which seems to be a continuation of the 'sea' at the left, but shadowed by, and corresponding to, the apocalyptic red sky above. This is not the bright land of *Battle of Britain*, but a dark country, incoherent even before the attention of the bombers.

Unlike *Battle of Britain*, the view here appears to be a multiple one. The upper two-thirds of the picture look across to a horizon, while the lower third, differentiated by colour and smallness of shape, seems to offer a bird's-eye view of a landscape, in corresponding to the patchwork effect of fields rather than a view of a city.

Yet the image was of a city as Nash had explained, in the way that had become customary with his war pictures:

> The moment of the picture is when the city, lying under the uncertain light of the moon, awaits the blow at her heart. In the background a gigantic column of smoke arises from the recent destruction of an outlying factory which is still fiercely burning. These two objects, pillar and moon, seem to threaten the city no less than the flights of bombers even now towering in the red sky. In contrast to the suspense of the waiting city under the quiet though baleful moon, the other half of the picture shows the opening of the bombardment ... In the central foreground, the group of floating discs descending may be part of a flight of paratroops or the crews of aircraft forced to bale out.[7]

Alongside the self-absorbed reference to his earlier transcendental painting, *Pillar and Moon*, begun in the 1930s and worked on until 1942, it is difficult to avoid the excited voice of the schoolboy in Nash's own words, with attacks on factories, and crews baling out. This city is not a place where thousands of civilians will shortly die, but in a suitably detached way 'awaits the blow at her heart'.

Nash wrote to Kenneth Clark that in this picture 'forms are used quite arbitrarily and colours by a kind of chromatic percussion with one purpose, to suggest detonation and explosion'. Clark's response was to confess 'Alas, I can't understand it ... it is sad to find oneself so little able to appreciate what is new'.[8] One recent and less bemused writer, building on the artist's own account, refined a few details, to suggest that the picture showed:

> ... a great German city just before a major air onslaught descends on it. A subsidiary raid has already started large fires in the left background; anti aircraft fire in the foreground has caused some aircrew to take to their parachutes, and take their chance of a lynching when they land. It is not necessarily Berlin – it might be Augsburg, or Munich or Frankfurt-am-Main...[9]

Despite it posing difficulties of interpretation, the picture works well as a big, bold semi abstract design; indeed both pictures, a half century on, and after recent cleanings, are impressive to see at first hand. Both exhibit Nash's inconsistency of surface. In both paintings there are areas which are barely sketched in – the enemy shore to the left in *Battle of Britain* and much of the horizon in *Battle of Germany*, for example – and other areas, notably explosions and smoke, which are relatively thickly encrusted.

However striking the two pictures, and, it should be said, this is mainly because of their large size, it is difficult to see them as 'major' war paintings; they are worthy but not 'classic' successors to *We Are Making a New World* and *Totes Meer*.

John Rothenstein, writing nearly half a century ago noted, in an otherwise appreciative essay, 'Nash's slender talent ... and the remarkable fact that he had managed to assemble a body of decent pictures ...[10] He had a point. Nash was, with Ben Nicholson, the best British artist of the inter-war period, he was a prolific painter as well as illustrator, photographer and theatre designer, but he did not make good art effortlessly. The worst of Nash, in which he seems eager to appear imaginative and innovative, but to little effect, is no better than the work of a typical 1930s English Surrealist. Nash, like most artists, was bound by limitations, but they confined him more than most other artists, and did not extend to the basic artistic skill of being able to cope with the human figure. There are few Nash pictures which are not weakened by the presence of a figure, and his leading actor is more likely to be a vegetable or inanimate form.

A comparison between the excellent *Totes Meer* and the relatively confused and inarticulate, though admired, *Menin Road* with its badly drawn and unhappily conceived soldiers shows how Nash was far stronger when non-human objects are the principals in the drama. It is possible to defend *Menin Road* on the grounds that the stiff machine-like soldiers set in a rigidly geometric landscape conformed to the fashionable Vorticist thinking, stressed the problems of human beings in existing in such a world, and gave scale to the scene. Nevertheless, it remains a poorly conceived painting.

Nash was near the end of his life when the two *Battle* pictures were painted and many of his late pictures have an elegiac quality, acknowledged at times in the titles of pictures. At the end of the essay 'Aerial Flowers' he wrote:

> But it is death I have been writing about all this time ... Death, about which we are all thinking, death, I believe, is the only solution to this problem of how to be able to fly. Personally, I feel that if death can give us that, death will be good.[11]

He was ill, often tired and lacking the energy to work, and though working for the Air Ministry, unable, because of his asthmatic condition, to go up in an aeroplane.

Denied the involvement of aerial combat experienced by the painter Sydney Carline in World War One,[12] Nash had to rely on photographs, and on his long practice of seeing and thinking imaginatively. In the midst of an epic conflict, he wanted to produce work of fittingly epic scope; 'I am passionately anxious to strike a blow on behalf of the RAF ... I have always believed in the power of pictorial art as a means of propaganda.'[13]

In the two *Battle* paintings, a number of comparisons suggest themselves. Firstly they have to be seen alongside Nash's other Second World War pictures which include pictures of British aeroplanes in flight and in or outside their hangars, pictures of crashed enemy aeroplanes including *Totes Meer* and the *Bomber* series of defeated German planes seen not merely *in* the English landscape but vanquished, it seems, by features of that landscape; and the undeveloped and untypical images of the satirical *Follow the Führer* paintings, which are sketches, in effect, for what might have become powerful works. All of these are vested with importance in Nash's oeuvre because they constitute a series of images, but it must be said that each individual picture tends to disappoint. Like *Follow the*

Führer, they are too frequently interesting ideas in need of a stronger vehicle.

Comparison can also be made with Nash's pictures from World War One: some of these paintings, for example *Ypres Salient at Night* and *Night Bombardment* (1919-20) were, in the rather self-conscious translation of flares and explosions into simplified and dynamic forms, precursors of the near abstract geometry of *Battle of Germany*.

What were Nash's fellow war artists doing? The conventional wisdom is that the art of the 1939-45 war was less good than that of the 1914-18 war. In truth the art of both wars is varied in subject and patchy in quality. For a major artist, Nash's own output was neither unified nor consistent.

There are, it should be said, relatively few pictures of battle, in any area of wartime activity. In 1942 Oxford University Press published *War Pictures by British Artists* as a series of booklets. Number three: *RAF* features only two pictures of combat out of a total of 48 illustrations. There are pictures of crashed planes, and one of a plane on patrol, but more typical are portraits – air marshals in decorated uniforms, flyers in flying gear – planes being constructed or repaired, planes being fuelled or armed, pictures of life at aerodromes.

Of the six Nash pictures illustrated, four are from his series of crashed German bombers, the fifth is *Whitley Bombers Sunning*, and the most interesting, if only because it is a picture whose title, effectively, does most of the work, is *Wellington Bomber, Drawn on the Day Hitler Invaded Belgium*. Nash has turned the shrouded nose of this plane into a predatory beak, and given it a wrathful eye.

As with the RAF book, so with other areas of activity. *War at Sea* has harbour scenes, a parade, shipbuilding, scenes on board ship (on the bridge, in the mess), and again, there are portraits of celebrities, and of serving sailors. *Army* includes the customary portraits, construction work, equipment, soldiers drilling, a gymnasium, and Ardizzone's gentle fun-poking at army stereotypes. There were other books in the series, and in these, and in other wartime books, as well as in exhibitions of war art, the mix is much the same. The impression is of a breadth and variety of subject matter, of a body of work which stresses the virtues of comradeship, organisation, and human values. Civilisation is shown not merely to be surviving, but to be thriving in difficult circumstances. Eric Newton was again perceptive in writing that ' ... the high-pitched cry of "Up Guards and at 'em!" has been replaced by the dogged slogan "Go to it!" ... The age of heroics is over ...'.[14] All of this makes the ambition and the apocalyptic character of the two Nash paintings discussed here more striking. A comparison can be made with Richard Eurich's panoramic pictures of conflict.

Eurich, born in 1903 in Bradford, and trained, like Nash, at the Slade, by the 1940s was living near Southampton and identified with the naval activities that he witnessed on the south coast. By 1942 his war paintings had secured his election as an A.R.A. As a war artist attached to the Admiralty, as Nash was to the RAF, he produced a series of panoramic pictures which reference the art of centuries long past. Compared with the two Nash paintings, they appear glazed and jewel-like, and are crowded with small scale detail in the manner of many a Renaissance picture. The stylisation of forms and the solving of problems of depiction in these Eurich paintings is strangely like an early Renaissance artist trying things for the first time – witness the rhythmical waves, soft but frozen, in *The Withdrawal From Dunkirk* (1940). Eurich avoids both academicism and a modernist spirit. Eurich himself said ' ... It seems to me that the traditional sea-painting of Van der Velde and Turner should be carried on to enrich and record our heritage.'[15] For all his preoccupation with the minutiae of war, Eurich, like Nash, was well aware that he was not working in a realist manner. Writing about his painting *Preparations for D-Day* (1944), he commented 'The funny part about it is that the whole thing is a creation of my own and has no relation to facts at all ...'.[16]

In addition to the D-Day scene, Eurich painted many wartime panoramas, including *The Withdrawal from Dunkirk* (1940), *Night Raid on Portsmouth Docks* (1941-1942), *The Raid on Bruneval Radio Location Station, 27-28 February 1942* (1943), and *Midget Submarine Attack on the Tirpitz, 22 September 1943* (1944).[17] The last two paintings have precise dates of events depicted in the titles. They thus reinforce historic specificity as does the Nash picture whose full title is *Battle of Britain August-October 1940*. In one picture *Air Fight over Portland*, commemorating an action in September 1940, Eurich was to parallel Nash in at least two other ways. Firstly Portland was the site of Nash's *Defence of Albion* (1942), in which a Sunderland flying boat defeats a U-Boat, and, secondly, Eurich, in dealing with German planes attacked by English fighters, features vapour trails as had Nash. 'The white condensation trails in the sky show where the fighters have been at work', is the satisfied report of the anonymous writer of the 'Notes on the Pictures' in *War at Sea*. The Eurich painting, however, differs from the two Nash pictures in its assumption of a viewpoint only just above ground level. We look down on frozen waves like those in the Dunkirk picture, but could quickly join the scurrying and gesticulating figures around the sandbagged gun emplacement on the hill.

That Nash's two *Battle* paintings continue the themes of much of his pre-war work, and parallel the themes of his other wartime paintings is not in doubt, but there are significant differences. In many of the 'Personality of Planes' pictures, for example, large scale aeroplanes were set against cubo-futurist backdrops, but in the two large *Battle* paintings the events, however great their import, become secondary to, and are rendered as small, against the landscape. In *Battle of Germany*, though the effect of their presence determines a large part of the picture, it is hardly possible to make out the planes. What made Nash depart from the format of, for instance, *Target Area, Whitleys over Berlin* (1941), or to take one which is more 'illustrative' in the manner of *Battle of Britain, The Augsburg Raid* (1942)? The former anticipates *Battle of Germany* in its fragmented and patchy action, and in the way in which it might be thought to imply the confusion of battle. Nash had written that 'machines were the real protagonists of this war', but in the two *Battle* pictures it is the land which has assumed vital importance.[18]

The land is *two* lands; the first, the south-eastern corner of Britain in which Nash had made his home for many years, and which is shown in the heatwave of 1940, over which much of the Battle of Britain took place; the second, Germany, not drawn from knowledge but rather from the imagination. It is a symbolically dark country, alien and confused even before the bombers come.

Which is the better picture? What makes a good painting, and what makes a good war painting? Here there are no ready answers, but it may be that the two *Battle* paintings belong in and perform better in different categories. In all of Nash's war paintings, from both wars, is manifested the resolve of a 'serious' artist to go beyond mere technical illustrations, and the implicit belief in the superiority of the imaginative powers of a creative artist. Nash's almost wilful distortions of aircraft, like the enormously enlarged tailfin of the Sunderland in *Defence of Albion*, were to upset not only his employers, but also more informed observers. Rothenstein might claim that 'The ready-made perfection of aircraft generally eluded his grasp ...'[19] but mechanical symmetry was not one of Nash's interests. But Rothenstein also wrote that 'No artist ever showed a slighter awareness of his fellow men,'[20] and in Nash's work there is little trace of the human aspects of war. Nash's London, seen under attack in *Battle of Britain*, is far from the London seen in the film *Fires were Started*, and his Kent is not the evocative landscape of Powell and Pressburger's *A Canterbury Tale*. These films, and many others like them, were rich in human detail. Nash's pictures plainly are not. But perhaps he was wise not to have attempted to include the tiny humans of Eurich's wartime panoramas, and to conclude that Nash's two *Battle* pictures don't succeed in engaging with a wartime spirit would be oversimplistic.

Battle of Britain, inferior to *Battle of Germany* as pure painting, is a compelling evocation of a land being protected from threat. The abstract forms of *Battle of Germany*, however, don't sustain Nash's detailed written account of its subject, and for me, it is more successful as a modern abstract work, with landscape references, than as a war picture.

By the time *Battle of Germany* was painted in 1944, and exhibited, the greater battles of World War Two had been won. There was no longer a compelling need for rallying cries, and Nash, having to rely partly on the accounts of airmen for something which he hadn't experienced, was able to experiment. At the end of the war, Nash wrote 'As an artist for the Air I was encouraged to regard myself as the imaginative interpreter, as a complement to the factual recorder, my opposite number ...'.[21]

Nash may not have always caught 'the mood below the surface', which Eric Newton thought the sign of the best war art, but on many occasions he did. His imaginative interpretations of the war affect the senses in multi-layered ways – then and now – far beyond the 'factual' recordings of war.

NOTES

[1] Uncredited foreword to each booklet in the series *War Pictures by British Artists*, Oxford University Press, Oxford, 1942.
[2] Eric Newton, *War Pictures at the National Gallery*, Trustees of the National Gallery, London, 1942.
[3] Letter dated 13 November 1917, but portion including extract is headed 'Three days later', quoted in Paul Nash, *Outline*, Faber, London, 1949.
[4] Newton, *op.cit.*
[5] Paul Nash, 'Aerial Flowers', *Counterpoint Magazine*, 1945. Reprinted in *Outline*, 1949.
[6] Paul Nash, note c, November 1941. Quoted in Meirion and Susie Harries, *The War Artists*, Michael Joseph, London, 1983.

[7] Paul Nash, note dated 1 October 1944. Reprinted in Alan Ross, *Colours of War*, Cape, London, 1983.

[8] Kenneth Clark, letter, 3 October 1944. Quoted in Harries, *op.cit.*

[9] M.R.D. Foot, *Art and War*, Headline, London, 1990.

[10] John Rothenstein, *Modern English Painters*, MacDonald, London, (1st edn), 1952.

[11] Nash, 'Aerial Flowers'.

[12] As an artist attached to the Royal Flying Corps, Carline wrote with clinical matter of factness of his experience of aerial combat. 'On patrol with two others we saw a Hun 2 seater taking photos 5000 ft. below us (we at 10,000). We dived on him. He put up no show, the pilot was shot and the observer leaning over tried to dive for home but he was shot and the machine crashed into the river ...' Letter February 1918. Quoted in Richard and Sydney Carline, Exhibition Catalogue, IWM 1973.

[13] Paul Nash, quoted in Penelope Curtis, *World War Two*, exhibition catalogue, Tate Gallery, Liverpool and London, 1989.

[14] Newton, *op.cit.*

[15] Richard Eurich, letter to WAAC, 10 June 1940. Quoted in *The Edge of all the Land*, exhibition catalogue, Southampton, 1994.

[16] *Ibid.*, letter to S. Schiff, 3 July 1944.

[17] Of Eurich's *Attack on a Convoy seen from the Air*, c. 1940, Newton wrote, on this occasion not very perceptively, that it was ' ... a purely descriptive document, bound together by no imaginative rhythm and therefore incoherent as a picture but interesting as a pictorial description ...' This seems unfair: Eurich's pictures may be less convincingly modern than Nash's but they do not lack a persuasive imaginative obsessiveness, like that of a miniaturist. Newton, *op.cit.*

[18] Paul Nash, 'The Personality of Planes', *Vogue*, March 1942.

[19] J. Rothenstein, 'Paul Nash as War Artist', in Margot Eates, *A Memorial Volume*, 1948.

[20] *Ibid.*

[21] Paul Nash, 'Aerial Flowers'.

Henry Moore's 'Shelter Drawings': Memory and Myth

Adrian Lewis

The 1939-45 World War saw the re-institution of the war artists scheme which had been instituted in the 1914-18 war. The War Artists Advisory Committee (WAAC), established in November 1939, patronised artists by means of either salaried fixed-term employment or specific commissions. Its chairman was Kenneth Clark, Director of the National Gallery, Controller of Home Publicity in the Ministry of Information during the blitz, and member of a range of wartime committees.

Henry Moore's major 'presentation-drawings' on the theme of London's anti-blitz underground shelters are generally regarded as the most striking artworks produced in response to the WAAC scheme. London's underground railway stations had been used briefly as shelters during the First World War and they began to be used again for the same purpose when the blitz began in September 1940, to the initial displeasure of the authorities. However their spontaneous occupation was soon accepted as a *fait accompli* and from December 1940 they became more organised and hygienic places of shelter.

Out of Moore's overall production of about 75 large finished 'shelter drawings', WAAC took 28 in all, commissioning these in batches. Moore's preliminary work was done in three or four sketchbooks, two of which survive. The one belonging to the British Museum was broken up for exhibition purposes. The other was taken apart by the Henry Moore Foundation in order to distribute its sheets to various museums[1]. This study aims to examine the production and reception of Moore's 'shelter drawings' and to consider the art historical text on

Moore as ideological representation.

The outbreak of war was disastrous for Moore's career as a sculptor because of the impossibility of buying materials, the cessation of the art market and finally, in October 1940, the bombing of his studio. Indeed, only one sculpture was begun in 1940 and Moore was not to resume sculpture until 1943. Moore had good reasons therefore for turning to another medium. Consider however Moore's own story of how he began these drawings in response to an early bombing raid on London in September 1940:

> Kenneth Clark had been made chairman of the War Artists' Committee and invited me to become an official war artist ... [but] I volunteered instead for the [Chelsea Polytechnic] course in [precision] tool-making ... When the Blitz started I was still waiting to hear from the Polytechnic ... One evening ... we returned home by Underground, taking the Northern Line train to Belsize Park station. It was a long time since I'd been down the tube. I'd noticed that long queues were forming outside Underground stations at about seven o'clock every evening but hadn't thought much about it, and now for the first time I saw people lying on the platforms at all the stations we passed ... When we got out at Belsize Park we were not allowed to leave the station because of the fierceness of the barrage. We stayed there for an hour and I was fascinated by the sight of people camping out deep under the ground ... I purposely went by tube to various parts of London to see what differences there were between the stations ... Kenneth Clark saw some of these sketches and pointed out that I now had no excuse for refusing to be an official war artist.[2]

Moore refers in his account to Clark 'seeing' the initial sketches. Turned around to put the agency on the artist, it is clear that Clark saw them because Moore made a point of showing them to him in order to take up the offer of official patronage.

The function of Moore's account is to suggest some problematic for himself around the notion of becoming a war artist. The text implies some serendipidous 'real-life' encounter impelling him to unpremeditated artistic creation, followed by external persuasion to become an official war artist. However, a different picture emerges if we fill in the gaps. Unlike his painter-contemporaries, Moore as sculptor was denied being a practitioner in his chosen medium by the war and on paper was not eligible for WAAC patronage. He needed to become a war-artist if he was to continue artistic practice, the more so since he had recently decided to give up his teaching at Chelsea School of Art rather than evacuate to Northampton with the art school. Here was an artist in search of a wartime motif and a financial *modus vivendi* without his becoming too locked into the official scheme.[3] Here also was an art administrator anxious to win Britain's most prominent artist for the war art scheme.

Moore was making drawings back at Much Hadham in Hertfordshire with a view to coming up with the goods for both himself and Clark. Why show Clark the shelter drawings if Moore did not want to persuade him into that 'invitation'? The function of Moore's account is to turn upside-down the order of prompting and motivation. Moore effaces his own worldly career moves from his own self-image as others are made to perform the task of organising and promoting his work. Moore's storyline of the chance origination of the shelter drawings is reproduced in all texts on Moore, reminding us of the extent to which, as John Glaves-Smith noted, the 'history of Henry Moore on both levels [of scholarly and popular writing] has been almost entirely an official one'.[4]

It has often been claimed that the shelter drawings bear some close unmediated relationship to a pre-existent visual/social reality. For example, the American critic Martha Davidson in 1943 assumed Moore had 'sat working in the air raid shelters'.[5] Nikolaus Pevsner, the renowned art and architectural historian, described Moore in 1944 as representing the 'truth of the shelters'.[6] British critic David Sylvester in 1946 characterised the shelter sketchbooks as 'the products of immediate observation and apperception'.[7] In a work of recent history entitled *The Blitz* (1957), Constantine Fitzgibbon used these images literally as documentary illustrations.[8] Similarly Joseph Darracott, keeper of art at the Imperial War Museum, was still claiming in 1975 that these were 'marvellous documents'.[9] We know that Moore visited various stations including Cricklewood and was fascinated by the huge warehouse 'Tilbury' shelter in London's East End near the junction of Whitechapel Road and Aldgate. He was especially interested in the Liverpool Street extension, where the track had not yet been laid but where two lines of sleeping figures could be found. However, we know from Moore's later explanation that his shelter drawings were not made in the shelters:

> I never made any sketches in the Underground ... Instead of drawing, I would wander casually past a group of people half a dozen times or so, pretending to be unaware of them. A note like 'two people under one

Figure One: Henry Moore, *Tube Shelter Perspective* (1941), chalk, pen and water-colour. Courtesy of Tate Gallery, London.
Copyright Henry Moore Foundation.

Figure Two: Henry Moore, *Pink and Green Sleepers* (1941), chalk, pen
and water-colour. Courtesy of Tate Gallery, London.
Copyright Henry Moore Foundation.

blanket' would be enough of a reminder to enable me to make a sketch next day ... I went up to London for two days each week, spending the nights in the Underground ... Then I would go back to Much Hadham and spend two days making sketches in the tear-off pad. The rest of the week I would be working on drawings to show to the War Artists' Committee.[10]

In other words, the finished drawings such as Figures One and Two were worked on over a long period at home as were the less 'finished' images on which they were based in the drawing books. They are certainly not documentary in the sense of being direct transcriptions of reality. *Tube Shelter Perspective* (Figure One), is a typical example of Moore's finished drawings presented to WAAC. We know that its production involved a roughing out stage, preparatory drawings and a transfer-process to more than one final image.[11] Moore's drawings of shelter motifs involved considerable distance, artifice, and trans-formation.[12]

Bill Brandt's photographs taken for the Ministry of Information[13] reveal a wide variety of shelters (underground garages, wine merchants' cellars, church crypts, railway arches, department stores) and different types of sleeping arrangement (platform surface, deckchairs, bunks). We see various types and patterns of bedding, informal family groupings, suitcases and bags, occasional pets, and makeshift arrangements for hanging clothes. Efforts were made to make things as homelike as possible.[14] Yet Moore's images lack particularisation of these sorts and in that sense do not speak of the creativity of others. What Moore sees, in his own words, is 'hundreds of Henry Moore Reclining Figures stretched along the platform'[15] and tunnels 'like the holes in my sculptures'.[16] What is surprising is the total absence of critical commentary (in terms of problems of closed circuitry) such statements, together with Moore's statement that he lost interest in the motif once the shelters became better organised and more sanitary,[17] have received.

We are fortunate to have detailed descriptions of shelter life amassed by the pioneer social research organisation Mass Observation, co-founded by Tom Harrisson and Charles Madge in 1936.[18] Initially a makeshift informal 'bagging' of family space took place, with part of the platform kept free until the end of the running of the tube at night. Later bunk-beds and a ticket system for spaces appeared. Tom Harrisson details activities in the Tilbury shelter which Moore visited frequently. They included a high level of knitting, reading and talking in the evening, before attempts at irregular sleep took place. Wakefulness and talking resumed in the early hours, and 'at no time were over two-thirds of the shelterers sleeping at once'. Eating dominated between 7 to 8pm and resumed at 5am.

Moore's images are dominated by sleep or stoic wakefulness without social interaction or family activities. Images of knitting appear occasionally, but ultimately these become portentous images evoking the three fates, emblems of time and mortality. In Moore's hands the scene at Liverpool Street extension with its 'intermingled bodies with the hot, smelly air and continual murmur of snores'[19] becomes a formally monotonous double line of generalised recumbent figures, more dead than alive (Figure One). The human particularity of awkward arm positions appears in his focused images of sleep, but drapery and body-forms are generalised in the extreme.

In other artists' images of the tube shelters, sleep also predominates over the social activities revealed in the photographic and written records. Ease of recollection and representation presumably went hand-in-hand with the dramatic unusualness of this aspect of the panorama of shelter life. However, there are significant differences between Moore's images and those of other visual artists represented in the Imperial War Museum. Edmond Kapp represented a greater variety of sleeping situations and details of state of dress.[20] Topolski's *The Tube* (October, 1940, IWM), a wash drawing of the Leicester Square tube, rhythmically generalises much of the visual information but lettering identifies the locale and the image is constructed around the contrast of familiar tunnel and unfamiliar human usage.[21] One sleeping figure sits upright on the station seat while another corpulent one is unable to sleep and standing wardens converse in the distance. The other artist apart from Moore to produce a substantial body of shelter images was Edward Ardizzone, who produced various images of families trundling off to the shelter as well as shelter scenes.[22] While his figures all tend to an affectionate dumpiness and are contained in convenient boxed spaces, he observes many particularities of physiognomy and dress, impromptu sleeping positions, and different levels of nocturnal restfulness.

Before 1939 there were panicky forecasts of the effects of aerial bombardment and sheltering. City-wide conflagration and mass entrenchment in the tubes, followed by disease, regression, and madness, were predicted and the Mental Health Emergency Committee reported in 1939 that psychiatric disturbance would be three times more prevalent than physical injury as a result of mass bombardment.[23] In the event, psychological reactions to the blitz as recorded by Mass Observation included fear and anxiety (and occasional exhilaration) but not the widespread hysteria or breakdown predicted in the immediate pre-war years. Harrisson concluded that 'the subsequent picture has been distorted' by removing these normal human responses from the images of the blitz 'spirit' of courage and fortitude.[24] A pattern of shock, recovery of a sense of reality, intense interpersonal communication, ego-enhancement and a gradual return to 'normality' and a determination to 'make do' is discernible in Mass Observation reports on how people responded to the blitz.

How do Moore's images relate to this typical pattern of experience? It is normally claimed that Moore's shelter drawings are warm humanistic statements. Pevsner in 1945 considered that the facsimile sketchbook images established 'once for all' Moore's 'tenderness and compassion'[25] while Roger Berthoud, Moore's authorised biographer, talks about their 'strong sense of compassion, and even of indignation'.[26] However, if we look at *Pink and Green Sleepers* (Figure Two), it does not take too much historical imagination to see that such images involved different interests from those of the shelterers themselves. The colours are a sickly yellow-green and cold red, colours which suggest disease and fear rather than human resilience and social warmth. The remnants of sectional drawing on the drapery evoke sepulchral stone and sarcophagal immemoriality.

One contemporary poet, Sheila Shannon, found Moore's images not triumphs of humanistic vision but 'soulless megaliths' incapable of human emotion and only 'half-alive'.[27] For Shannon, these figures were 'half patient, malleable, enduring rock' though she was clearly sympathetic finally (as another artist) to the sculptor's self-engrossing vision. In 1941 Eric Newton described Moore's images as 'unearthly studies of a white, grub-like race of troglodytes swathed in protective blankets'[28] in terms which conjure up pre-war fears of regression to the level of primeval life or primitive anthropoids skulking around in the underworld. Yet in the end, this art critic was committed to professional admiration of Moore's project.

Fortunately one record of 'popular' reaction to Moore's work (albeit indirect) survives to measure against continuing claims, reiterated by Susan Compton in 1988, that 'Londoners were able to identify with Moore's vision of their plight'.[29] That record comes in Keith Vaughan's 1943 review of a National Gallery display of war art:

It is a tragedy, nevertheless understandable, that so many Londoners confronted with these drawings feel baffled and insulted. Here is a whole new underground world from which they feel themselves totally excluded, though the elements were all so familiar ... I have heard people call these drawings morbid and unreal.[30]

The experience of coping in the shelters as described by Harrisson seemed unconnected with these stoic statues. By what process did this alienating imagery of immemorial long-suffering and passive endurance become 'the most enduring work of war art' in Angus Calder's words, the key image for him and others of a putative 'people's war'?[31]

Moore's shelter drawings were exhibited at the National Gallery in London as part of its displays of commissioned war art, signifying (in the absence of the permanent collection stored in caves in North Wales) the continuation of artistic life and playing a part in boosting morale. The person responsible for these displays was Kenneth Clark, in his dual capacity as Director of the National Gallery and Chairman of WAAC. Clark was also Controller of Home Publicity and a nakedly useful civil servant. Indeed his functionality lay precisely in his movement between state gallery, government committee and artist's studio. Clark had been a patron of Moore's since his early career and a close friend from around 1938.[32] He had certainly been resistant to Moore's early sculpture[33] and he described himself as being thought of in the late 1930s 'as the spokesman of the "new romantic movement" '.[34] Neo-Romanticism constructed a sense of national cultural identity based on heightened emotional response to the land and its history, in order to create a sense of specifically British interests worth valuing and protecting, to unify public opinion around a sense of national endurance in the face of external threat. Clark's presentation of Moore's drawings at the National Gallery, however, needs to be seen within the context of presenting British culture not only as deeply conscious of tradition but also as progressively modern.

As Renaissance scholar and Director of the National Gallery, Clark was well placed to mediate those selected aspects of contemporary art which he found amenable. In terms of British cultural life, Clark's function was to rework modernism both as tradition and as potentially popular in appeal. Clark produced a catalogue essay on Moore's drawings for the Buchholz Gallery, New York exhibition in 1943 and was eventually to produce a full-scale study of Moore's drawings in

1974 which compared them to those of the Renaissance, reproducing 26 drawings from his own family collections.[35] Indeed it was Clark's wife who was given by Moore his first shelter sketchbook.[36] Nothing is made of this gift in art history texts other than to affirm the closeness of friendly relationships between the Clarks and Moore. However Moore could have anticipated fairly easily that such a gift, while registering private appreciation for support and promotion, would be put to good use in making publicly available his 'private' artistic processes, as happened when Clark's wife bequeathed his sketchbook to the British Museum in 1977. This sketchbook was published in facsimile and broken up to display its sheets publicly as intriguing individual works of art.

Indeed the distinction between private and public breaks down here. In 1944, for example, Editions Poetry published *Shelter Sketchbook: Henry Moore*. The conventional connotations of the word 'sketchbook' suggested some glimpse into private artistic process. Such insights seemed guaranteed by both Moore's copious written notes referring to details of shelter life and exhorting himself to various artistic investigations, and by the different types of drawing included (brief idea, 'study', technical experiment, compositional design, and squaring up for enlargement). Arguably the two sketchbooks, of which this volume is an unstated and highly selected amalgam, were conceived as artistic objects in themselves designed to signify artistic process. However it is probable that the most preliminary artistic stages were not represented.

It is important to recognise that Moore already had considerable artworld prestige in 1940, although it was largely the British Council's active promotion of his career from 1947-8 onwards which made him world famous. Before this process could take place the discursive basis for Moore's 'greatness' as a universal 'modern master' had to be established by blending his modernist experimentation with reference to old master tradition and human epic subject matter, and part of this operation already took place during wartime.

One text where we can see this process happening is Geoffrey Grigson's *Penguin Modern Painters*, a 1943 monograph on Moore which reproduced six shelter images. Moore's move towards abstraction in the 1930s and his wartime move back towards greater naturalism were both seen as a 'gain'. Moore is presented as seeing 'everything' from pebbles and caves to megaliths and cathedrals and giving a symbolic order to the 'mess and muddle and fecundity of life', following 'his road between the theorem and the heart'. This artist is clearly ancient and modern, analytic and intuitive, particular and universal. The discursive function of the shelter drawings is to create the image of an artist caring for the plight of humanity. Examples of the mediating role played by the shelter drawings are his return to sculpture before the end of the war after the Rev. Hussey saw these drawings and commissioned the Northampton *Madonna*,[37] and the Italian critic Argan's contacts with Moore and authorship of the first foreign language monograph on him in 1947 as a result of buying a copy of the 1944 *Shelter Sketchbook*.[38]

Moore's shelter images played their part in raising American awareness of the plight of Londoners during the blitz, when they were shown in the 1941 exhibition *Britain at War* at MOMA, New York, amid various efforts to dramatise the actuality of war, to consolidate the supportive climate of Lend-Lease (by showing Britain's national defence) and to strengthen the claims for American involvement in the war. When shown in his 1943 Buchholz Gallery exhibition, these images seemed to one critic to represent England's 'solid stand'.[39]

One Polish Jewish victim of the concentration camps, Gena Turgel, found after the war that the British would automatically refer to the tube shelters as evidence of British wartime hardship in response to her own harrowing account of the experience of the death-camps.[40] Moore's shelter pictures were valued in subsequent decades as part of a phenomenal investment in the myth of the blitz, culminating in its recent incorporation by the 'heritage industry', with the Imperial War Museum creating a simulated shelter in *The Blitz Experience* (created in 1989) and a mock tube station with platform bunks appearing in the *Britain at War Museum* opened in 1992.

Moore's images of passive suffering and active endurance by an anonymous collectivity might have its ideological roots in interwar British socialism[41] but was reshaped as part of a blitz mythology of fundamental importance to both Labour and Conservative parties. Kenneth Morgan has described the function of this myth as preserving an illusion of great-power status, reinforcing national identity during a period of traumatic change, and producing 'legends of social solidarity and common citizenship'.[42] It is important to remember that over half the London population never used the communal shelters and over one quarter did not generally. The middle classes generally preferred their domestic shelters. Only 4 per cent used the tubes regularly and 9 per cent the other public shelters.[43] Nevertheless, the image of the shelters took on a symbolic importance that extended far beyond the numbers involved. The image of the public shelters in the post-war myth of the blitz involved not collective lower-class sheltering but collective endurance and solidarity. Moore's shelter drawings achieved later pre-eminence within war art because they dealt with a theme which came to symbolise a time of trial for the British citizenry within the representation of the emergence of a new post-war consensus. The shelter image performed a key function in the myth of the blitz, a period nostalgically reconstructed as a bedrock of 'British identity' when uncertainties prevailed later.

NOTES

[1] F. Carey, *Henry Moore: A Shelter Sketchbook*, London, 1988, is a facsimile of the British Museum sketchbook. Eighty pages from the second sketchbook were printed as collotypes by the Ganymede Press, Berlin, in 1967 for Rembrandt Verlag. Moore (Carey, p10) started one or two other sketchbooks 'but a lot of the pages were torn out and used for other purposes and they are no longer in existence' although he still had 'a school exercise-book with a few scribbles in it' (Carey, p10). (It is worth speculating on whether motives of ambition and career may have led in some way to these instances of dismemberment and 'loss', if they contained more preliminary or 'undercooked' efforts.) J. Darracott, *Henry Moore: Wartime Drawings*, Imperial War Museum, London, 1975, lists the post-war distribution of the 28 WAAC shelter drawings.

[2] Carey, *op.cit.*, pp8-10. Moore's recollection that it was the first night of significant anti-aircraft barrage allows us to date the incident precisely to the night of 11 September 1940, five days (and nights) into the blitz. (C. FitzGibbon, *The Blitz*, London, 1974 ed., p111.)

[3] He was not commissioned as a war artist for the duration but only for batches of work, and when commissioned to treat subjects to which he could not relate, civil defence and medical aid post subjects, he diplomatically accepted the brief but let the notion drop quietly. See the letters from WAAC secretary E. Dickey to Moore, 2/1/41 and 11/8/41, in the Imperial War Museum Art Dept. Moore 1941-48 correspondence file GP/55/104.

[4] J. Glaves-Smith, 'Henry Moore', *Art Monthly*, Number 19, 1978, p8.

[5] M. Davidson, 'Mountainous sculptor draws: exhibition, Buchholz Gallery', *Art News*, 15 May 1943.

[6] 'The Truth of the Shelters' was the title of Pevsner's review of the 1944 *Shelter Sketchbook: Henry Moore, Architectural Review*, 1945, XCVIII, p147.

[7] A.D.B. Sylvester, 'Henry Moore: The Shelter Drawings', *Graphis*, 2, 14, March-April 1946, p127.

[8] An apparently documentary photograph captioned 'Henry Moore looking at sleepers in the Underground' was published opposite *Tube Shelter Perspective* (1941, ill.1) in the catalogue of Moore's 1946 retrospective at the Museum of

Modern Art, New York. However, the photograph is dated 1944 and was connected with Jill Craigie's film about the work of war artists, *Out of Chaos*, released in December that year. The footage shot in September 1943 in the Holborn underground station represents Moore in the position of direct gazing and conspicuous note-taking. The photographic still was taken by Lee Miller for a *Vogue* story on the making of the film (A. Penrose, *The Lives of Lee Miller*, London, 1985, pp111-112). So the photograph which mediated the 'truth' of the shelter drawings to an international audience was a staged recreation from two years later.

[9] Darracott, *op.cit.*, p4. Can we at least say that the two shelter sketchbooks were drawn at the time of the blitz, which lasted from September 1940 to May 1941? The first certainly goes back to 1940 but the second shelter sketchbook was dated to March-October 1941 in the 1946 MOMA retrospective catalogue (p91). Moore was still delivering finished shelter drawings to WAAC in September 1941 and he went on producing shelter-derived images into 1942.

[10] Carey, *op. cit.*, pp9-12.

[11] This image appears about one third of the way through the first shelter sketchbook (p21). Moore tried a variety of compositional schemes here, looking down the wide tunnel or sideways on. If this image was in his mind by late winter 1940, it also reappears on p10 of the second shelter sketchbook, implying some time-lag. Specific body-forms have now been extracted from the earlier figural mass and the tunnel is deeper and narrower. This squared-up image with its right foreground sleepers at right angles to all the others was the basis for two works in private collections in which the tunnel really sucks the eye in. Another squared-up drawing on p24 of the second shelter sketchbook curves the tunnel and removes the two sleepers at right angles to the others. This drawing becomes the basis for the Tate's *Tube Shelter Perspective*. A. Wilkinson, *The Drawings of Henry Moore*, Tate Gallery, London, 1977, pp31 and 110 illustrates all these works except p10 of the second shelter sketchbook (repro. *Shelter Sketchbook: Henry Moore*, 1944, p35) and the Roland collection *Tube Shelter Perspective* (repro. W. Grohmann, *The Art of Henry Moore*, London, 1960, p107).

[12] To track the development of *Pink and Green Sleepers* (1941, fig.2) is even more complicated, given Moore's focus on sleeping figures and their positions. Groups of figures sharing blankets, depicted from a low viewpoint, appear in the first shelter sketchbook and a variety of related drawings can be found in the second sketchbook, focusing on gaping mouths and raised arms. At one point, the appearance of a wide-awake figure suggests that he used someone to model the pose *Shelter Sketchbook: Henry Moore* (1944), p79. (Other relevant pages are pp34, 48-9, 51, 69-71, 78.) The definitive squared-up composition appears on p67 of the second sketchbook, but there are various intermediary stages sharpening facial features and tightening body and drapery rhythms, and seven related compositions have been counted (Wilkinson, *op.cit.*, pp111-13).

[13] By working with their documentary potential, I do not mean to imply that they are not constructed from a set of interests, a combination of social and artistic concerns. One image of a crippled old woman sleeping upright has a hook above her head like a question-mark. The oddity of the social scene

draws on Brandt's surrealist interests, while he tilted sleepers to create a dream-like eroticised image of sleep (D1575). See N. Warburton (ed), *Bill Brandt: Selected Texts and Bibliography*, Oxford, 1993, pp29-32 and 47-55. The photographs are to be found in the Imperial War Museum (D1503-25, 1566-83).

[14] D1596 is the best example.

[15] Quoted in C. Lake, 'Henry Moore's World', *Atlantic Monthly*, 209, 1, January 1962, Boston.

[16] Carey, *op.cit.*, p9.

[17] Carey, *op.cit.*, p12.

[18] T. Harrisson, *Living Through the Blitz*, London, 1976, 1990 ed., pp109ff, esp. p124. Harrisson was drawing on the Mass Observation Archive deeded by him finally to Sussex University, which published a sampling and analysis of these reports in 1976.

[19] The words are Bill Brandt's from 'Shelter Pictures by Brandt and Henry Moore', *Lilliput*, December 1942, caption to *Liverpool Street Extension*.

[20] Imperial War Museum, London, collection, LD796/798/802/817.

[21] IWM LD672.

[22] IWM LD467/472/474/477/478/479/480/481/484/862/866/871.

[23] FitzGibbon, *op.cit.*, pp22-3, 30-31; W. Ramsey (ed), *The Blitz Then and Now: Volume 2*, London, nd., p114; A. Calder, *The People's War*, London, 1969, pp179-87. The 'deep-shelter' debate from 1938 onwards took place within this discursive formation. The Communist Party and sections of the Labour and Liberal Parties believed that the working class in the East End would suffer most from bombardment and that deep-shelters should be provided. The Government feared the development of a 'deep-shelter mentality'.

[24] Harrisson, *op.cit.*, p305.

[25] Pevsner, *op.cit.*, p147.

[26] R. Berthoud, *The Life of Henry Moore*, London, 1987, p176.

[27] S. Shannon, 'The Artist's Vision: A Shelter Picture by Henry Moore', *The Spectator*, 23 June 1944, p568.

[28] *Sunday Times*, 18 May 1941. We are reminded of the words of Vera Brittain: 'some parts of the city have temporarily lost the ordinary facilities of civilised living; there are rumours of shelter epidemics ... Soon, I reflect, London's poorer population, like melancholy troglodytes, will spend its whole life in the Underground.' (Quoted in R. Hewison, *Under Siege*, London, 1977, 1979 ed., p40.) Similarly H.G. Wells' *The Fate of Homo Sapiens* (1939) had predicted a return to a Dark Ages as a result of planetary war and images of such holocaust had been engraved on the public mind by the 1935 film of his *The Shape of Things to Come*. These fears soon disappeared and schemes for boring tunnels in chalk hills and even using mines as shelters were mooted in 1941 but abandoned as diversions from immediate tasks. Cave/tunnel came to signify instead the womb-like protection and nurturing of the 'land'.

[29] S. Compton, 'Drawing and Sculpture: A Timeless Art of Our Time' (*sic*) in *Henry Moore*, Royal Academy, London, 1988, p32.

[30] K. Vaughan, 'War Artists and the War', *The Penguin New Writing*, Number 16, January-March 1943, pp112-114.

[31] Calder, *op.cit.*, p638.

[32] K. Clark, *Another Part of the Wood*, London, 1974, pp224-5. Berthoud,

op.cit. pp157-8, implies that Clark predates the period of both real friendly intimacy and aesthetic appreciation.

[33] Kathleen Sutherland believed Clark appreciated Moore's drawings before he did his sculptures and remembers him likening the sculptures to 'hot-water bottles' (Berthoud, *op.cit.*, p157).

[34] K. Clark, *The Other Half*, London, 1977, p44. Clark, for example, was turned to as the obvious person to open a 1941 exhibition at Temple Newsam, Leeds, in which Moore was bracketed with Neo-Romantic painters Piper and Sutherland.

[35] K. Clark, *The Drawings of Henry Moore*, London, 1974.

[36] Clark (1977), *op.cit.*, p42. Issues of prestige, public service probity and financial legacy clearly explain why Moore refers to the sketchbook as being in Kenneth Clark's collection while it was treated by the couple as a gift to Clark's wife. The date of the gift is not recorded at the British Museum, so another level of precise signification is occluded from view.

[37] J. Sweeney, *Henry Moore*, Museum of Modern Art, 1946, p77.

[38] Berthoud, *op.cit.*, p213.

[39] M. Riley, 'Exhibition: Buchholz Galleries', *Art Digest*, 15 May 1943, pp4-6.

[40] G. Turgel, *I Light a Candle*, London, 1987, p138.

[41] See A. Barnett, 'The Shape of Labour', *Art Monthly*, Oct. 1986, pp4-8.

[42] K. Morgan, 'The Second World War and British Culture' in B. Brivati and H. Jones (eds), *From Reconstruction to Integration: Britain and Europe Since 1945*, Leicester, 1993, pp33-46.

[43] These figures, based on a shelter census in early November 1940, are found in FitzGibbon, *op.cit.*, p143.

Section 4: Popular Pastimes

Pulp Versus Penguins: Paperbacks Go To War

Steve Chibnall

The War produced artificial conditions in the book industry which have no permanent significance.
Arthur Calder-Marshall 1947[1]

The buffeting which the British fiction market received between 1940 and 1947 as a result of paper rationing was Adolf Hitler's gift to the paperback book.
Brian Stableford 1993[2]

The great advantage which historical analysis has over contemporary criticism is hindsight. In the euphoric exhaustion of a hard won peace, Arthur Calder-Marshall could dismiss the war as a temporary disruption which accelerated the pre-war trajectories of the publishing industry;[3] but hindsight has enabled the historian of publishing to see that the most significant influence upon popular book publishing between 1914 and 1950 was war.[4] The 1939-45 conflict set in motion a chain of events which would transform the business, opening up new markets, introducing fresh blood into the publishing industry, and establishing the legitimacy of the late twentieth century's dominant book format – the paperback.

The paperbound book was not a creation of the Second World War. Its origins can be traced back beyond the nineteenth century.[5] In Britain, paperbacks had long been a staple of working-class reading and they made considerable progress into more bourgeois markets before the First World War via the railway station bookstall. But, by the 1920s, paperback pioneers like Chatto & Windus were experiencing a dramatic decline in sales as first the cinema and then the radio lured away readers.[6] A steady demand for cheap romances, detective stories and thrillers kept paperbacks in publication during the 1930s but few were granted the privilege of bookshop distribution, being branded as juvenile, feminine, lower class or morally suspect.[7] Condemned to the same distribution channels as magazines, they shared the same depressed market conditions – victims of the poverty created by unemployment and the competition from new leisure pursuits and imported American 'pulp' magazines.[8] By 1935 the paperback was firmly ghettoized and glibly dismissed by the literary establishment as a gaudy distraction for proletarian readers. The Leavisite chauvinism of letters gave no credence to popular taste and circumscribed the circulation of cheap paperbacks as surely as any concentration camp.[9]

Paperbacks were not classed as 'literature' because they supposedly made few intellectual demands on the reader. They offered escapist entertainment and were viewed by both their detractors and consumers as disposable commodities to be passed on, or thrown away, after reading. 'Real books' could be bought from bookshops, assembled to display the cultural capital of their owner, and had cloth covers. Even paper dust-jackets were suspect, particularly if their function moved beyond the purely utilitarian to the realm of decoration. Public librarians promptly removed them, lest they exert too great an influence on borrowing decisions.

Public and private libraries flourished in the interwar years. The free public library system catered for the educational and intellectual needs of a predominantly male, middle-class clientele. For fiction aficionados there were the commercial subscription libraries run by retailers such as W.H. Smith and Boots, the Chemist. Their customers were also mostly from social classes B and C, but predominantly female. At the bottom of the book borrowing hierarchy were the 'tuppenny libraries' that sprang up in working-class districts to pedal romances, thrillers and westerns. Books here kept their jackets on so that the appeal of the latest Annie Swan or Ethel M. Dell could be properly assessed by the neighbourhood's romance readers. These exchanges were the video rental emporia of their day – functioning as centres of sociability and enlivening drab terraces with their colourful window displays.[10]

Many publishers came to regard libraries as their primary customers. The direct sales market came a distant second for companies like Mills & Boon which had quickly abandoned an experiment with paperbacked fiction to concentrate on 'library editions'.[11] The effect on the literary product was stultifying and homogenising – 'nothing flashy, nothing bizarre, nothing scandalous or obscene'.[12] The flashy and the bizarre remained in the paperback ghetto, appearing sporadically in the output of Irish-based publishers, Mellifont Press, and the 'Piccadilly Novels' produced by Fiction House. Contrary to the common wisdom that cheap books had to be reprints, many of these works were original novels bought at modest rates. The 'scandalous' and 'obscene' existed too, mainly salaciously moralising exposés of white slave trafficking and loose Parisian living. Prolific wordsmiths Ernest McKeag and Richard Goyne, writing under the pseudonyms Roland Vane and Paul Renin (respectively) became the leading authors of this erotica which shady companies like Gramol Ltd distributed through broadminded stationers and specialist Soho bookstalls.[13]

PICK UP A PENGUIN

Allen Lane's speculative launch of Penguin Books in 1935 shook up the complacent world of publishing, but did not fundamentally alter the status of most paperbacks. Lane's much vaunted 'paperback revolution' was a bourgeois revolution which left working-class publishing further denigrated. Penguins were not entirely innovative. Their severe, undecorated covers with their bird symbol and genre colour-coding followed the modernist formula invented by the European publishers of Albatross Books.[14] Penguins were cheaper than Albatrosses but so were the paperback reprints of Newnes, Wright & Brown, and the ubiquitous Hodder & Stoughton. What was unique about Penguin was Lane's willingness to combine an evangelical modernism of almost Reithian proportions with techniques of commodity marketing which had rarely been seen in the book industry. His slogan was 'Good Books Cheap' and his mission was to provide an opportunity for discerning consumers of modest means to elevate their taste and build a private library of classic texts – old and new.

> There are many who despair at what they regard as the low level of the people's intelligence. We, however, believed in the existence in this country of a vast reading public for intelligent books at a low price and staked everything on it.[15]

Challenging the equation between soft covers and disposability, Penguins were marketed as chic left-of-centre collectibles for the young intelligentsia. Dust-jackets increased their resemblance to 'real books' and emphasised their permanence. Three million copies of fifty titles were sold in the first year, leading to comment that 'everybody finally bought Penguins'.[16] But, although they straddled the divide between Woolworths and the bookshop, their universality was largely illusionary. The D class reader rarely picked up a Penguin. Their carefully nurtured power as a commodity sign made little impression on a reading culture which valued paperbacks almost exclusively as utilitarian objects.[17]

Thus, on the eve of World War Two, reading and publishing remained organised around divisions of class. In a finely graded hierarchy, books were classified by price. Book publishing was still considered a gentlemanly pursuit, although professional methods of commodity marketing were gaining ground.[18] In fiction publishing, cheap reprints dominated the retail market, 55 per cent of production in 1939. Original novels were swallowed up by the burgeoning library sector, leaving a residue of 'mill girl romances' and sexually suggestive novelettes to populate the newsagent's window.

BOOKS FOR THE BLACKOUT

The war reshaped the world of popular literature. New conditions weakened the paternalistic grip of bourgeois publishers, challenging the ethos of gentility and good taste propagated by the literary establishment, and provided opportunities for the launch of new commodified publishing businesses. They also undermined the established habit of book borrowing, stimulated a developing market of young male working-class and lower middle-class consumers, and aided the widespread acceptance of the paperback as a legitimate commodity form.

The Mass Observation survey of 1944 revealed people to be reading less overall, and detected a note of hostility to the activity among some working-class women.[19]

> I got enough to do as it is. It's only people who got nothing better to do that do all the reading.[20]

> I think your time's better employed knitting than reading.[21]

The demands of running a home in wartime reduced leisure time available for reading[22] and the war effort interfered with pleasure and leisure.[23] Tiredness, distraction, and the paucity of light during the blackout affected most sections of the population but there were significant social groups whose war experiences increased the time and inclination for reading. These consisted chiefly of 'young people in the forces and factories, who have been largely non-readers or small readers up to now ... those who are "mobile" and are billeted in new factory towns, or stationed in camps far from home'.[24] By 1942-43 library borrowing figures were increasing, particularly for novels,[25] and significant numbers of working-class readers began to venture into the foreign territory of the bookshop.

> There's quite a new interest in books on the part of the less educated section of the community – factory hands and so on ... a lot of young people ... are quite unused to bookshops and feel awkward at first.

> The factory workers ... are all going mad on buying books, and the ARP and demolition squads ... buy books too.[26]

Much of this new buying was of technical books and literary classics but the war also legitimised frankly escapist reading, particularly for women. As conditions on the home front became increasingly intolerable, the interests of morale demanded temporary respite.

> There's enough tragedy in real life not to want to read about it, and that's one of the reasons I *never* read a war book.[27]

For a 35 year old stenographer a residual guilt remained:

> I take light literature as I do cigarettes: nothing so potent as a drug, merely a harmless bromide. I've only done this in the past two years or so. Until then I took reading very seriously, but now I feel I can afford a little frivolity mixed in. In honesty I ought to say I am sometimes rather snobbishly ashamed of being seen with my current 'bromide'.[28]

Selling books was not a problem but obtaining them was. Paper rationing was introduced with the Control of Paper Order in February 1940. Supplies to publishers were restricted to 60 per cent of their 1939 usage and soon to 30 per cent. A low point was reached in 1943, with supplies from Norway cut off by the German invasion and Canadian paper taking up valuable shipping space.[29] Recycled paper had become so low in quality after repeated pulping that fresh materials were urgently required. The Ministry of Supply's salvage trawl netted a staggering fifty-six million books, of which fifty million went to the pulp mills with diligent librarians rescuing the remainder to replace bombed stock or to send to the Forces.[30] Frustrated publishers saw the lion's share of new paper disappear into the ravenous jaws of government ministries. The War Office alone used more paper than the entire publishing trade. The response of the book producers was the voluntary negotiation of the Book Production War Economy Agreement of January 1942. Volumes bearing the statement 'This book is produced in complete conformity with the authorised economy standards' were thinner, with smaller type and narrower margins. Even this was not enough for some newspapers which campaigned to outlaw dust-jackets.[31] Production costs soared and labour became scarce as compositors and bookbinders were called up. By 1943 the number of new books published had fallen from the pre-war figure of 15,000 to just 6,700.[32]

As supplies dwindled, the paperback which saved on materials and was light for ease of shipping to servicemen, could be seen as a patriotic and pragmatic necessity. Merchandising opportunities opened up at the lower end of the market as established publishers concentrated on more expensive books with higher profit margins. It is one of the ironies of the war that, as the publishing industry was starved of raw materials, the number of publishers in Britain and Ireland increased from 320 to 412.[33] The key to this conundrum lies in the doubling of the value of book sales during the period from £10 million to £22 million pounds.[34] More money was being spent on fewer books as prices were forced up by shortages. Penguins doubled their price during the war, with no apparent effect on demand, and other paperbound imprints moved above the one shilling barrier. 86 new bookshops opened in 1941 alone.[35] Books needed no coupons and as war work swelled disposable incomes customers flocked to buy. Part of this bonanza, however, was at the expense of the commercial libraries, particularly the tuppenny libraries which were killed by conscription, lack of capital and the blitz. Only the large concerns tended to survive the disruption of distribution channels and the rising costs resulting from the destruction of wholesalers' stock.[37] It was the vacuum left by the tuppenny libraries that the new pulp paperback houses rushed to fill.

THE MOBILE MALE MARKET

In the early months of the war, 92 per cent of Class D respondents told Mass Observation that they never or seldom bought a book.[38] Two years later, approximately nine out of ten books read in this class were borrowed, with almost one person in five using the tuppenny libraries.[39] Borrowing, however, relies to a large extent on permanency of residence and there was an increasing number of people in all classes who were increasingly 'mobile', particularly younger males. What the new paperback publishers discovered was not so much a mass working-class market but a large niche market of mobile men in uniform or overalls. There was clear evidence, even from the tuppenny libraries with their largely female clientele, that there was a substantial market for male-oriented genre fiction, particularly detective and western stories.[40] Not only did men devote more time than women to reading but with more money in their pockets and fewer competing attractions, they also bought their books.[41] In 1940 working and lower-middle class men were slightly less than twice as likely as women to say that they bought books; but, by 1947, they were three times more likely to do so.[42]

Mass Observation greeted this expanding market for books with the enthusiasm one might expect from an organisation which shared Allen Lane's zeal for adult education and social improvement. It advocated propaganda to break down reverence for the cloth-bound book and represent the buying of books 'for oneself' as 'something normal for these people' (i.e. manual workers).[43] Here was an opportunity for Penguin to boldly go where no respectable paperback publisher had gone before, to penetrate working-class enclaves as the literary stormtroopers of social engineering. The firm was quick to grasp the opportunity presented by mobile male readers. Book donation boxes for servicemen appeared in Post Offices when Allen Lane launched his Forces Book Club in October 1942. These special military editions which, like other Penguins, fitted perfectly into that pocket in the army uniform intended for an entrenching tool, were given an official seal of approval with an additional paper allocation of sixty tons per month. Print runs were set at 75,000 copies as patriotism and commerce joined hands.[44] However, there remained two obstacles, the first associated with genre, the second with cover style.

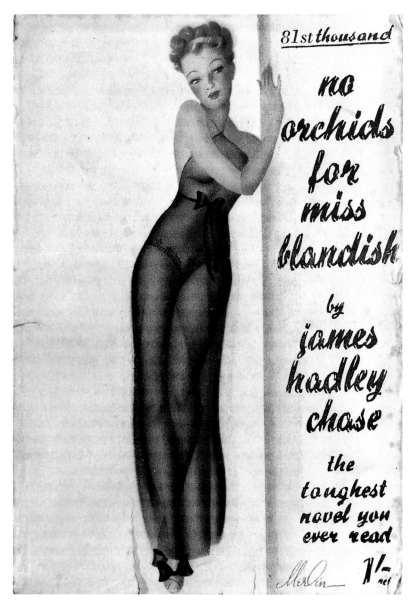

Figure One: No Orchids For Miss Blandish, described by Orwell as 'plainly aimed at Sadists and Masochists'.

Figure Two: Dames Spell Trouble!
'Dames ... and Tough-Guys in a collection ... that will Thrill and Shock the
most hardened reader'.

139

GENRE

Allen Lane's mission to raise the literary tastes of the common reader meant that Penguin's concessions to populism stopped at the whodunnits of Erle Stanley Gardner, but men exposed to the carnage of the battlefield and the daily brutalities of service life found little relevance or stimulation in the genteel machinations of 'golden age' detective mysteries, preferring the blood and guts realism of hard-boiled crime fiction. What might have seemed an exotic fantasy in the pages of imported American pulp magazines before the war, now acquired a social and psychological truth – the experience of violence transposed into a foreign location.[45]

After just six months of hostilities, the *Daily Express* suggested that soldiers wanted only thrillers, 'the gorier the better',[46] while the most popular novel with the troops, and probably the best selling novel of the whole war, was James Hadley Chases's pseudo-American gangster story, *No Orchids For Miss Blandish* (Figure One). The novel was typical of what *The Bookseller* described as 'drunk and disorderly reading',[47] its notoriety sealed when George Orwell singled it out as a prime example of popular fiction's degeneration into a 'cesspool'. Describing books like *No Orchids* as violent power fantasies, 'plainly aimed at Sadists and Masochists', Orwell deplored their atmosphere of moral ambiguity and glorification of brutality, and likened their psychological appeal to that of fascism and totalitarianism. Given the choice between the American 'jump on his testicles' school of writing and the refined snobbery-with-fisticuffs stories of E.W. Hornung's Raffles, Orwell preferred Raffles.[48] His opinions found more favour among Mass Observation's largely middle-class panel of reporters than among working-class readers. As one panel member opined, 'I don't buy books of the calibre of *No Orchids* because I cannot bear the poor style in which they are written, and so far as the sexual experiences contained in them are concerned, I consider my own private life far more interesting'.[49] But with sales in excess of half a million, it seemed more people preferred the private life of Miss Blandish. The book defined the borderline of pornography, and the less salubrious Charing Cross Road dealers could not keep up with demand. As one observer reported:

> A young girl comes into a shop to sell an armful of second-hand books. Amongst them is a copy of *No Orchids for Miss Blandish*. She smiles

rather shamefacedly at the assistant. 'It doesn't matter about that one if you don't want it' she said (*sic*) nervously. 'Maybe *we* don't want it' answers the assistant, 'but if you are not doing anything tomorrow morning come round here and watch the queue for it.'[50]

Surveys noted an increased demand for 'suggestive and pornographic literature' and a number of specialist shops opened in London, attracting a largely male working-class clientele with a 'noticeable sprinkling of servicemen'.[51] Their stock-in-trade was the spicy paperback and they seemed to have no trouble in acquiring[52] these books which were shunned by libraries, threatened with prosecution and, consequently, always in demand.[53] In the early years of the war, the need to boost morale had loosened censorship restrictions, with *Men Only* supplying a steady stream of barrack-room pin-ups.[54] *Men Only* was tolerated as a saucy but respectable diversion for the officer corps and the sergeants' mess, but, as 'suggestive' materials for other ranks began to proliferate, action was taken. In May 1942 James Hadley Chase (Rene Raymond) and Jarrolds, his publishers, were prosecuted for obscenity at the Old Bailey, effectively suppressing his latest blockbuster, *Miss Callaghan Comes To Grief*.[55] A second writer in the American hard-boiled style, Harold Kelley, and his publishers, Wells, Gardner, Darton, were also fined for Darcy Glinto's *Lady Don't Turn Over* and *Road Floozie*.[56]

Prosecutions slowed rather than halted the spread of 'tough' thrillers. Rene Raymond suspended writing his steamy novels during a period in the RAF, but Kelley simply changed his pseudonym and cracked on with *It's Only Saps That Die* and *The Bronsville Massacre*. If anything, the court cases boosted interest in a genre which conflated sex, violence and the American way.[57] The visceral delights of 'tough' fiction were graphically summed up by a commercial traveller who told Mass Observation:

> I prefer to have my murders good and gory. Not to have the whole book devoted to the putting right of just one murder, but to have horror piled on horror until the whole book is swimming in blood ...[58]

The lifestyle of commercial travellers, as 'men on the loose' away from the surveillance of wives or mothers had long been the subject of saucy seaside postcards, but, as the war made more men mobile, a physical, temporal and psychological space was opened up for the consumption of erotic literature. Working-class males began to experience the freedom which bachelor apartments and college rooms had offered to bourgeois men before the war. Barracks, billets and lodgings meant that 'illicit' materials did not have to be hidden from parents or partners.[59]

The attitude of many women to the growth of masculine pulp fiction was captured by one female reader when she told Mass Observation, 'I am very chary of trying recent novels, as I have no time for anything sexy or unpleasant',[60] but there was a minority female interest in the violent and erotic.

> I like a murder story – the more blood spilled the better, or a dirty book!
> I like thrillers – *Not at Night* is lovely, all about horrors.
> Oh, my dear, I can give you the lowdown on those American shockers. I've read them all – priceless, aren't they?[61]

Clearly, the 'subversive longing for all that is not nice',[62] was present in both sexes,[63] although romance continued to be the favoured genre of women readers. The retail market for romantic fiction grew much more slowly than that for the masculine genres of hard-boiled crime and cowboy stories, as demand continued to be met by a library sector which offered the pleasures of sociability and the recommendations of knowledgeable librarians.[64] Sales were also retarded by women's habit of circulating their books within family and neighbourhood networks.[65]

COVERS

Whereas most popular paperbacks were produced for what Robert Escarpit terms 'consumer reading', Penguins were designed for 'connoisseur reading'.[66] The thoughtful contemplation of the text was complemented by the cultivation of pride in ownership through careful point-of-sale display and modernist book design. Brand-loyal Penguin buyers were likely to be middle-class Labour voters, socially and politically active, with a passion for reading and a desire to build a library of books.[67] Allen Lane's design philosophy appealed to them:

> I think it is the attractiveness of Penguin and Pelican books in their *form* which always makes me stop and look at any display of them, to see if there are any titles I want. Certainly I do not feel drawn in the same way to other cheap books.[68]

Mass Observation's panel represent the quintessential Penguin public and it is clear from their discourse on book jacket design that they appreciated the tasteful, the unobtrusive and the understated: 'I like them to look pleasant. And I don't like lurid jackets.' 'Sometimes if it's rather gaudy I don't get it.' Only one in ten of the panel mentioned the importance of the jacket in choosing a book, and most of these were more likely to be put off than encouraged by a cover design.[69] Tasteful and agreeable covers were also vital in breaking down the prejudice of booksellers against stocking paperbacks.[70]

The austere and standardised design of Penguin and its imitators, however, cut little ice among working-class readers. Book covers for this market had always been the province of illustrators rather than graphic designers and typographers, and the evocation of fantasy and mood through realist representation rather than symbolism and abstraction was the key to sales. Moreover, 73 per cent of D Class readers claimed to be influenced in their choice of book by its look (against 32 per cent of B Class readers).[71] Legend has it that the buyer for Woolworths, well versed in the tastes of this class of consumer, almost rejected Penguin books on sight[72] and many newsagents certainly did:

> ... a little more attention to the covers would help sales. There's very little design or illustration to suggest to the customer what's in the book. I'm talking about Penguins now, not this stuff with nude women on the front. You can see at a glance what's in them, and in a way they've got the right idea. Why don't they do something like it in good taste?
> —Aston newsagent[73]

LITERARY BARROW BOYS

The people who put nudes on book covers were largely a new breed of publisher. They realised that, with paper rationed, new markets could not be exploited by the established book trade. Many came from working-class backgrounds and had experience in retailing. They knew about selling, and understood the ordinary consumer. Whereas Penguin was publishing from above, this was publishing from below – naked populism.[74]

Typical of the new breed, and first off the mark, was Gerald Swan. His rise from market vendor of second-hand books to major force in popular publishing was meteoric. Swan issued everything from children's comics to steamy novelettes but judiciously abandoned his gangster fiction series after the James Hadley Chase ruling. The brother of 'tough guy' author Harold Kelley, and publisher of his 'Buck Toler' books, had a base in the secondhand trade that thrived in wartime. His Everybody's Bookshop in the Charing Cross Road advertised for used paper-covered fiction at 4d each. It even took books without covers, such was the shortage of reading material; 'Every book that does its job twice is helping the vital "Save Paper" campaign.'[75] Another market trader was Sydney Pemberton who began publishing paperback romances in 1941 and soon produced westerns and gangster thrillers. There were many more blue collar entrepreneurs who tried their hand at publishing as well as employees of the publishing industry who struck out on their own:

> The 'mushroom' publishers were usually small operations … Any sort of paper was used, and some products looked as if they had been printed on toilet paper (appropriately enough, in some cases) but that didn't matter to the publisher because it would still sell.[76]

Published by Bear Hudson Ltd., at one shilling, *Dames Spell Trouble!* by Michael Hervey is a typical product: 'Dames, Hoodlums, Snow-Peddlers and Tough-Guys, in a collection of Gripping, Fast-Moving Yarns that will Thrill, Amuse, and Shock the most hardened reader'. On the cover, the guy in the dressing gown with the 'dame' on his knee has just been shot through the heart. Inside the mayhem continues in no less than thirteen stories in the space of forty pages of type of the size required to put the Lord's Prayer on a postage stamp.

Bear Hudson was just one of several companies established by two related families of Jewish refugees, the Assaels and the Babanis, which became a major force in the publication and distribution of popular fiction in the immediate post-war years. For the Assaels and Babanis and their legions of Grub Street competitors, paper was more vital to survival than stories. Wheeling and dealing in paper was a constant preoccupation, and supplies came from the strangest sources – in one case a wholesale grocer's quota for wrapping margarine.[77] Ironically, the commodification of publishing was hastened by the shortage of its most basic commodity as considerations of literary quality took a back seat to black market paper supplies.

THE BOMBS THAT FELL ON PATERNOSTER SQUARE

If 1935 had been the paperback's bourgeois revolution, the Second World War was a period of proletarian upheaval in popular publishing. Like all revolutions, it was not without its critics. The rise of paperback barons with 'no literary or cultural gloss' provoked one struggling author to suggest that 'they could quite easily have been mass producing stockings of doubtful quality for the barrow trade'.[78] Some consumers were shocked that while textbooks and classic novels remained unobtainable, *Shipwreck Passion* and *Yankee Science Fiction* were in plentiful supply.[79]

The war had created a new book market. Social visionaries like Allen Lane and Arthur Calder-Marshall hoped for an 'active' rather than 'passive reading public' seeking books for 'information and understanding rather than escape into fantasy'.[80] However, the desire for fantasy was fuelled by the experience of war and for the growing body of male paperback consumers, the fantasy took an American form. When Mass Observation surveyed reading in Tottenham in 1947 and asked people to indicate, from a list of established genres, those which they liked to read, one male factory worker commented that 'None of them subjects is interesting to me. All I like is gangster stories'.[81]

A year before, an aspiring young publisher and writer named Stephen Frances had been told that westerns and gangster stories were the hot sellers. Frances was an idealist – a pre-war communist and a wartime conscientious objector – but as Hank Janson he became the bestselling author of the postwar paperback boom with his hard-boiled tales of crime in America, a country he had never visited.[82]

Joseph McAleer is only partially correct when he writes that 'paperback publishing on a mass scale in Britain was not introduced until after the Second World War, and only then after the creation of consortia which could underwrite the considerable costs of production and marketing'.[83] While this may be true of Pan and Corgi Books, many of the most prolific paperback imprints of the 1950s, such as Digit, Panther, Ace and Badger Books, had their origins in the underworld of wartime mushroom publishing, and prospered because of the changed market conditions created by the war.

When the Luftwaffe bombed Paternoster Square, the headquarters of London publishing, in December 1940, they did more than destroy the offices of Collins, Hutchinson and Longman and five million books; they helped to open up a cosy and elitist game to new players. Although the publishing business survived, Hitler's gesture was more than symbolic, it truly was his gift to the paperback book.

NOTES

[1] Arthur Calder-Marshall, *The Book Front*, The Bodley Head, London, 1947, p30.
[2] Brian Stableford, foreword to Steve Holland, *The Mushroom Jungle*, Zeon Books, Westbury, 1993.
[3] Calder-Marshall, *op.cit.*
[4] Joseph McAleer, *Popular Reading and Publishing in Britain 1914-50*, Oxford Historical Monographs, Clarendon Press, 1992, p247.
[5] Holland, *op.cit.*, Chapter 1; McAleer, *op.cit.*
[6] Anon, *Sixpenny Wonderfuls*, Chatto & Windus, London, 1985.
[7] For evocative descriptions of the retailing of paperbacks in the 1930s see Winifred Holtby, 'What We Read and Why We Read It', *Left Review*, Volume 1, Number 4, 1935; or Q.D. Leavis, *Fiction and the Reading Public*, Chatto & Windus, London, 1932, Chapter 1.
[8] The historical development of the pulp magazine is discussed in Ron Goulart, *Cheap Thrills*, Arlington House, New York, 1972; Lee Server, *Danger Is My Business*, Chronicle Books, San Francisco, 1993.
[9] See also Leavis *op.cit.*
[10] Calder-Marshall, *op.cit.*, pp15-16, bemoans the commodity orientation of tuppenny libraries: 'Most people running two-penny libraries have little interest in literature. It is merchandise like sweets or cigarettes.' They were seen by some public librarians as a godsend, relieving them of the need to stock pulp fiction and allowing them to concentrate on 'good books'.
[11] McAleer, *op.cit.*, Chapter 4.
[12] Calder-Marshall, *op.cit.*, pp17-18.
[13] The directors of Gramol Ltd were convicted of obscenity charges in 1931.
[14] Piet Schreuders, *The Book of Paperbacks*, Virgin Books, London, 1981, pp7-12; Kenneth C. Davis, *The Paperbacking of America*, Houghton Mifflin, Boston, 1984, Chapter 4; Hans Schmoller, 'The Paperback Revolution' in Asa Briggs (ed.), *Essays in the History of Publishing in Celebration of the 250th Anniversary of the House of Longman*, Longman, London, 1974.
[15] Allen Lane, 'Books for the Millions', *Left Review*, Volume 3, Number 16, 1938.
[16] Calder-Marshall, *op.cit.*, p26.
[17] 'To many working people, books are outside their economic scheme, and the only books bought are paper-covered ones to while away the time – they have no conception of buying books for the sake of owning and displaying them.' Mass Observation File Report, M.O. FR 1332, *Report on Books and the Public*, 1942, p12. If Penguins made any headway with working-class readers, it was largely through their detective fiction reprints, M.O. FR 2545B, *Penguin World*, 1947.
[18] McAleer, *op.cit.*, Chapter 2.

[19] I am indebted to the staff at the Mass Observation Archive at the University of Sussex for their help in researching this paper.
[20] F25D (Female, aged 25, D class), M.O. FR 2018, *Books and the Public*, 1944, p14.
[21] F35D, *ibid.*, p15.
[22] 'I never read – I've far too much to do, what with factory work, shopping and managing the flat', F25D, M.O. FR 1332, *op.cit.*, p114.
[23] M.O. FR 2018, *op.cit.*, p15.
[24] *Ibid.*, p68.
[25] *Ibid.*, p66.
[26] *Ibid.*, p70. Mass Observation's survey of 1942 suggests that working-class buyers were perhaps more conspicuous than numerous. M.O. FR 1222, *Book Reading Survey*, Interim Report, 1942.
[27] F35C, M.O. FR 2018, *op.cit.*, p78.
[28] *Ibid.*, p85.
[29] McAleer, *op.cit.*, pp60-61; Holland *op.cit.*, pp10-12.
[30] Norman Longmate, *How We Lived Then*, Hutchinson, London, 1973, pp286-7.
[31] *Ibid.*, p448.
[32] Holland, *op.cit.*, p12. Working from the *Bookseller and the Publishers' Circular*, McAleer *op.cit.*, p52, offers this dramatic comparison:

	1936	1944
New (adult) Fiction titles	1,046	1,095
Reprint (adult) Fiction titles	2,862	160

[33] McAleer, *op.cit.*, p47. The latter figure almost certainly ignores some of the smaller firms founded during the hostilities.
[34] Calder-Marshall, *op.cit.*, p30.
[35] McAleer, *op.cit.*, p62.
[36] M.O. FR 1332, *op.cit.*, p70a.
[37] M.O. FR 2018, *op.cit.*, p65.
[38] The figure for Class C (clerical) was 86 per cent. M.O. FR 48, *op.cit.*, p26.
[39] M.O. FR 1322, *op.cit.*, p21.
[40] M.O. FR 48, *op.cit.*, p23.
[41] M.O. FR 1332, *op.cit.*, pp10-16.
[42] M.O. FR 47, *Wartime Reading*, 1940, p18; M.O. FR 2537, *Reading in Tottenham*, 1947, p7. Moreover, men were displaced by women as the main users of public libraries during the war. M.O. FR 1222, *op.cit.*, p7.
[43] M.O. FR 1332, *op.cit.*, p43.
[44] Holland, *op.cit.*, p12. Penguin's initiative was almost a year ahead of the American Council of Books in wartime's more ambitious non-profit making programme involving 'Armed Services' and 'Overseas' editions of books. Schreuders, *op.cit.*, pp47-51.
[45] Steve Holland, *op.cit.*, pp82-83, has argued that the British version of hard-boiled crime offered principally discourse on violence rather than sex: 'The overriding impresson from reading these novels constantly is that the time spent between violence is meaningless.'
[46] *The Bookseller* 7/3/40, quoted in McAleer, *op.cit.*, p77.
[47] *Ibid.*, p74.

[48] George Orwell, 'Raffles and Miss Blandish', *Horizon*, 1944. See also Brian Stableford's critique, 'James Hadley Chase and No Orchids For Miss Blandish', *Million*, Number 4, 1991.

[49] M.O. FR 2545B, *op.cit.*, p141.

[50] M.O. FR 1332, *op.cit.*, p52.

[51] *Ibid.*, p51, '17% of all D class people observed in and about bookshops were at these pornographic shops, as compared with ... only 1% of B'. An earlier study had suggested that B Class men were the main customers. M.O. FR 1222, *op.cit.*, p4.

[52] M.O. FR 1332, *op.cit.*, p52.

[53] As one tuppenny library manageress put it, 'We get lots of enquiries for any banned books', *ibid.*, p7b.

[54] Paul Ferris, *Sex and the British*, Michael Joseph, London, 1993, pp138-40.

[55] It is perhaps ironic that this plebeian porn was written by a Squadron-Leader W.O.G. Lofts and D.J. Adley, 'Collecting James Hadley Chase', *Book and Magazine Collector*, Number 85, April 1991.

[56] Holland, *op.cit.*, p111.

[57] M.O. FR 1332, *op.cit.*, p52. Tuppenny libraries had American sections even before the GIs arrived in 1943, *ibid.*, p70.

[58] M.O. FR 2018, *op.cit.*, p88. This 35-year-old-insomniac's diet of gore consisted of at least six books per week.

[59] 'Best laugh I ever had was a thing I got in Woolworths ... it had a girl with legs on the cover and bloke looking through a window. I thought, that's a bit of alright, and it was. I never finished it though, had to hide it from the missus and never found it again ...'
Middle-aged man from Notting Hill, M.O. Reading Box 8 File C, 9-10 Sept. 1943.

[60] M.O. FR 1332, *op.cit.*, p129a.

[61] *Ibid.*, F30D p70d, F25C p107, F35C p163.

[62] Geoffrey O'Brien, *Hard-boiled America: The Lurid Years of Paperbacks*, Van Nostrand Reinhold, New York, 1981.

[63] There is some evidence that the reading of pulp paperbacks was shared by men and women. M.O. FR 2018 *op.cit.*, p8 contains a description of a couple reading *The Tragedies of the White Slaves* together in Leicester Square. The man was a serviceman home on leave, aged about thirty. The woman (F30C) was 'overdressed in a black fancy costume, with long scarlet fingernails, a simpering voice and she [did] a terrible lot of giggling'.

[64] M.O. FR 1332, *op.cit.*, p708.

[65] Men were probably more likely to pass their pulp novels on to workmates, *ibid.*, p114.

[66] Robert Escarpit, *The Book Revolution*, Harrap, London, 1976.

[67] M.O. FR 2545B, *op.cit.*, pp38-53.

[68] M.O. FR 1332, *op.cit.*, p146.

[69] M.O. FR 2018, *op.cit.*, pp102-104.

[70] As one Oxford Street bookseller stated: There is a lessening objection to paper-bound books when they're good. Penguins have bound their books neatly and attractively. There's a growing demand for good material if presented in attractive and satisfactory Penguin format. M.O. FR 2545B,

op.cit., p229.

[71] M.O. FR 1332, *op.cit.*, p147. The visual orientation of C and D Class readers was also apparent in their enthusiasm for novels which had been filmed, the text becoming valued for its ability to revive fantasies already created by another medium, *ibid.*, p59.

[72] Davis, *op.cit.*. For an alternative account see J.E. Morpurgo, *Allen Lane, King Penguin: A Biography*, Hutchinson, London, 1979.

[73] M.O. FR 2545B, *op.cit.*, p237. Penguin's American branch complied with this suggestion in 1943, causing considerable dismay to the doctrinaire Allen Lane. Davis, *op.cit.*, p101.

[74] See Holland *op.cit.* and Philip Harbottle and Stephen Holland, *Vultures of the Void*, Borgo, San Bernardino, 1992.

[75] Advertisement in Buck Toler, *It's Only Saps That Die*, Everybody's Books, London, 1944.

[76] Harbottle and Holland, *op.cit.*, p19.

[77] Holland, *op.cit.*, pp13, 15. Author and publisher Steven Frances supplies an illustrative anecdote in his unpublished autobiography, *Whatever Happened to Hank Janson?*: 'I knew where I could buy a certain type of paper. My printer friend knew a buyer in Scotland. We pooled our resources and scraped up the cash to buy the paper and sent it off. That night there were heavy air raids. I rang my printer friend in the morning. 'Tell me, did you insure that paper?' ... 'No' he admitted huskily ... For eight days neither of us had a good night's sleep. We'd both borrowed money right and left and were in debt well over our heads. The good news came. The paper had got through safely – the wages bill for that week was ensured.'

[78] Holland, *op.cit.*, p15.

[79] Longmate, *op.cit.*, p449.

[80] Calder-Marshall, *op.cit.*, p39.

[81] M.O. FR 2537, *op.cit.*, p8.

[82] Frances, *op.cit.*

[83] McAleer, *op.cit.*, pp59-60.

Cross-Dressing in Wartime: Georgette Heyer's *The Corinthian* in its 1940 Context

Kathleen Bell

Georgette Heyer's *The Corinthian*, her second novel of 1940 and published in November of that year, negotiates and addresses a number of social and political debates current at the time, which it may have been difficult to consider overtly. At first glance, *The Corinthian* seems to merit the adjective 'escapist', fulfilling a need to take refuge in fantasy from such anxieties as the black-out, the blitz, food shortages, rationing and the fear of German invasion. This label would seem to be endorsed by the subject of the book; both principal characters and many minor characters directly enact escapes of various kinds and the words 'escape' and 'escapade' occur frequently in the text. Moreover the story, set in the early nineteenth century, seems at first consideration far removed from World War Two. Its two main characters, the Corinthian Richard 'Beau' Wyndham and the 17-year-old heiress Pen Creed, are both under pressure to enter into marriages that will further their families' interests. Wyndham, hours away from proposing to the frigid Melissa Brandon, is wandering home, drunk, when he observes what he at first takes to be a young man escaping from the upstairs window of a house. The 'youth' turns out to be a young woman, Pen Creed, who has donned masculine clothing in order to travel safely to meet her childhood sweetheart, Piers Luttrell, whom she has not seen for five years. They travel cross-country by stagecoach, heading for Piers' home, with Richard acting in turn as Pen's tutor, guardian and uncle. The plot is complicated by a series of episodes concerning the upper-class but impoverished Brandon family, bringing Pen into contact with a thief, a Bow Street runner, a stolen necklace and a murder. When Piers is finally discovered, it turns out that he has entered into a secret betrothal with the ultra-feminine and unadventurous Lydia Daubenay – a discovery that frees Pen who realises that she is now in love with Richard.

Certain staple elements of romantic fiction are present – the young woman slowly realising her love for the older, protective man and the need to assert freely-chosen love over compelled marriage – as well as detective story puzzles about the theft of the Brandon necklace and the murder of Beverley Brandon. These offered a degree of escape in that they were familiar plot elements pointing to reassuringly familiar conclusions. At the same time, however, comparisons with wartime circumstances are frequently implied, as, for example, when Pen, perpetually hungry, eats her apples core and all.[1] Indeed, the novel offers the fantasy of a constant supply of large meals ranging from a hamper on a coach to a breakfast of 'lavishly' buttered bread with 'several slices of ham' – goods that were rationed in 1940.[2]

The era in which *The Corinthian* is set suggests further comparisons with 1940. Military service in Wellington's Peninsular Army is offered as a means to personal redemption, drawing on the further parallel of Napoleon's conquest of Europe and threatened invasion of Britain with contemporary fears of invasion – a parallel frequently invoked at the time.[3] Comparisons with the Napoleonic Wars also offered the happy conclusion of Allied victory at Waterloo. Heyer's first novel of 1940, *The Spanish Bride*, had been a fact-filled historical romance set in the same period. Based on Harry Smith's marriage to the 14-year-old Juana, it recounted hardship shared in campaigning, the separation of the married couple and finally victory at Waterloo. The book was a best-seller[4] and therefore Heyer's regular readers could be expected to pick up the significance of *The Corinthian*'s occasional references to the Peninsular Wars.

More intriguingly related to the events of 1940 is the introduction of a cross-dressed heroine at a time when the suitability of women for war-work, as well as femininity itself, was a subject of public debate.

Heyer had created two cross-dressed heroines more than a decade previously: Léonie in *These Old Shades* (1926), her first big success, and Prudence in *The Masqueraders* (1928), who was, less usually, accompanied by her cross-dressing brother, Robin. Tales involving cross-dressing were not unusual in the inter-war years[5] and its resonances varied from the erotic to the political. The heroines of *These Old Shades* and *The Masqueraders* used their masculine disguises to enter male territory; Léonie, serving as the Duke of Avon's page, accompanied him to brothels and gambling clubs and relished lessons in sword-fighting, while Prudence, disguised as an adult male, encountered men as equals in the world of male clubs, joining them in drinking, gaming and – less successfully – fighting. In these two novels the assumption of male clothing is concealed from other characters for a long time and even, to some extent, from the reader. Ambiguity about gender, and doubt about the hero's knowledge of the heroine's true identity, adds a layer of erotic interest to their encounters.

But Pen Creed is different from earlier transgressive heroines. Her assumed masculine identity brings her few of the advantages or erotic encounters afforded the others. She willingly places herself in a subordinate position in relation to the older Richard, adopting the role of pupil or ward. Apart from a few scenes of farcical confusion in which she enacts the role of Lydia's would-be seducer, Pen's assumption of masculine identity allows her no more freedom than the indulgence of a healthy appetite and the occasional walk at night, with Richard as protector always close at hand. Even the erotic possibilities of the scenario are limited by Richard's (and the reader's) immediate identification of Pen as female. Instead of being put forward as a figure whose gender is uncertain, Pen is quickly established as the boyish girl, able to fit into the male world – but never quite as an equal. While Heyer novels were not noted for their emphasis on sexuality, even within Heyer's *oeuvre* the romance between Richard and Pen is signally lacking in erotic interest. When it is suggested that Richard and Pen (at this stage travelling as schoolboy and tutor) should share a room,[6] there is not any embarrassment in their laughter; they are simply amused at the impossibility of the situation and Richard rapidly puts forward an alternative suggestion.

This surprisingly unadventurous combination of elements may derive from popular uncertainty about what role women were to be given as their country waged war. While in the later war years younger, childless women were conscripted and others encouraged to seek paid employment, the beginning of World War Two saw an increase in female unemployment.[7] Employers reportedly preferred cutting back on production to engaging women workers, provoking an active lobbying campaign from the Federation of Business and Professional Women.[8] In January 1940, Winston Churchill appeared to endorse their aims in a widely-reported speech, although he also offered reassurance to any who feared the permanent loss of the pre-war status quo:

> Nearly a million women were employed in the last war in 1918 under the Ministry of Munitions. They did all kinds of things that no one had ever expected them to do before and they did them very well.
> But after the war was over they went back home and were no obstacle to the resumption of normal conditions of British life and labour.[9]

Churchill's speech stimulated national debate, but he did not become prime minister until May of that year and it was not until 1941 that women were subject to conscription. Instead the emphasis was on women selecting themselves as capable and volunteering for service – as civilian workers and as soldiers.

As the debate continued, questions raised included national need, the rights of women to equal treatment and, inevitably, the danger that female sexuality posed to men.[10] Pre-war prejudices against women working continued to surface. On 13 July *Time and Tide* reported an incident which it considered representative of the country's unwillingness to allow women to take on 'unsuitable' jobs despite the anticipation of invasion:[11]

> Cornering women out of the war has become a regular fetish with officialdom. The latest evidence comes from a town in the Eastern Counties, where women who responded to the 'dig for defence' appeal to civilians were told to go back home. Women, it seems, are not fit to dig or fill sandbags. They are not fit to co-operate with I.D.V.s. In some districts they have even been deemed unfit to hold important A.R.P. posts. Meanwhile women are deluged with 'pep' talks on the radio, designed on special homely lines which it is hoped no doubt will penetrate to their sub-human understanding.
> What a mercy the bold Mrs. Cardwell did not have to ask officialdom before she arrested an armed parachutist. It certainly would have been forbidden ... unseemly, unsuitable and quite beyond her powers.[12]

Time and Tide goes on to praise the action of Churchill in cutting through the usual red tape to secure an OBE for the intrepid Mrs Cardwell. Here, as elsewhere in *Time and Tide*, Churchill functioned as a hero despite its largely feminist and left-leaning agenda. Yet Churchill's call for female labour and female involvement in the war effort had been couched in conservative terms; similarly Heyer's representation of Pen Creed can be read as an attempt to allay male concerns while praising certain of her qualities as 'unique'.

> 'I am afraid,' confessed Pen, 'that I am not very well-behaved. Aunt says that I had a lamentable upbringing, because my father treated me as though I had been a boy. I ought to have been, you understand.'
>
> 'I cannot agree with you,' said Richard. 'As a boy you would have been in no way remarkable; as a female, believe me, you are unique.'
>
> She flushed to the roots of her hair. 'I *think* that is a compliment.'
>
> 'It is,' Sir Richard said, amused.[13]

In the context of 1940, Pen's assumption of a masculine character posed little danger to the established order. However, for the female reader of the time and/or the would-be wartime volunteer, Pen legitimises difference, exceptionality and the desire to function in a male world. But the limits to female aspiration are clearly defined. As a boyish woman, Pen is marked out as praiseworthy because she achieves the virtues of an average, unexceptional boy and, within a system of values which views men as superior to boys as well as women, there is never any danger of her competing with or equalling grown men. Nevertheless, her aspirations are endorsed precisely because they relate to masculine virtue. It is important to note that this is not a fixed scheme throughout Heyer's work. In novels as diverse as *Devil's Cub* (1932), *Sylvester* (1957) and *Frederica* (1965), men are seen as in need of the domesticating and civilizing force of femininity while *Faro's Daughter* (1941) and *The Grand Sophy* (1950) allow their powerful and active heroines a combination of conventional feminine attributes with an understanding of and adherence to aspects of the masculine ethos. It seems reasonable, therefore, to link the attitudes to masculine prowess and, by implication, feminine weakness in *The Corinthian* to the situation in contemporary England.

While boyishness is treated as praiseworthy in *The Corinthian*, it is set against two other, less approved models of femininity: the masterful woman whose qualities are thrown into relief by the weak men around her and the more conventionally feminine woman who uses her appearance of weakness to manipulate people. These types are common both to Heyer and the genre but are treated less sympathetically than usual. Louisa, Wyndham's sister, who falls into the first category, may possess a 'leavening gleam of humour'[14] but has no rapport with her brother, being chiefly concerned to push him into an unwelcome marriage. Melissa Brandon, the bride chosen for Wyndham by his family, is described as 'hard', 'contemptuous' and an 'iceberg'.[15] Lady Luttrell alone, making a belated appearance in the final chapter, redeems the model of this type, but only by endorsing Wyndham's judgement and taking more interest in his love-match with Pen than she does in the elopement of her own son.

More conclusively dangerous is the exaggerated and manipulative femininity of Lady Wyndham, using her apparent frailty as a 'subtle way of getting her wishes attended to'. The 'delicate state of her nerves', indicated by handkerchief, vinaigrette and hartshorn, has, we are warned, a 'sinister message'.[16] As she fades from the plot, another feminine manipulator intervenes in the love story. Lydia Daubenay's frilled garments[17] indicate her concentration on her own desires. Having run away and fainted at the sight of violence, Lydia attempts to use tears to win the support of Pen, only to be condemned as an 'unprincipled' liar.[18] In the younger woman feminine weakness is significantly connected with a lack of that important wartime quality, public spirit.[19]

Yet this public spirit, which Lydia is condemned for lacking, proves an elusive concept in *The Corinthian*. While this novel lacks the adherence to the strict standards of social etiquette proclaimed in most other Heyer novels – Pen is the only Heyer heroine to effect a successful escape from her bedroom window while Piers and Lydia set off to commit the *faux pas* of a Gretna Green marriage – social hierarchy and class interest still prevail. At the end of the day public interest (represented by the magistrate and the Bow Street runner) is at odds with and subordinated to the needs of the upper classes to maintain their public image.[20] Richard, acting as the text's ethical arbiter, is prepared to co-operate with the magistrate over the murder of Beverley Brandon but, openly preferring class solidarity to public justice, he works to cover up Beverley's earlier crimes thus averting public disgrace for his family. Although public-spiritedness is seen as a masculine virtue to which women should aspire, the degree to which it is genuinely public is a matter for men to determine. Women must take their part in public-spiritedness at second hand; Richard defines what is best for the proper ordering of society while Pen and Lady Luttrell defer to his judgement.

This concentration on class may echo concerns about changing class relations in wartime. While government-backed propaganda did not deny class difference, a new emphasis was placed on classes working together.[21] In practical terms people from different classes were asked to work alongside each other; the officer class, for example, was enlarged to include those with relevant ability and experience. Objections were raised to the preservation of narrow peacetime hierarchies in the wartime situation.[22] But against this concern that ability be given priority over social standing was the fear that women who had achieved professional status in peacetime (a status barely open to women of working-class or lower middle-class origins) should lose that status as unqualified women were taken into the workforce.

Set in the context of this debate, Pen Creed's position is that of the very young, enthusiastic, aristocratic amateur. Her class origins, which are the same as the hero's, hark back to an older world in which aristocratic position is the best guarantor of intelligence and the security of the aristocracy the only surety for a happy and well-ordered society.

For the first part of the novel Richard and Pen escape from society and its rules; as Richard observes, 'it was good for a man to be removed occasionally from civilisation'.[23] But the use of Richard to represent civilisation in the latter half reveals a deep fissure in the novel since he stands both for the values of civilisation and the need to escape from it; indeed, it is only his escape and his refusal to make the socially-approved marriage with Melissa Brandon that enables him to function as protector of the Brandon family's reputation. There are two reasons for this. Firstly, the civilisation from which Richard is escaping is a world of female rule and dominating domesticity. This was, of course, the very 'escape' being asked of men recruited and conscripted into the armed forces as well as an 'escape' which some women were also demanding for themselves. Given the heterosexual conventions of the genre, female escape can best be achieved by a romance whose heroine has been brought up by her father and who dresses, thinks and acts like a boy. But she is represented as an immature male; s/he defers to Richard as her/his superior and is dependent on his advice and commands. The relationship Pen and Richard achieve is asexual; Pen's chief attraction is her boyishness –

which partly denies her sexuality. Athough Pen is at one point accused by Richard of a 'feminine trick'[24] (the word 'trick' is significant) there is no traditional transformation of the 'tomboy' into a beauty in petticoats. But she does get her man, romance and, the reader is given to assume, sex; the last reference to the couple is to a 'golden-haired stripling ... locked in the Corinthian's arms being ruthlessly kissed'[25] to the amazement of a stagecoachful of passengers. The text implies that feminine women are powerful and dangerous but women prepared to be lesser men can be trained to obey male commands and absorbed into male hierarchies without danger. They also get some rewards.

Secondly, the journey of escape undertaken by Richard and Pen, which introduces them to experiences not usually encountered by members of their class, can be related to a journey recommended to the British wartime population as a whole. They journey away from civilisation and their customary comforts in order that civilisation (or the pre-war status quo) may be restored. Discomforts are made light of while the benefits of the journey are lauded. Men escape from the powers of womanly women into an arena in which they can take control while women who give up the delights of femininity are promised its conventional rewards.

NOTES

Page references to *The Corinthian* follow the 1948 edition.

[1] *The Corinthian*, pp46 and 137.

[2] For details of rationing, which began in early 1940, see Norman Longmate, *How We Lived Then*, Hutchinson, London, 1971, chapter 13, pp140-155.

[3] For instance in many press references and in Winston Churchill's enthusiasm for and conviction of the propaganda value of the film *Lady Hamilton* (1941).

[4] The 'In the Bookshops' column in *The Observer*, 14 April 1940, lists *The Spanish Bride* as the book most in demand from libraries and as one of the seven top-selling novels of the week. Present-day readers may be startled by early passages in the book which depict British soldiers in disorderly activities ranging from looting to raping nuns but the conduct of the troops undergoes a marked improvement in the course of the novel.

[5] Examples of novels include: D.K. Broster, *Mr Rowl* (1924), Virginia Woolf, *Orlando* (1928), while notable instances of cinematic cross-dressing can be found in *Queen Christina* (1933), *Morocco* (1930), *Sylvia Scarlett* (1936) and *First a Girl* (1935).

[6] *The Corinthian*, p59.

[7] For a detailed analysis of changing employment patterns in World War Two and their causes see Penny Summerfield, *Women Workers in the Second World*

War, 1984, especially Chapter 3.

[8] This is chronicled in the editorial pages and correspondence columns of *Time and Tide* for 1940.

[9] Churchill's speech, given in Manchester on Saturday 27 January 1940, was fully reported in *The Observer*, 28 January 1940.

[10] The concern that women's irregular sexual activities may weaken the resolve of their soldier husbands by causing 'trouble at home' is expressed by an article sent to *Time and Tide* by 'the Archbishop of York who vouches for the writer' and published on 31 August 1940, p886.

[11] After the fall of France the Government was concerned to advise the population of how to react when the Germans landed. George Orwell's letter to *Time and Tide* (22 June 1940, p662) recommending arming the populace in response to the 'almost certain' invasion of Britain stimulated debate about the possible arming of Britain, including calls that women be equipped with hand-grenades.

[12] 'Time and Tide Diary', *Time and Tide*, 13 July 1940, p727.

[13] *The Corinthian*, p58.

[14] *Ibid.*, p6.

[15] *Ibid.*, pp20, 22 and 13.

[16] *Ibid.*, p6.

[17] For a midnight assignation, Lydia is described as wearing 'a white muslin dress, high-waisted and frilled about the ankles, and with a great many pale-blue bows of ribbon with long fluttering ends.' (p128). Needless to say one of her major concerns is that the grass might stain her dress.

[18] *The Corinthian*, p132.

[19] Pen and Richard happily assume that she would be unwilling to perform the public duty of identifying Captain Trimble. (p164).

[20] In the detective novel of this period the reader would expect that while the magistrate and the Bow Street Runner might not be able to ascertain the truth without the aid of the amateur sleuth, the sleuth would share their value system. In the detective sub-plot Richard functions as aristocratic sleuth but clearly separates his value system from those held by the forces of law and order.

[21] In such films as Humphrey Jennings' *London Can Take It* (1940) the stress is on the shared experience of Londoners regardless of class. Other films dealt less happily with the need to address all social classes as Jeffrey Richards and Dorothy Sheridan's, *Mass Observaton at the Movies*, RKP, London, 1987, illustrates, especially in Section D 'Ministry of Information Shorts', p424ff.

[22] For example, *Time and Tide* was concerned that 'the recruiting of officers for the W.R.N.S. has taken place practically entirely from the wives and daughters of existing naval officers' and expressed particular concern that commissioned rank had been recommended for 'a schoolgirl barely eighteen'. 'Families in Uniform', *Time and Tide*, 30 December 1939, p1647.

[23] *The Corinthian*, p83.

[24] She does no more than pat her curls into order before the mirror (p162). The comment may seem a trifle unfair from a man who requires the minimum of an hour in which to dress himself.

[25] *Ibid.*, p207.

Murder in Wartime

Stephen Knight

For literary criticism, it was not a good war. In comparison with the traditionally vaunted heights of military glory and national spirit, commentators on the novel felt they faced a featureless plain relieved only by the restrained sentiment of Elizabeth Bowen or the moderate gloom of Graham Greene. The conventional wartime novel did not even manage the modest level of military elevation found in the poetry of Kenneth Douglas and Alun Lewis.

Critics themselves seemed flattened by the featureless prose: for W.W. Robson this was 'one of the worst periods' in the English novel and in *Under Siege*, Robert Hewison gathered a range of negative views of this 'depressing' time in a chapter entitled 'There is no Such Thing as Culture in Wartime'.[1] The rationing of paper has sometimes been suggested as a basis for the novel's unheroic performance, but the real cause may lie in the mistaken expectations of those who perceive such a literary defeat.

Incisive military fictions are normally recollected in tranquillity, from *The Song of Roland* to the not dissimilar *The Naked and the Dead*; our own period has seen many *post factum* appropriations of the Vietnam conflict, from jingoism to critique and back again. And what is written after a war may well be more concerned with the ideologies of a present than the practices of the martial past. In *Dockers and Detectives*, Ken Worpole exposed how English military fictions of the 1950s worked to restore, or reinvent, an English national hierarchy.[2]

But there was more to war fiction than the languid art novel of 1940-45 or later fantasies of heroism. There was a wartime boom in demand for books and in spite of constraints like paper rationing, the loss of stock in bombing raids and the widespread recycling of second-hand material, substantial sales were enjoyed by all forms of literature. As in peacetime much of this was in the various genres of popular fiction. This is not noticed in the standard literary accounts, but Angus Calder, though writing an avowedly popular history, still felt able to say 'much of this output of course was low-grade fiction' and Tom Harrisson, who wrote a survey of all contemporary fiction for *Horizon* in 1942, felt able to describe it, in tones of even more canonical confidence, as 'a cataract of tripe'.[3]

Much of this tripe was in the mode of crime fiction. John Creasey, the champion of all producers in the genre, published at least seventy-five thrillers during the war, allied to which were some westerns (as 'Tex Riley') and a few love stories under the suitably Gallic name of 'Elise Fecamp'. Some other big names were elsewhere – Leslie Charteris moved to America in 1935 and only a few Saint-as-counterspy novels appeared for the embattled UK audience; 'James Hadley Chase', with the *succes de scandale* of *No Orchids for Miss Blandish* (1939) behind him and many diluted versions in the peacetime years ahead, was occupied for the duration as Squadron Leader Rene Raymond. But Agatha Christie, though working in a London hospital, was in full production with her usual two novels a year and the least-remembered name may well have been the most successful: in 1944 and 1945 Peter Cheyney released audited sales figures of over two million a year.

Many other crime writers followed the path of the major figures, but their work and its reception has gone quite unnoticed. This is unlike the treatment of the genre in other periods: it has become commonplace to search the emergent crime fiction of the *fin de siècle* to find in Doyle, Stevenson, Futrelle and Freeman the scientistic narcissism that bespeaks bourgeois hopes and fears; it is the merest conventionality to trace in 1930s thrillers the privatised results of economic strain in Britain and America; contemporary crime stories are today acknowledged as bearing the clearest traces of our own period's sense of the body in crisis. The crime fiction of World War Two deserves comparable analysis. In the light of acknowledged massive sales, and as an obvious way of displacing the widespread sense of physical threat, it seems a potentially positive process to explore how crime fiction mediated the notion of a nation at war.

Agatha Christie, it has often been remarked, was a staple item of reading in the air raid shelters, and cheap reprints, even separate editions of short stories, were produced for this kind of context. Most commentators have thought this phenomenon was no more than escape, that as the sirens howled and explosions reverberated, people turned over page after page of fey investigations of bloodless crime in what Colin Watson has wittily called Mayhem Parva. But this is not

162

quite the case. In various ways Christie's wartime novels do recognise aspects of the contemporary world – though not in the naive reflective way that many naively unreflective critics have thought appropriate. It is some time now since Jane Austen was criticised for not representing the Napoleonic Wars: the modern tendency would be to see a deep-laid contemporaneity in her realisation of a largely male-free world, where the meretricious attractions of quasi-soldiers like Frank Churchill or Mr Fairfax are set against the absent verity of a Captain Wentworth. Through her displaced focus, it can be argued, Austen gives a veridical and even moving account of the period and its problems from a domestic and feminine viewpoint.

Christie's *Towards Zero*, published in 1944, has a remarkably similar structure. Without overt reference at all to the war, it presents a world of weak, selfish men, whose inability to control what they think of as their inheritance is exposed in part by the resistance of women of courage and principle and in particular by a police detective who goes by the appropriate wartime name of Superintendent Battle – though he was used as long ago as *The Secret of Chimneys* (1925), Christie shows a special fondness for him in the war period.

Christie's wartime mysteries superintend contemporary battles from a distance and with an Austenesque pattern of radical displacement, not recognising the war as itself, but representing its effect in terms of disruptions to the normal balance of gender and social power – *Sad Cypress* (1940) and *The Moving Finger* (1943) are good examples, as is the most powerful of all her novels from this period *The Body in the Library* (1942), which not only deals sharply with male narcissism and social mobility in women, but also parodies her own previous forms of certainty by returning to the world of *Murder in the Vicarage* with nothing now secure for Miss Marple and her systems of inquiry.

It is notable that the less well known and less successful, in both market and critical terms, of Christie's wartime texts do not displace the war so completely, but represent it as a part of the criminal setting. This is the case in *One, Two, Buckle My Shoe* (1940) which presents the crime as being involved with threats to the stability of the country and involves several of the characters in espionage. This sense of political melodrama was improbably emphasised when the book was in America retitled *The Patriotic Murders*. But that title is actually, and not – playfully – misleading. The crime is ultimately shown to be entirely personal not political – and Christie deals overtly in those terms as if justifying her displacing technique. The novel is not clearly

set in wartime and the leisured London lifestyle of the characters
provides a sense of wish-fulfilment much to be valued as rationing,
black-out and utility in all aspects of life quenched the consumerist
excitements some had enjoyed, or at least aspired to, in the 1930s. That
combination of stylish fantasy, apparent politics and acutely private
threats remains Christie's basic style throughout the war as is indicated
in *Sparkling Cyanide* (1945), which also refers to foreign fiendishness
as a possible but eventually negligible disruption to London leisure.
We may suspect someone of being both a villain and an arms dealer,
but in fact he is a spy loyal to both Britain and the heroine. More
focused than they usually are, these political threats are ultimately no
more than part of the cloud of suspicion that Christie always sets up.

She does, however, give the war a full place in the process of crime
and detection in what seems perhaps her least successful wartime
mystery, *N or M?* (1941), which to a modern eye positively creaks with
antiquity, unlike the titles discussed above. It uses the already ageing
couple Tommy and Tuppence Beresford, whose breathless pursuit of
national enemies had started in *The Secret Adversary* (1922) and
received a highly unlikely comeback in extreme old age in *Postern of
Fate* (1973). *N or M?* is basically in the tradition of jingoistic
pot-boilers, like the series produced by J.M. Walsh, an Australian
writer based in London (he actually used 'Haverstock Hill' as a
pseudonym), who favoured heart-stopping titles like *Spies from the
Skies* (1941) or *I Stand Alert* (1943). In much the same mood, in *N or
M?* we are in mid-1940s England, under threat of invasion. Tommy, a
retired colonel, is summoned back to the ranks of espionage; Tuppence
is ignored. But secretly she joins him at a south-eastern English resort,
where they pluckily expose what they would no doubt call a nest of
traitors, proving their enduring skills and courage to readers and their
own children. This is a fantasy of action for those uninvolved in
military life, and some other attitudes of interest emerge: Christie
continues, as in her early adventure stories, to suggest there is a core of
anti-British people close to the centre of power in the country. Where
before some of them were internationalists, seen in a xenophobic light,
they are now high-placed Nazi sympathisers of impeccably English
origin. In the light of the later national myth of pro-Churchillian
unity, it is striking how firmly Christie stresses that the real 'enemy
within' is not German nationals undercover, and especially not the
rather noble IRA sympathisers represented quite fully in the novel, but
echt pukka sahibs. Christie, of course, tended to make British officers

and their girlfriends into her villains ever since 1926 when Colonel Christie himself decamped with his secretary, but she also specifies a distinct doubt about the national hierarchy; in fact this scepticism about the commitment of the propertied classes to the war effort is a widespread feature of wartime crime fiction, which has been obscured through selective memory and the impact of post-war popular war films and fiction with their anodyne sense of patriotic coherence.

Apart from its engaging element of anti-ageism and this notion of dissent within the respectable ranks, *N or M?* is a threadbare piece of jingoism. At the time and since, success for Christie appears to have depended on a major process of displacement as a central mechanism of response to the war. The same pattern is clear in the work of Peter Cheyney. He died in 1951; reasons for his present oblivion must include his absence from the publishing scene, his dated slang and attitudes and, it may be, the combination of marked sexism with an almost complete lack of violence (unlike Chase and Spillane, for example). Yet he held a major position as a popular author, seemed highly exciting for teenagers, and tends still to be remembered with bemused nostalgia by readers over fifty.

Of Irish origin, wounded at the Somme, Reginald Peter Cheyney was a journalist about town in the 1930s.[4] He began producing real crime stories for the *Sunday Graphic* and these interests were transmuted into fiction with his creation in 1935 of the character Lemmy Caution, an American private eye related to Hammett and Chandler, but so stylised in language and mannered in plotting as now to be almost unreadable (though he had a brief renaissance in Godard's film *Alphaville* where, no doubt with conscious irony, he was addressed as M. Cochon). Perhaps the most bizarre thing about this strange creation is that Cheyney prided himself as being a realist,[5] and he – and apparently his audience – saw Caution and his various versions as a credible account of transatlantic crime and its treatment. This would be all the more surprising if it were not the case that all major mythographers of crime, from Poe to the creators of Kojack, appear to have shared the view that they were basically realists.

Apparently criticised for being too pro-American,[6] Cheyney in 1938 created a British – or rather Irish – version of the tough but engaging hero. Slim Callaghan is broad-shouldered, narrow-hipped, devoted to silk pyjamas and silkier women. A heavy hand with a drink and a light touch on financial trickery, Callaghan became the star of a very successful series of high-life adventures.

They were hardly mysteries, though there is usually a half-concealed twist at the end. Cheyney, as befits a Sunday journalist, wrote easily and let the action flow well, most unlike the moralising intensity of Chandler or the knotty enigmas of Hammett. There were gestures at culture at times, but the major thrust was towards a world of elegant consumption. The social level of the action was crucial: this was the private eye story reshaped for Mayfair and the elegant home counties. Developed as he was for the still depressed late 1930s, Callaghan's suaveness and style had an even greater fantasy value in the England of wartime repression. There was Callaghan's appearance to enjoy:

> He was wearing a sea-green silk undervest and shorts. One foot sported a blue silk sock and well polished shoe; the other merely a suspender which hung precariously from the big toe.
>
> His hands were folded across his belly. He slept deeply and peacefully. His broad shoulders, which almost covered the width of the settee, descended to a thin waist and narrow hips. His face was thin and the high cheekbones made it appear longer. His black hair was troubled and unruly.
> (*You Can't Keep The Change*, 1940, p9)

Cheyney famously appealed to women readers, but for the gentlemen there was something equally inspiring, if less immediately lubricious:

> She looked exquisite. She wore a plain black crêpe de Chine dinner frock with a small diamond buckle at its belt and soft beige ruffles at throat and wrists. Her hair, loosely but artistically dressed, was tied at one side with a black watered silk ribbon.
> (*Sorry You've Been Troubled*, 1942, p62)

Most well provided for of all were foot-fetishists among the audience. In the time of army boots and utility shoes, Cheyney's characters of both genders reveal slim ankles, they wear either tight kid pumps or suave leather loafers and the blacked-out streets of London are redolent with the hiss of fine leather and the click of tiny heels.

In the same tone the action flickers through sophisticated Mayfair clubs, whisks in the Jaguar down to home counties mansions, pauses in the louche luxury of Callaghan's bedchamber or the scented air of a lady's sitting room. After 1939 the wartime context is occasionally touched on: now and then the sirens go; occasionally a crêpe de Chine clad heroine mentions her absent soldier husband, but, as in Christie, the plotting is extraneous to the war and involves quite complicated dealing in bonds, jewels, wills and cash, all suggesting that a world of pre-war money, from property and business, has come into contact with wartime forces of black market and get-rich-quick merchants, and the ladies are left with all their problems and only Slim to help.

The Cheyney novels read like a Ruritanian fantasy of wartime elegance and thoroughly displaced danger; they clearly held a remarkable spell – as a fantasy of sophistication, with sensuality taken as far as it then could go, and also offering a charismatic model of ironic heroism in a most unmilitary figure. Slim was an unclassed version of the Saint or the Toff, more sexually aware than either and much more worldly-wise – he comes from the world of Mayfair corruption Cheyney had handled for his newspaper. There are obviously strong elements of identification and attraction – Rupert Patrick Callaghan's initials are the same as Cheyney's. The world-weary tough guy element clearly lived on in James Bond, and both that and the trace of a caddish stud which is relished in the texts make of Slim Callaghan a hero who is the exact opposite of what we are led to believe was the ideal wartime figure, the wimpish star of 1950s war films.

Like Christie, Cheyney did not only use this mode of total displacement, highly successful though it was. In some fiction he approached the realities of war more closely. The Callaghan figure mutated easily enough into spy fiction, and Cheyney undertook different versions of heroic adventures in this mode in his 'Dark' series, but here, also as in Christie, elements of realism seem to have been felt unsatisfactory, and were essentially abandoned or restricted as Cheyney continued in this form.

Dark Duet (1942) was consciously oriented towards the war. The dedication read 'To my step-son A/C2 Walter'. Just like the world of an aircraftman second-class, the office in the opening of the story is 'sombre and unassuming'. The police who appear are skilful and realistic, not the clowns outwitted by Slim Callaghan. The world of West-End party-going is still a major part of the setting, but the bombing and the blackout ominously surround those glittering oases. Kane, the leading counter-spy, has like Callaghan 'the sensitive mouth, the humorous and Celtic cut of the cheekbones' but he also has 'a peculiar indefinable grimness' (p12).

The pattern of plotting is also more realistic. Bombs have fallen, people have been killed, and Mrs Marquis, a leading party-goer, is suspected of espionage. Most strikingly, instead of Callaghan's comical Canadian assistant well-named Windy, the hero's partner is Ernie Guelvada, a short, tough Belgian who speaks seven languages and lost his parents at German hands. This deadly version of Poirot is keen to use his knife, and his attitudes also permit Cheyney to deploy a grisly version of his usual voyeurism – Guelvada speaks of Nazi horror in terms of a woman's breast used as a tobacco pouch. Based firmly on an espionage plot, *Dark Duet* does offer a reasonably realistic representation of the uncertainties, dangers and moral obliquity of wartime life, with no rejection of the sadomasochistic possibilities of such verismo.

However, although he prided himself on the 'psychological' element in this series,[7] Cheyney did not maintain this degree of darkness. In following novels in the same sequence the more simplistic elan of Slim Callaghan was worked into the new format: *Dark Street* (1944) is dedicated much less tensely to 'My Wife, Companion in Adventure' and it introduces the superheroic Shaun Aloysius O'Mara, who takes over the action from the unreliable Ricky Kerr. Behind them looms the omniscient figure of Quayle, the mysterious and patriotically authoritative spy master. Without the disturbing elements of *Dark Duet* – both its realism and its prurience – *Dark Street* is a mainstream patriotic thriller with an obvious structural resemblance to a James Bond novel and perhaps other submerged resonances: Ricky Kerr the weak link and O'Mara the huge handsome hero are curiously like Ricky Tarr and Jerry Westerby in John Le Carré's *The Honourable Schoolboy*.

Those connections may testify to the impact that Cheyney once had, before his work and name were swallowed by different forms of sophistication and modes of the thriller that at least appeared new. The success he had in wartime presumably arose in part because of the exotic lifestyle he offered in a world of blackout and rationing, but also because, in his most popular work, he like Christie used the wartime setting as no more than a context against which to continue exploring the issues of human betrayal and various forms of inter-personal crime; when he ventured into fairly realistic espionage stories, he soon withdrew from sharp and sadistic realism into a mildly political variation of his fantasies of suave detection.

If the patterns of both Christie and Cheyney suggest that the most successful forms of crime fiction in war-time were those that both recognised and extensively reprocessed the reality of war, there existed a number of less well-known writers who worked steadily and in less fantasised ways in that essentially displacing mode, whose work deserves to be noted as long-overlooked examples of war-time crime fiction.

Patricia Wentworth was a well established writer of thrillers; her series character Miss Silver had appeared before the war in 1937 (*The Case is Closed*) and 1939 (*Lonesome Road*), but she became a mainstay of Wentworth's fiction during the war, appearing in six of the nine more novels published by 1945. One of the most interesting is *Miss Silver Intervenes* (1944), though the American edition of the previous year had the more effectively descriptive title *Miss Silver Deals with Death*. From the 'little old lady' school of detection, presumably influenced by Christie's Miss Marple (first appearing in 1930), Miss Silver is an amateur who takes on cases out of interest and reasons her way to an infallible conclusion, being capable of both ingenuity and intervention in the process.

In *Miss Silver Intervenes*, this Jane Austenish character 'deals with death' in two ways – first, there are the immediate murders in a block of flats in wartime London. But more particularly death in war stalks the story: Meade Underwood, the cool heroine who is the observer of events, took her brother's children to America after he was killed in France, but on her return the ship was torpedoed and her new fiancé, an army officer she met in America, was lost. As in Christie's *Towards Zero*, there is an absence of active, decisive men throughout the story – a pattern that helps explain why Wentworth turned so much to Miss Silver in wartime. There is also a consistent context of wartime reality. Miss Silver herself is always knitting for servicemen; fish cakes and Ovaltine are characteristic refreshments, the blackout plays a significant part in the development of the mystery and, perhaps most emotionally important of all, when Meade's fiancé returns without a memory she will not accept a ring from him in wartime.

The mystery itself is based on a plot about blackmail and assumed identity, both stalwart features of prewar social anxiety, though the blackmailer allegedly derives not money but saleable secrets from her victims. The criminal is a woman: this book mediates in many ways a world without men, and a world of personalised danger. Less flamboyant than Cheyney and more intimately realistic than Christie, *Miss Silver Intervenes* is a fine example of the way crime fiction could both represent and displace the actual strains of living through the war in England.

These elements come together most impressively in one of the best-organised and ultimately far-reaching examples in this mode, Christianna Brand's *Green for Danger* (1945). The novel is set in a hospital in the south-east of England during the V1 bombardment towards the end of the war. The doctors and nurses have been enlisted from many places and a sense of disrupted normality dominates from the beginning – a major activity is tending those wounded in the bombing. As in Christie and Wentworth the viewpoint is continuously female, and an especially strong concern is the love lives (or their absence) of the nurses and rather few male doctors.

The mysterious deaths occur in the operating theatre and are eventually traced to the murderer's device of repainting the green cylinders of poisonous gas with the black and white reserved for oxygen. It is a simple but ultimately suggestive motif: just as the title has a strangely ironic note, suggesting that green, the most positive of colours, can be the most deadly under certain circumstances, so the underlying plot shows that under the circumstances of wartime strain a nurse can turn her skills against life, and that itself occurs through a malign misdirection of feeling. She is avenging her mother, who, she believes, was left for dead by a rescue squad who abandoned her bombed house because of danger to themselves.

This complex pattern of protection and betrayal, danger and emotion is a high-order version of the displaced tension found in varying degrees in other war-time crime fiction. But Brand does not only displace anxiety from military to domestic circumstances: she has the imaginative skill to link them through the events and the symbolic structures of the novel. This book was filmed in 1946 and though a somewhat humorous frame was constructed, with Alastair Sim as a whimsical detective, its impact was quite unlike the simplifying national propaganda Worpole found in postwar fiction. Through their ultimate fidelity to Brand's structure and language, Frank Launder and Sidney Gilliat (the director) represent well the way in which an allegedly trivial art form like crime fiction can be the medium in which to realise highly charged responses to danger and disturbance.

Broken romance, sudden death, unbearable strain, a sense of lost normalities: crime fiction has at its most effective the power to mediate those tensions into a tolerable emotive medium. The interpretative and expressive potential of culture in wartime is exemplified by a novel like

Green for Danger, which is both well shaped and satisfying as a formulaic fiction and also subtly responsive to various levels of contemporary need and, even, guilt. Well chosen for the Pandora Women's Crime Writers series in 1987, and so still available in second-hand bookstalls, this novel exemplifies the possibilities of the mystery genre in war time to displace threats, personal and national, into a form both recognisable and negotiable.

Crime writers as well-known as Christie and Cheyney or as apparently minor as Brand and Wentworth worked at various ways of accommodating the wartime reality into their fictions. The variety and complexity of their renovations of the crime form in wartime, as well as the strong public response to the genre in that period is both a narrative worth revisiting and also an indication of how little is understood about the role of culture in context by those who feel that literature was dull and uninspired in the early 1940s and in particular that popular fiction fulfilled no significant role in wartime.

NOTES

1 W.W. Robson, *Modern English Literature*, Oxford University Press, Oxford, 1970, p146; Robert Hewison, *Under Siege*, Weidenfeld and Nicholson, London, 1977, Chapter 8, pp167-81.

2 Ken Worpole, *Dockers and Detectives*, Verso, London, 1983, Chapter 3, 'The Popular Literature of the Second World War,' pp49-73.

3 Angus Calder, *The People's War*, Cape, London, 1969, p512; Tom Harrisson, 'War Books,' *Horizon*, December 1941, p418.

4 The only biography, which has little about the novels, is Michael Harrison, *Making Crime Pay*, Spearman, 1954.

5 *Ibid.*, pp258-9.

6 *Ibid.*, p273.

7 *Ibid*, p254.

Listening Through: The Wireless and World War Two

Tim O'Sullivan

> Those who have grown up in the television age can have little
> appreciation of the place of radio in everyday existence in Britain during
> the war.[1]

The history of British radio – 'the wireless' – in the Second World War,
remains tightly stitched into accounts of the more general conditions
and crises experienced between 1939 and 1945.[2] Radio occupies a
significant and often mythologised position, in mediating news from
the battlefronts in the 'world out there', to the inner, private and
situated cultures of wartime home, locality and workplace. This
mediating power is not viewed as confined simply to the controlled
relay of events and information to domestic and overseas populations.
It also encompasses the provision of wartime entertainment, variety
shows and music, those other galvanising factors in the battle for
morale, for 'hearts and minds', especially on the home front. In both
the broadcasting of information and of entertainment, radio is
recognised as an essential 'part' of the British experience of the Second
World War – at times intense in the foreground, more generally a
background accompaniment to the dislocations and uncertainties of
everyday life.

There is general agreement that the period marks a watershed for
British broadcasting,[3] and that the requirements of 'total war',[4]
prompted fundamental transformations in both the place and the
purposes of radio broadcasting in the national public sphere. The
values and practices of public service broadcasting were redefined in a

period when *radio*, not television, was the dominant, *everyday* broadcast medium.[5] This was not a war 'without pictures', the press, magazines, and the newsreels supplied their visual versions of the national conflict and efforts, at home and abroad. It was, however, a war when the characteristics and intensities of the '*blind*' sound-only medium – the wireless – assumed a commanding position in the daily processes of 'making sense', of establishing, following and coming to terms with 'what was going on', as events unfolded. The widespread *domestic* presence of the radio receiver, and the capacity of the medium to achieve simultaneous and nationwide forms of speech- and sound-based contact and authority, do single out radio as deserving special attention.[6] For many of the people in Britain, especially those living in urban locations:

> The Second World War began with a broadcast and an air raid warning. On Sunday 3rd September, at 11:15, in carefully measured tones, Neville Chamberlain, the Prime Minister, told listeners, most of them well prepared for the news, many of them anxious to have it confirmed, that Britain was at war with Germany and was fighting against 'evil things'.[7]

The importance of the 'intervening' presence of radio broadcasting in the war has been acknowledged but relatively little has been written on radio and its everyday place. Histories of radio in the war tend to be histories of the BBC – that 'most important instrument of domestic propaganda',[8] and its efforts to renegotiate a place for itself in response to the wartime challenges and changes. These accounts rightly focus upon issues of institutional concern and power, on the changed controls, requirements and conditions faced by BBC producers and policy managers.[9] They tend to be 'inside stories', culled from memos, minutes or biographies, with a pronounced focus on BBC production policy. Rarely apparent, or indeed active, in this picture are other, equally important 'inside stories' – those of the *listeners* – who are, by and large, conceived of as the subordinate partners in the production-reception relationship. In short, there are histories of radio in the war, but they do not easily admit or accommodate the stories of radio listeners – of wireless owners and users. The aim of this essay is to develop some foundations from which more detailed oral histories of radio listening and use in the war might be pursued.

The changing role of radio in the war needs to be set against developments in the preceding two decades, which saw the technical and social establishment of radio in Britain and its transformation from 'the miraculous toy'[10] of the early 1920s – the masculine preserve of experimenters, hobbyists and amateur 'boffins' – into an institutionalised and domesticated, recognisably modern, public service broadcast medium. By the late 1930s, it had become a part of the accepted routines of everyday life. A central part of this expansion involved the entry and acceptance of radio into the home, into the living room, a process of 'capturing' both domestic space and time.[11] Moores' study of memories of radio in this period highlights several important issues.

The first concerns the ways in which radio was implicated in the more general move towards home-based leisure and private domestic culture. Radio broadcasting and listening to radio played a part in 'a general move away from the occupation of exterior space towards a family grouping which had withdrawn to interior space'.[12] In order for this to occur, several preconditions had to be met. The form, reliability and technology of the domestic receiver had to be improved and refined. The crystal sets of the 1920s, often limited to individualised, headphone reception and powered by cumbersome batteries, gave way to electric, mains supplied and valve-powered wirelesses in the 1930s. The tuning and loudspeaker arrangements allowed for group or family listening in the home, workplace or barracks. Radios became part of the geography of the living room in the 1930s and manufacturers began to take design seriously.[13] By 1935, the British radio industry was producing 1.9 million domestic receivers per yer.[14] In 1938, the *Radio Times* was selling almost three million copies per week at a price of 2d and there were in excess of 8.8 million wireless licences issued in that year.[15]

The modalities of British radio – what it offered, and in what tones and terms – also played a central part in these changes. Prewar broadcasting was organised into two services, the National and the Regional programmes. Moores points to the formation during this period of broadcasting discourses which addressed members of the family group, individually and collectively, citing the emergence of *Children's Hour*, and daytime radio features which addressed the mother as the manager of the domestic sphere. Cardiff and Scannell also note that during the 1930s[16] BBC programming started to allow more popular, family entertainment formats, serials, quizzes, variety shows and music, designed to achieve what Frith has called, 'the pleasures of the hearth'.[17] By the late 1930s, BBC policy had also, in limited ways, begun to embrace the idea of fixed daily and weekly schedules, in order to establish regular and routine listening habits in audiences.

These developments were subject to considerable debate within the BBC because they ran against the grain of some key elements of pre-war policy and the ethos associated with its first Director-General, John Reith. The establishment of the Listener Research Department in 1936[18] met with opposition but the necessity for systematic insight into the public use of radio services proved too strong even for major detractors:

> The real degradation of the BBC started with the invention of the hellish department which is called 'Listener Research'. That Abominable Statistic is supposed to show 'what listeners like' – and of course, what they like is the red-nosed comedian and the Wurlitzer organ.[19]

Reith left the BBC in June 1938, having wielded considerable influence over the nature of the broadcast services made available to listeners on the National and Regional services. He had also established an uneasy degree of distance from direct government intervention. It is in the shadow of his legacy of an 'improving' and 'uplifting' public service broadcasting system – with its formality and middle class preoccupations – that subsequent changes in wartime radio have been largely understood.[20]

In spite of the fact that in the event of war, the complete shut-down of domestic radio services had been briefly contemplated as late as June 1938,[21] a special supplementary edition of the *Radio Times*, 4 September 1939, proclaimed 'Broadcasting Carries On':

> That is the slogan of the BBC in this hour of national endeavour, when the British nation is nerving itself for the greatest effort it has ever made. In every department of life the British people are steeling themselves for their great task. Broadcasting intends to help in the work, what ever the difficulties may be.[22]

The emergency editorial outlined its vision of the key functions of the radio services during the war. First and foremost was the insistence that:

> The Government can speak to the people – news can reach the remotest village – instructions can be issued by the Ministries – warnings can be given of approaching attacks.[23]

But entertainment was also stressed.

> Broadcasting can help take our minds off the horrors of war as nothing
> else can ... Even in the dislocation of the first few days, some of your
> favourite talkers have been coming to the microphone, and the BBC
> Theatre Organist has been at his post to entertain you.[24]

The editorial also informed listeners, that London, the centre most
vulnerable to attack, had ceased to be the centre of British
broadcasting.[25] Thus the *Radio Times* sought to reassure listeners of
the planned and effective transition from peacetime to wartime radio
services. This first wartime edition also contained important
information about changes in the wavelengths and frequencies of
programme services. Changes in the organisation of programming
followed. From the declaration of war in September 1939, the old
Regional Programme was suspended and the National Programme
renamed the Home Service. For several months, this was the only BBC
channel available to listeners.[26] In February 1940, the Forces
Programme came on air, with a remit to provide a 'lighter', alternative
schedule.

> In a world starved of entertainment, it provided the kind of
> entertainment designed to appeal to very large numbers of people, and
> by the end of 1942 the audience listening to it was nearly half as large
> again as that which listened to the Home Service.[27]

When the ill-fated British Expeditionary Force returned to Britain
following Dunkirk in June 1940, the Forces Programme rapidly
established itself as *the* popular radio programme, attracting 65 per
cent or more of the adult, civilian audience. Its success, and that which
greeted some of the subsequent changes in the Home Service, lay in the
way it aimed at *pleasing* listeners, first the armed services and later the
domestic wartime workers at home and in the factory. This was in
stark contrast to the ethos which had driven the prewar BBC
programming policies.[28]

The Forces Programme was at first broadcast only in the evenings,
and even when a 6.30 am to 12.00 pm schedule was established, it made
use of selected, often simultaneous Home Service programming.
However, the blend of popular records, live dance band music, variety
shows and popular features proved very successful in 'reaching out' to

people. The BBC claimed that the Forces Programme was accomplishing important work in maintaining national morale. Cardiff and Scannell argue that the Forces Programme epitomised a broader shift in BBC programme policy, and two particular tendencies are worth noting. The first relates to the changed styles of continuity, presentation and scheduling which marked the Forces Programme as different to anything which had gone before – at least in BBC terms, although overseas commercial channels such as Radio Normandie, Radio Luxembourg and Radio Fécamp International, which closed down in the war, provided models for change. Prior to the war, in order to discourage what was known as 'tap' listening (turning on the radio like a tap as background accompaniment to work or domestic activities) and to insulate contrasting programme items, the BBC had used intervals of silence lasting up to five minutes. Presenters had adopted highly formal, impersonal modes of address. In contrast to this, the need to communicate with and appeal to the popular audience, required new, less formal, more fluent, American derived techniques of continuity and presentation – a more friendly, even regional and less impersonal mode of address. This accompanied a clearer sense of daily and weekly scheduling and routinisation of programming, so that listeners could anticipate and plan the structure of the day's programmes.

The second innovation related more to the content and tenor of programmes and their changed mode of engagement with the audience. This, it has been argued, involved a move towards:

> a democratisation of the content of entertainment, with more audience participation, a nurturing of performers who would be accepted as the representatives of ordinary men and women and the creation of more topical, mildly subversive forms of comedy.[29]

Programmes which embodied some of these shifts were transmitted on both the Home and Forces networks and they included several aimed at maintaining the morale and output of workers in factory production – *Music While You Work* (June 1940), *Works Wonders* (October 1940) and *Workers Playtime* (May 1941).[30] Programmes from the Variety Department of the BBC assumed greater significance; shows like *Monday Night at Eight, ITMA*.[31] *Band Waggon, Ack-Ack, Beer-Beer, Happidrome* and many others represented new forms of highly popular, engaging radio entertainment, as well as evidence of the shifts between the BBC and its wartime audiences.

These changes in the forms of radio – what programmes were broadcast, how, and in what kinds of scheduled 'flow' – represent part of the currency of the realignments between broadcasting institution, radio producers and radio listeners in the war.[32] To extend this analysis it is important to begin to trace the changing fortunes of the radio industry and the wireless set. The main index for the diffusion of UK domestic radio receivers during the war is generally calculated from the number of wireless licences in circulation each year. These point to a pattern of increase from 1938 to 1946, with a slight dip in 1942. At the outbreak of war, some 8.8 million licences were in operation, by 1945, 10 million.[33] It is clear that the domestic radio industry grew considerably during the war, although its primary stimulus was *not* the production of wirelesses for the home. In fact, production and sales of radio receivers for domestic use fell rapidly from a total of 1.2 million in 1939, to a low point of 50,000 by 1943. By 1945 however, with the impetus of utility set production, this figure had risen to 245,000.[34]

Foremost among the reasons for the decline in the manufacture of wireless sets was the switch to military production, to deal with the problems of an obsolete or non-existent capacity which characterised British services radio and communications equipment in 1939. The industry's priority from the outbreak of war was the production of military communications and radar equipment. Domestic demands for new wirelesses soon became hard to meet. For many listeners and retailers, repair, refurbishment and secondhand sales became the order of the day. As early as the summer of 1940 retailers began to report their inability to accommodate the pressure for set repairs. By February 1942, estimates suggest that 75 per cent of retailers and repairers were failing to meet the rising demand for repairs to domestic sets and that about 10 per cent of all domestic radio receivers were estimated to be out of order.[35] About one third of all households at this time were without mains electricity, and for those reliant on batteries to power their sets, these were soon in short and variable supply. This national shortage was officially recognised and in 1943 the War Cabinet Production Planning Radio Committee recommended production of a War-Time Utility Civilian Receiver, non-branded and using standardised valves and components. Production began in June 1944, with a design attributed to D.G. Reynolds of Murphy Radio, and in excess of 250,000 sets were sold on the domestic market by the end of the war.[36]

Radio listening became an important focus for BBC researchers during the war. The findings played an important part in planning schedules and programme policies in the Home and the Forces Services and the undertaking had a clear impetus from the internal demands and requirements of the BBC. More generally, the investigation of attitudes towards radio programmes or coverage of topical wartime issues became a significant part of the analysis of public opinion and wartime morale, which was an obsession of the Ministry of Information and its Home Intelligence Reports.[37] BBC Listener Research had commenced in 1936, and Robert Silvey, the first Head of Research, had visited America just before the outbreak of war, and had been impressed by the systematic advances in radio audience research in the different, commercial contexts of the USA.[38] By late 1937, under his direction, the Listener Research Department had experimented with a number of statistical techniques which culminated in 'The General Listening Barometer' – a largely quantitative means of plotting what number and type of people had listened to the programmes broadcast on the previous day. It had been proposed to establish this as a permanent daily monitoring system from September 1939. Events in that month considerably strengthened the case for this, and by December, the *Daily Survey of Listening*, involving a minimum of 800 interviews, commenced – many carried out under the 'difficulties' of wartime conditions.[39]

The Listener Research Department of the BBC employed three principal methods in the war. The first was the *Daily Survey*, which aimed to establish quantities of listening. Each daily quota sought to measure the size and patterns of the previous day's listening and over time this enabled more general patterns and profiles to be analysed.[40] Until 1943 the interviews were carried out under contract by the British Institute of Public Opinion and while they were designed to elicit quantitive data, the use of additional questions at the end of the schedule explored topics as diverse as public attitudes towards 'blue jokes' in radio variety, and towards German propaganda broadcasts.[41]

The second method of enquiry used *Listening Panels*, selected largely from volunteers and designed to assess the reactions of listeners to programmes. By means of questionnaires, the panels were used to establish more qualitative insights into the levels of appreciation or response to programmes and programming.[42] The final 'tier' of analysis employed a network of *Honorary Local Correspondents* and about 2000 were employed throughout the war. There was also a parallel system of correspondents in the Army, Navy and Air Force to gather and assess the views of non-civilian listeners. Correspondents were:

listeners who, by the nature of their normal activities, are *well placed to hear and sound the opinions of listeners* – rural store-keepers, welfare workers, insurance collectors, club secretaries, trade union secretaries, for example.[43]

This was a much more broad ranging system which allowed for more qualitative insights to be drawn from listeners' accounts.

These three methods were employed throughout the war and generated considerable amounts of data and analysis.[44] Recurrent issues which Listener Research was asked to report on included; listeners' tastes, the characteristics of different 'taste publics', evaluations and consumption of news programmes and reports, audiences for entertainment, sectional patterns and fluctuations in listening, and attitudes towards BBC policy. For Silvey, reflecting on this wartime work many years later, the power of radio in the war was, above all, as the main source of *news*:

> The news bulletins invariably stood out as peaks as in the daily listening curve: the largest were at six and nine pm when on a typical day their audiences would be anything from 30 to 50 per cent of the population. On special occasions, as when it was known that the Prime Minister would speak, the listening audiences would be even greater – usually over 60 per cent. On the evening of D-Day, by which time it was known that the Allied Armies had at last landed in Normandy, 80 per cent listened at 9 pm.[45]

The reorganisation of radio services in the war and the shifts in the forms of programming made available to the listening public during the prolonged national crisis undoubtedly changed the nature of British radio broadcasting and set a pattern for postwar services in a number of decisive ways. In a period when multiplying television screens, rather than radio loudspeakers, dominate the domestic sphere,[46] it may seem perverse to call for a reconsideration of the place of the wireless in wartime Britain. Perhaps the suggestion quoted at the opening of this discussion – that it is impossible for generations born into postwar television culture to comprehend the everyday place and power of radio during the war – has to be accepted. The generations of (post)modern times may never be able fully to reconstruct or to capture many aspects of past media history and cultural experience. But we can at least recognise the need for a more adequate historical analysis of the place of radio in wartime life. In the face of assumptions concerning the widespread power of radio as an instrument of national propaganda, morale and 'victory', and behind the nostalgic, mythical representations of wartime life, there are a number of themes which remain relatively unexplored. This essay has suggested several, linked issues as worthy of special attention. Analysis might productively be focused on 'the place' of the wireless and broadcast programming in terms of the homes, factories, pubs, barracks and many other wartime situations into which it was received. This entails considering the wireless set as an industrially produced commodity, its production, marketing, and diverse appropriation and domestic or other use by listeners in the period. In short, we need to know more about 'the place' of the wireless set in terms of its conditions of reception. Despite the use of oral history and other sources,[47] much remains to be accomplished here before the emphasis to date on production and policy can be matched. Such a focus not only holds out the possibility of 'humanising' or 'socialising' the history of radio in the war, but also of testing out assumptions concerning the ideological power and significance of radio broadcast culture during the crisis of war. From the 'inside stories' of listening – the accounts and memories of listeners – we can begin to come closer to a more adequate understanding of what was at stake, and what it was like, to be 'listening through' in radio's 'finest hour'.[48]

NOTES

[1] R.J.E. Silvey, *Who's Listening?*, Allen & Unwin, London, 1974, p121.

[2] See for example: A. Calder, *The People's War*, Jonathan Cape, London, 1969.

[3] S. Barnard, *On the Radio: Music Radio in Britain*, Open Univesity Press, Milton Keynes, 1989, p17.

[4] See, for example, D. Cardiff and P. Scannell, *Radio in World War II*, Unit 8, U203, Popular Culture, Open University, Milton Keynes, 1981, p35.

[5] The BBC began broadcasting the world's first regular Television Service to restricted audiences on 2 November 1936. It was closed down for the duration of the war, reopening in June 1946.

[6] See P. Scannell, 'Public Service Broadcasting and Modern Public Life', *Media, Culture and Society*, 1989, Volume 11, Number 2, pp135-166, where he estimates that 75 per cent of all British households had a radio by the outbreak of war. The total population of Britain at the outbreak of war is estimated at some 45 million. Approximately three and a half million households, representing thirteen and a half million people, mainly the poorer sections of the population, had no access to radio. J. Stevenson, *British Society 1914-45*, Penguin, Harmondsworth, 1990, p408.

[7] A. Briggs, *The History of Broadcasting in the United Kingdom: Volume III, The War of Words*, Oxford University Press, London, 1970, p77.

[8] J. Curran and J. Seaton, *Power Without Responsibility*, Routledge, London, 1988, p136.

[9] Of particular note are the relationships, throughout the war, between the BBC and the Ministry of Information which had official responsibility for the regulation and guidance of home broadcasting.

[10] S. Briggs, *Those Radio Times*, Weidenfeld and Nicholson, London, 1981.

[11] S. Moores, ' "The Box on the Dresser": Memories of Early Radio and Everyday Life', *Media, Culture and Society*, 1988, Volume 10, Number 1, pp23-40.

[12] *Ibid.*, p25.

[13] M. Pegg, *Broadcasting and Society 1918-1939*, Croom Helm, London, 1983, p56, notes: 'At first, design was limited to the improvement of control facilities, such as clearer tuning dials and illuminated panels ... From then on, firms decided to give designers their head. Using traditional materials, or more often exploiting the flexibility of new materials like Bakelite, a whole new vista was revealed. Murphy employed a furniture designer ... whilst Ecko employed architects.

[14] K. Geddes, *The Setmakers: A History of the Radio and Television Industry*, BREMA, London, 1991, p260.

[15] A. Briggs, *op.cit.*, Appendix B, p736.

[16] D. Cardiff and P. Scannell, 'Broadcasting and National Unity', in J. Curran, *et al* (eds), *Impacts and Influences: Essays on Media Power in the Twentieth Century*, Methuen, London, 1987.

[17] S. Frith, 'The Pleasures of the Hearth', in T. Bennett *et al* (eds), *Formations of Pleasure*, Routledge & Kegan Paul, London, 1983.

[18] See R.J.E. Silvey, *op.cit.* and D. Chaney, 'Audience Research and the BBC in the 1930s: A Mass Medium Comes into Being', in J. Curran *et al* (eds), *op.cit.*

[19] A. Briggs, *The History of Broadcasting in the United Kingdom: Volume II, The Golden Age of Wireless*, Oxford University Press, London, 1965, p261. The quotation is attributed to Lionel Fielden.

[20] On Reith see: D.L. LeMahieu, *A Culture for Democracy*, Oxford University Press, 1988; I. McIntyre, *The Expense of Glory: A Life of John Reith*, HarperCollins, London, 1993; and J.C.W. Reith, *Into the Wind*, Hodder & Stoughton, London, 1949.

[21] A. Briggs, *op.cit.*, p77.

[22] *Radio Times*, Volume 64, Number 831A, 4 September 1939.

[23] *Ibid.*

[24] *Ibid.*

[25] 'Far away in other parts of the country, in new premises especially reserved for this time of need, are the centres from which your programmes come. At one centre is a team of Variety favourites and expert producers. At another centre, far removed from the first, is another 'Radio City', whose inhabitants are a team of actors and producers capable of putting over any number of plays and features. A third team will include the leading members of the BBC Symphony Orchestra, *plus* an assemblage of star players of light music; *plus* the Theatre Orchestra, the Variety Orchestra – in fact a total force of musicians

WAR CULTURE

capable of filling the ether with music for days on end', *ibid.*

26 In its early days, gramophone music interspersed with news bulletins and official instructions accounted for a large amount of the output and Calder notes initial hostility to this diet. See A. Calder, *op.cit.*, pp56-62.

27 A. Briggs, *op.cit.*, p47.

28 D. Cardiff and P. Scannell, 'Good Luck War Workers: Class, Politics and Entertainment in Wartime Broadcasting', Chapter 5 in T. Bennett, C. Mercer, and J. Woollacott (eds), *Popular Culture and Social Relations*, Open University Press, Milton Keynes, 1986.

29 *Ibid.*, p110.

30 'Since 1940 factory installations have increased at the rate of over one thousand a year and now over eight thousand factories, covering more than four and a half million workers, receive programmes daily'. Wynford Reynolds, organiser of *Music While You Work*, BBC Year Book, 1945, BBC, p60.

31 *It's That Man Again*, one of the 'classic' wartime programmes, had commenced just before the outbreak of war but gained considerable popularity in the war years. See A. Briggs, *op.cit.*, p564 for data and history. A. Calder, *op.cit.*, pp65-66 also provides a useful account.

32 See A. Briggs, *op.cit.*, pp301, 595-7, for useful analysis of data concerning programming and schedules.

33 The extent to which licences indicated a firm basis for analysis is questionable and there may be a considerable 'hidden' additional figure or multiplier needed to adjust these statistics to obtain a more realistic picture of diffusion.

34 A. Briggs, *op.cit.*, p69 and K. Geddes, *op.cit.*, Chapter 4 for relevant data.

35 K. Geddes, *op.cit.*, p277.

36 *Ibid.*, p279. See also A. Briggs, *op.cit.*, p68. Some have argued that the production and cheapness of utility sets allowed for more working-class ownership of radio sets. Earlier popular Philco models had been dubbed the 'people's sets'.

37 A. Briggs, *op.cit.*, p124.

38 R.J.E. Silvey, *op.cit.*

39 'Ever since December 1939 a daily quota of 800 interviews have been made for the survey. The quota is so distributed as to be representative in terms of sex, socio-economic class, age and geographical distribution of the whole adult population of Great Britain. Save for a break of ten days during the first week of the blitz – when the department was "bombed out" of its headquarters – the continuity of the survey has been maintained. It so happened that Coventry was included in the schedule for investigation at the time of its severe bombing. The investigator working there carried on and he never failed to turn in his quota: though he confessed to finding the work "a little difficult" the morning after the great raid.' R.J.E. Silvey, 'Radio Audience Research in Great Britain', in P.F. Lazarsfeld and F. Stanton (eds), *Radio Research 1942-1943*, Essential Books, Duell Sloane and Pearce, New York, 1944, p157.

40 Towards the end of the war, the contours of the typical day's listening (Thursday, May 24, 1945) indicates four main 'peaks'; 8:00 am (with 28 per cent of the adult civilian population listening), 1:00 pm (34 per cent), 6:00 pm

184

(33 per cent), and 9:00 pm (46 per cent). From T. Gompertz, *What's the Use of Wireless?*, Army Bureau of Current Affairs pamphlet, Number 97, 1945. See also Silvey, *op.cit.*

[41] R.J.E. Silvey (1974), *op.cit.*, p98, pp105-7.

[42] In 1942-43, there were five panels in all; those dealing with Serious Music, Talks and Discussions, Features and Plays numbered 600 members, while the Light Entertainment panel had 1,100 members.

[43] R.J.E. Silvey, *op.cit.*, p160-161.

[44] The records of this research, together with the reports and recommendations which emerged as a result are held at the BBC Written Archive Centre, Caversham Park, Reading. Another source worth consulting is The British Library National Sound Archive, 29 Exhibition Rd, London SW7 2AS.

[45] R.J.E. Silvey, *op.cit.*, p120-121.

[46] R. Silverstone, *Television and Everyday Life*, Routledge, London, 1994.

[47] Sources in addition to oral history research include the BBC Achive, Mass Observation Archive, Ministry of Information records, Radio Manufacturers records, Radio and Wireless Museums and Societies and other specialist agencies.

[48] I would like to thank and acknowledge the assistance of Mr Gerald Wells of the Vintage Wireless Museum, West Dulwich, London in researching this paper.

Professional Football In World War Two Britain

Pierre Lanfranchi and Matthew Taylor

Saturday afternoon football fever and the idea of competitive League matches and Cup Finals does not really fit with the game as played during wartime when the international matches, intended to create a fair hierarchy of nations and to express their real power and capacity, were replaced by an armed expression of that rivalry on the battlefields.

World War Two, like the First, was not just a *Blitzkrieg*, but modified the whole social life of the nation during seven years. However, the mood and interests of the population of Britain could not be exclusively concentrated on the front line, the war effort and the exceptional gravity of the situation. During the most intensive and apprehensive periods of war the life of the nation was focused on the battlefield or the home front, but in many other moments of the war there was a great desire for normal life. John Houston in his film *Escape to Victory* (1979) pointed out the impact a football match could have for prisoners of war. This was not just a fight for the victory of the prisoners over their guardians; the football match, with its codified rules, accepted equally by both sides, could be considered as a moment out of time, reminiscent of youth and of peace.

The declaration of war in September 1939 virtually marked the end of football in England, Wales and Scotland as well as in France. Three days after the official declaration, the Scottish Football Association suspended all football played under its jurisdiction and, on 8 September, the English FA followed suit, announcing that all football, except that organised by the armed forces, was entirely suspended 'until official notice is given to the contrary'.[1] Footballers were no longer full-time professionals; their contracts were declared void and they were effectively out of work. Thus, within a week of the beginning of the war, the football authorities had sent out the unambiguous message that football would subordinate itself to the interests of the nation. This was to be total war, a people's war in which every available human and material resource was to be directed to the war effort. Football was no exception.[2]

Football can be considered as a *trait d'union* between peace and war. It did not cease but continued throughout the war in a modified form, consisting of a mixture of representative matches, home internationals, inter-service matches and a limited League and Cup programme. The situation was different in Germany and Italy, where officials considered it essential to continue regular football activity throughout the war. Between September 1939 and November 1942, Germany played thirty-five official internationals against its allies, new satellite states such as Moravia, Croatia and Slovakia, and neutrals such as Switzerland and Sweden. In Italy a regular professional championship was organised until the summer of 1943 in order to persuade the population that the war did not affect their regular activities and passions. This tendency was, to a degree, also found in Britain. According to the FA's official historian, wartime football was not fundamentally dissimilar from its prewar variety: 'the rhythm may have been unfamiliar, but the tune was much the same'.[3] Yet the 'rhythm' of professional football in Britain had been a distinctive feature for over fifty years. The regularity of the Saturday afternoon fixture and the ritualistic and cultural meanings attached to it were crucial to the experience of watching and playing football. Mass Observation recognised the traumatic effect of the initial ban on competitive sport in the first few months of war, referring to the 'deep repercussions' which might follow from the breaking of well established routines.

It had been somewhat different during World War One. Throughout 1914 and much of 1915, professional football continued without alteration. It was consequently denounced by many as unpatriotic and counter-productive to the war effort and became a site for the expression of social divisions and class antagonism. Football proved to be 'the medium through which vocal elements of the middle and upper classes launched an embittered literary attack upon the working-class reaction to the national crisis'.[4] However, it was extremely popular at the front, making the lives of soldiers more bearable and some 'legends' tell of matches between the English, French and Germans.[5]

By contrast, football enjoyed an harmonious Second World War. It was more often the subject of praise than vilification in the press, with criticism largely restricted to the operation of the football pools. The FA even published a small pamphlet *Victory was the Goal* celebrating football's wartime achievements. In the foreword, FA President, the Earl of Athlone, paid tribute to 'the many ways in which football and The Football Association contributed to the war effort and ... that great army of footballers whose valiant service in many fields helped so materially to bring us victory and peace'.[6]

The changing external circumstances of war and the maturation of both governmental attitudes towards football and the attitude of the football authorities towards the war were crucial elements in this evolution. The situation in 1939 differed in two fundamental ways from 1914, both of which affected football: the immediate introduction of conscription, and the risk of air attack. During the first year of the Great War, the sight of the 'finest physical manhood of the country' engaging in a full programme of League football was anathema to many. MPs, clergymen and civic dignitaries all exhorted footballers to enlist, with little success. *The Times* vehemently criticised the clubs employing professional footballers for 'bribing a needed recruit to refrain from enlistment'. The Colonel of the Footballers' Battalion regarded the failure to enlist as a 'public scandal' and complained that by March 1915 only 122 professionals out of 1800 had joined 'the Colours'.[7] In 1939, conscription prevented a repeat of this situation.

Similarly, the risk of air attack in 1939 necessitated government control over the organisation of football. At first, the anticipated danger of mass gatherings prompted the Home Office to ban all football, but by 9 September permission was given for football grounds in low-risk areas to re-open. On 21 September the Home Office gave support to a revised programme of football, providing it did not interfere with national service and local industry. Even so, crowds were limited to 8,000 in evacuation areas and 15,000 elsewhere[8] and all matches were subject to authorisation by the local police.[9]

Despite such restrictions, the official attitude to football during 1939-45 was far more accommodating than it had been in 1914-18. The 1930s saw the partial rehabilitation of football's respectable image among the middle and upper classes, through its relationship with the popular media and the writings of J.B. Priestley and others. The game was increasingly seen as an intrinsic element of British life and 'seemed if anything to stand for much that was good in society'.[10] This change in perspective was reflected in the social value assigned to the game during the war. Mass Observation noted in 1940 that: 'Sports like football have an absolute major effect on the morale of the people, and one Saturday afternoon of League matches could probably do more to affect the people's spirits than the recent £50,000 Government poster campaign urging cheerfulness'.[11] Hence efforts were made by the Government and local authorities to encourage football at all levels. The Board of Trade assisted over 650 clubs by providing priority certificates for the manufacture of footballs and other equipment and as the war advanced restrictions on the size of crowds were eased.[12] No longer marginalised, football was encouraged to flourish, albeit under certain conditions, as at once a signal of normality and a practical resource in the war effort.

The football authorities had learnt the lessons of 1914. At the outbreak of war the FA immediately volunteered the services of a panel of coaches, trainers and masseurs to the Home Forces and clubs were quick to offer their grounds for military training and recreational purposes. The FA also co-operated with the War Office in preparing a list of footballers to be trained as army and RAF physical education instructors and, in addition, contributed together with the Central Council of Physical Recreation and the government to the *Fitness for Service* scheme and the establishment of training centres for the Civil Defence service. Indeed, the FA Secretary, Stanley Rous, became chairman of the Civil Defence Sports Committee.[13] Moreover, the FA and the Football League were instrumental in raising large sums of money for wartime causes. Particular matches were set aside, and some were organised specifically, to assist the Red Cross and St John's Ambulance Brigade Fund. By June 1943, football alone had channelled £58,120 in this direction. A single match organised by the League at Chelsea in May of the same year raised £8000 for the Navy Welfare Fund.[14]

The traditional prewar professional footballer was a kind of working-class folk hero. According to Critcher: 'He came from ... the same economic and cultural background as those who paid to watch him'.[15] Part of Stanley Matthews' attraction for supporters was that his physical appearance and persona symbolised not pre-eminence, but normality: '*You* could be him, with a bit of luck. You *might* have been if things had turned out differently. He was the epitome of the ordinary bloke who became a star'.[16] This association of the football hero with the normal citizen reached its peak during World War Two. While most continued to play on a part-time basis, for the first time in over fifty years the nation's premier footballers had other jobs. They were auxiliary firemen, reserve policemen, taxi-drivers or factory workers. Hundreds volunteered for the forces and many more were later conscripted. Newspapers were inclined to print photographs of famous footballers in uniform or doing civilian work more often than in their familiar guise as professional sportsmen. Footballers were paradoxically celebrated for the mundane rather than the spectacular; as ordinary everyday heroes rather than Saturday afternoon idols.

To many players the future looked bleak and uncertain. Even when regular football reappeared, the rewards for players were limited. They were to receive no more than 30 shillings per match without bonuses in England, and £2 in Scotland, in contrast with the prewar limit of £8 a week. The Players' Union considered this inadequate payment and received numerous reports of professionals in financial hardship. Few were prepared for 'working' life and had other skills to fall back on: it was reported that only one of Heart of Midlothian's eight internationals had an occupation other than football. Many decided to leave their clubs and find work elsewhere, often in the area they had grown up.[17]

Elsewhere, in cities like Birmingham and Coventry, work was quickly found in munitions or other local industries. One tube manufacturer in Oldbury was employing up to eighteen West Bromwich Albion players in early 1940. Some clubs – including Bolton Wanderers, Liverpool and Brentford – signed up *en masse* for one of the services, reporting immediately for training.[18] Matt Busby was one of the Liverpool players called up within days for full-time military service. As an experienced thirty-year-old Scottish international, Busby was soon recommended for training as an Army Physical Education instructor. He was sent initially to Aldershot where in November 1939, along with several famous players like Joe Mercer and Cliff Britton, he passed out successfully as a Sergeant-Major Instructor. In 1944 when the Allies invaded Italy, Busby was appointed Officer-in-Charge of the British Army team sent to entertain the troops in battle areas. He was responsible for the training, tactics and selection of the team and also for the general discipline of the footballer-soldiers under his command.[19]

Stanley Matthews also spent most of the war as a physical training instructor, but with the RAF. For the first few months of war he was employed by a local engineering firm in the Potteries. On joining the RAF Matthews was posted to Blackpool, where he ran a sports store on the pier and organised sporting activities for the troops. He also played plenty of football; mid-week matches for RAF teams, Saturday fixtures for Blackpool (and for Greenock Morton and Glasgow Rangers when posted to Scotland) and, remarkably, thirty 'unofficial' international matches for England.[20] He seems to have had a relatively comfortable and uneventful war. Billeted in Blackpool with his wife and child, he generally maintained as conventional a life as any footballer could expect under wartime conditions.[21]

Whereas established players were utilised to provide training and entertainment, the vast majority of footballers became ordinary servicemen. For younger players in particular, the experiences of football and war were intertwined from the very beginning. Tom Finney was one for whom the war years made a deep and lasting impression and his autobiography *Football Round the World* devotes no less than five chapters to the period. In January 1940, a seventeen-year-old Finney was signed as a part-time professional for Preston North End, and played regularly for the next two seasons in the regional wartime competitions. He was called up in April 1942 and in December of that year landed in Egypt with the Royal Armoured Corps. His next three years were dominated by the fulfilment of playing football for units and Combined Services teams and the fatigue of gruelling manoeuvres and the anxiety of waiting for action. Finney was particularly sensitive to accusations of dodging the column and the apparent incongruity of organised football so near to the front line: 'I often wondered if it was right that I should go on playing while others were fighting'. As the war intensified he experienced active service at first hand. Transferred as a tank driver to the Ninth Queen's Royal Lancers, he was engaged for months in the Eighth Army push up Italy in 1944. Only when the war in Italy was ending did Finney play football again.[22]

For those players left at home, football was cherished as a break from military duty and war work. It was also a unique experience in itself. The most distinctive feature of the wartime game was undoubtedly the guest player system. It broke down one of the principles of business-orientated professional football: players as the property of their clubs. Initial FA wartime regulations laid down that 'a registered player will be permitted to play for another League club within reasonable distance of his residence or work by consent of his club'.[23] But, in practice, players stationed locally, on leave or those simply passing through would often appear without prior approval from their own clubs. The change certainly gave football an unpredictable look. Teams changed substantially from week to week and favourably located clubs produced formidable sides. Third Division Aldershot, not surprisingly, often fielded six or seven international players because of the club's proximity to the army training centre. Although most clubs used guests only to replace players unavailable because of national service or priority war work, the system was abused by others. Bill Shankly was among those guest players who were constantly in demand: 'It was easy to be found out, even in big camps where there were maybe thousands of men ... I played for many teams and had a game every Saturday'.[24]

This system also gave the less experienced footballer a rare opportunity to play alongside established stars and internationals. George Fisher was a local Bermondsey lad signed by Millwall as a junior player during the 1942-43 season. Appearing for Millwall and representing RAF and Combined Services teams in Italy, he played alongside England internationals like Sam Bartram, and appeared at Wembley before a crowd of 90,000 in the 1945 League South Cup Final. For this teenager, the experience represented the pinnacle of a career.[25] Nat Lofthouse was only fifteen years old when war started. He worked as a Bevin Boy in the coal mines while playing as an amateur for Bolton's first team. Even for him, playing alongside guest footballers 'was really something ... I was playing with people I'd only ever seen before a hundred yards away when I was standing on an embankment. And people were *paying* to watch me'.[26] Although criticised, the guest player system had an equalizing effect on the professional hierarchy within football.

One of the most surprising effects of the war on football was the arrival of a number of foreign players. Bert Trautmann is the best known. A paratrooper in the Luftwaffe, he was captured near the Dutch border shortly after D-Day. Transported to a prisoner-of-war camp at Ashton-in-Makerfield in June 1945, he began to play as goalkeeper for the camp team in charity matches throughout Lancashire. Trautmann so impressed the talent scouts that he joined St Helens on his release in 1948 and a year later was signed by Manchester City as the replacement for retiring England international Frank

Swift.[27] While Trautmann's story is unique, other foreign players stationed with allied forces in Britain also began to appear for local clubs. Players from the Polish Resistance troops were particularly popular in Scotland and Alfie Lesz of St Mirren and Feliks Staroscik of Third Lanark were two who embarked on professional careers after the war.[28]

It was the football ground itself which best epitomised the links between football and the war world. Few grounds were left untouched by war. Some were entirely or partly requisitioned by military or defence authorities and many suffered some degree of bomb damage. Aston Villa had their Trinity Road stand converted into an air raid shelter and ammunitions store, while the offices were used by the police, fire brigade and First Aid divisions. Highbury became an ARP centre; a prisoner-of-war camp was built at Swindon's County Ground and Norwich City had their car-park turned into a machine gun emplacement manned by the Home Guard. The wartime football ground became a suitable resource for the state authorities and ceased to function purely as a sporting arena.[29]

In certain ways wartime conditions did affect the established bond between supporters and 'their' stadia, what John Bale has described as 'a sense of place' ('topophilia').[30] The closing down of a ground, and its use for purposes other than football, served to loosen the ties of familiarity and affection which came from a supporter's habitual attendance. Even where regular football continued, the atmosphere of the stadium and the context in which matches were played tended to change. One observer noted during a match at Preston in early October 1939: 'there was practically no conversation at all [and a] general impression of listlessness, very unlike the usual football crowd'.[31] Attendances fell, particularly during the first two years of war. The forty-one regional League matches played on 4 November 1939 produced an aggregate attendance of 101,000 as against the 685,000 who watched forty-four matches a year earlier.[32] People were less inclined to visit football grounds and hence probably less emotionally attached to them.

In areas where air raids were frequent, there is some evidence of a fear of visiting football grounds. In this case the stadium becomes an object of 'topophobia', a potential source of danger. For an international at Hampden Park, Glasgow, in May 1940, at least 6,000 ticket holders stayed away as a result of widespread rumours and German radio propaganda forecasting a Luftwaffe raid on the ground in the second half. In parts of London, heavy raids during matches were not uncommon. During a match at Charlton Athletic in September 1940, shrapnel fell onto the terraces and pitch and there were similar instances at nearby Millwall.[33] Yet even at the height of the bombing, inconvenience and apathy probably drove spectators away more than a diffuse fear. The Home Office had ordered that play must stop every time an alert was sounded – a situation which often led to long and frequent delays and even the abandonment of some matches. By the 1941-42 season, the adoption of the 'spotter' system on League grounds, which gave warning only of imminent danger, and the reduction in daylight bombing, led to a significant increase in attendances and a safer atmosphere at matches.[34]

Birmingham's case suggests that wartime stadia were not generally viewed as a source of 'topophobia'. The local Chief Constable decided to close the ground at the start of war due to the threat of serious casualties from air raids if crowds gathered there to watch football. Despite the fact that St Andrews was frequently hit by enemy bombs, his decision received little local support. A letter to the *Sport Argus* accused the Chief Constable of 'killing' people's Saturday afternoons and suggested that 'he would change his views if he had to work in a factory fifty or sixty hours a week'. On 12 March 1940 Birmingham City Council approved a resolution to re-open St Andrews and formally asked the Chief Constable to reconsider. A group of local workers summed up the view of many: 'if [we are] willing to take the risk of getting together in the factories for 5 days [a week, we] should be allowed to take the risk of watching twenty-two men kicking a football about on a Saturday afternoon'. Ten days later, they succeeded and the ground was re-opened. 12,000 spectators watched Birmingham's match against Walsall.[35] For them as for many others, the football ground was still a place of recreation and enjoyment.

All considered, football's contribution to the war was rather small. Up to eighty British professional footballers were killed during the war, according to recent estimation, although dozens more were wounded, captured and honoured alongside others as national heroes.[36] Contemporaries could not fail to recognise that the football community was uncomfortable with providing entertainment in austerity. Guest players, regional leagues and representative matches were tolerated as *temporary* features. In fact, when peace returned, football would begin where it had left off in 1939. On 27 April 1946, over 98,000 watched Derby County beat Charlton Athletic in the first postwar FA Cup Final. As *The Times* football correspondent noted, the parenthesis was closed: 'Here at last ... after seven years is the real thing again'.[37] Football was a kind of barometer of normality and of the morale of the population. Yet, in most official football memoirs and club histories, the war did not exist – regular life (i.e. the League) stopped in 1939 as did internationals, and the Football League, like Sleeping Beauty, needed a kiss of peace to re-emerge. This paradox is also one of the most interesting aspects of football's significance in World War Two Britain.

NOTES

[1] *The Times*, 9 September 1939.

[2] James Walvin, *The People's Game*, Allen Lane, London, 1975, p137.

[3] Geoffrey Green, *The History of the Football Association*, Naldrett, London, 1953, p365.

[4] Colin Veitch, ' "Play Up! Play Up! and Win the War": Football, the Nation and the First World War, 1914-15', *Journal of Contemporary History*, Volume 20, 1985, pp363-378.

[5] Gérard Bacconnier, André Minet, Louis Soler, *La plume au fusil: Les poilus du Midi à travers leur correspondance*, Privat, Toulouse, 1985, p252; Antonio Papa, Guido Panico, *Storia sociale del calcio in Italia*, Il Mulino, Bologna, 1993, p110-111.

[6] Green, *op.cit.*, p361.

[7] Quoted in Veitch, *op.cit.*, p371; Nicholas Fishwick, *English Football and Society, 1910-1950*, Manchester University Press, Manchester, 1989, p145; A.J. Arnold, ' "Not Playing the Game?": Leeds City in the Great War', *International Journal of the History of Sport*, May 1990, p113; Simon Inglis, *League Football and the Men Who Made It*, Collins Willow, London, 1988, p95.

[8] In the previous season, the League Champions Everton had an average home crowd of 35,039 and only one attendance below 10,000. Ivan Ross and Gordon Smailes, *Everton: A Complete Record*, Breedon Books, Derby, 1993, p286.

[9] *Birmingham Mail*, 9 September 1939; *Birmingham Post*, 21 September 1939.

[10] Fishwick, *op.cit*, p146.

[11] Quoted in Walvin, *op.cit.*, p144.

[12] Green, *op.cit.*, p367.

[13] *Ibid*, pp362-365.

[14] *Ibid*, p365; Inglis, *op.cit.*, p168.

[15] Chas Critcher, 'Football since the war', in John Clark, Chas Critcher and Richard Johnson (eds), *Working-Class Culture: Studies in History and Theory*, Hutchinson, 1979, p163.

[16] Tony Mason, 'Stanley Matthews', in Richard Holt (ed), *Sport and the Working Class in Modern Britain*, Manchester University, Manchester, 1990, pp159-178.

[17] *Birmingham Post*, 12 September 1939.

[18] Jack Rollin, *Soccer at War, 1939-45*, Collins Willow, London, 1985, p148; Brian Pead, *Liverpool: A Complete Record, 1892-1988*, Breedon, Derby, 1988, p267.

[19] Eamon Dunphy, *A Strange Kind of Glory: Sir Matt Busby and Manchester United*, London, Heinemann, 1991, pp80-83.

[20] The international matches of the home countries were not recognised by the respective FAs and players did not receive caps. Many internationals were played against army, RAF and Allied troops.

[21] *Birmingham Post*, 27 September 1939; Stanley and Mila Matthews, *Back in Touch*, Arthur Barker, London, 1981, p91; David Miller, *Stanley Matthews: The Authorized Biography*, Pavilion, London, 1989, pp68-77.

[22] Tom Finney, *Football Round the World*, Sportsman Book Club, London, 1955, pp17-43.

[23] *The Times*, 23 September 1939.

[24] Rollin, *op.cit.*, pp56-57.

[25] Interview with George Fisher on 15 July 1994; Richard Lindsay, *Millwall: A Complete Record, 1885-1991*, Breedon, Derby, 1991, p65.

[26] Arthur Hopcraft, *The Football Man*, Sportspages, London, 1988, p34.

[27] Alan Rowlands, *Trautmann: The Biography*, Breedon, Derby, 1990, pp43-71.

[28] Bob Crampsey, *The First 100 Years*, Glasgow, Scottish Football League, 1990, p128. Other examples include Icelandic international Albert Gudmundsson, who studied in Glasgow and played for Rangers first team and reserves during much of the war, before moving to Arsenal in 1946, and then to France and Italy, and later becoming an MP and ambassador.

[29] Tony Matthews, *Midland Soccer at War, 1939-46*, Sports Leisure Concepts, Warley, 1991, pp3-4; Fred Ollier, *Arsenal: A Complete Record, 1886-1992*, Breedon, Derby, 1992, p332; Rollin, *op.cit.*, p29. Stadiums had been used earlier in the 1930s by Mussolini and Hitler as essential venues for big crowd propaganda meetings, V. Ottani, 'Lo stadio di Bologna: Quando un campo è monumento da tutelare', in *Azzuri 1990 Storia del calcio a Bologna*, Meridiana, Rome, 1990, pp129-32.

[30] John Bale, 'Calcio e topophilia', in P. Lanfranchi (ed), *Il calcio e il suo pubblico*, ESI, Naples, 1992; J. Bale, *Sport, Place and the City*, Routledge, London, 1991.

[31] Quoted in McCarthy, *op.cit.*, p39; Stanley and Mila Matthews, *op.cit.*, p91.

[32] McCarthy, *op.cit.*, p40.

[33] Rollin, *op.cit.*, p42; Anthony Bristowe, *Charlton Athletic Football Club, 1905-50*, Voice of the Valley, London, 1992 (reprint), p49; Lindsay, *op.cit.*, pp316-17.

[34] Bristowe, *op.cit.*, pp49-50.

[35] *Sports Argus*, 4 November 1939; *Birmingham Mail*, 13 March 1940.

[36] McCarthy, *op.cit.*, p175.

[37] *The Times*, 27 April 1946.

Section 5:
Beyond the Pale:
Ethnic Minorities
and the War

Immigrants, Refugees, the British State and Public Opinion During World War Two

Panikos Panayi

During the last two decades, primarily under the influence of Arthur Marwick, British historical scholarship has recognised the fundamental importance of war on social, economic and political change.[1] More recently, as a result of the increasing movement of the study of minorities into the mainstream in British history, there has been a recognition that their positions also change in wartime.[2] The purpose of this essay is to examine the experience of minorities in Britain before and during the Second World War.

During the course of the nineteenth and twentieth centuries as many as five million immigrants and refugees made their way to Britain. The period from 1815-1945 saw an influx of as many as two million people.[3] Countries of origin included continental Europe and areas further afield but, for the pre-1945 years, Europe was of far more importance. For our purposes, the most reliable statistics come from the 1931 census which indicates that by far the largest minority grouping in Great Britain consisted of the Irish, whose numbers totalled over half a million.[4] They were a mainly working-class population, focused upon industrial districts, especially in Lancashire, Scotland and London. While assimilation may have taken place on a significant scale, their Irish ethnicity, together with sectarian conflict between Catholics and Protestants, remained alive.[5]

The second largest minority consisted of Jews – 370,000 by 1939.

There were three major groups. First, established Anglo-Jewry, whose origins date back to the seventeenth century, consisting mainly of an upper bourgeoisie. Second, the East European newcomers of the late nineteenth century and their children, originally living mostly in working-class areas of London, Leeds and Manchester, but, in the interwar years, moving into the suburbs. The third, and most recent, Jewish group consisted of refugees from Nazism, whose number may have reached 70,000, after the British government loosened its refugee policy just before the outbreak of the war. Many of the newcomers were professionals, including academics, lawyers, doctors and architects, although others came as children, or as domestic servants. A strong Jewish ethnicity remained but it needs to be remembered that distinct working-class and middle-class Jewish communities existed. In terms of the experience of Jewish people, British anti-semitism reached new peaks during the interwar years, as illustrated by the rise of the British Union of Fascists.[6]

Compared with the Irish and the Jews the other groups were relatively small. A few minorities numbered more than 20,000 in England and Wales, namely Americans, French, Italians and non-Jewish Germans, with many of them having lived in Britain from the nineteenth century. The Americans consisted almost entirely of people involved in middle-class occupations.[7] Primarily working-class, with a petty-bourgeois business community, the Italian community was the most well-established, with a rich social life and was mainly located in London, Glasgow and Manchester.[8] Finally, the (non-Jewish) German community had been reborn out of that destroyed by the vicious state and popular Germanophobia of World War One.[9] Although there were small numbers of ethnic groupings such as Indians, Africans, West Indians and Chinese who had settled in Britain before 1939, there was no sizeable non-European community.[10] The 86,963 Indians recorded in the 1931 census are overwhelmingly white Anglo-Indians.[11]

The effect of war upon flows of immigration is complex and it is difficult to come to any definite conclusions about them. On the one hand, an increasing labour demand, to help in the process of rearmament, suggests the need for the importation of foreign labour. The classic example of such a process is Nazi Germany which became dependent upon foreign workers between 1939 and 1945; by the end of 1944 one in every five workers employed in the German Empire was a foreigner.[12] In contrast, the mass immigration to the USA which had taken place throughout the course of the nineteenth century dried up during World War One because its major source, Europe, could no longer afford to give up its surplus labour. The labour demand consequent upon rearmament depended upon the Great Migration of black southerners northwards.[13]

The situation in Britain during both world wars was fundamentally different from either the German or US examples. During both conflicts, British women played a fundamental role in filling the labour demand created by the war economy and male conscription.[14] In neither case did large scale immigration take place. The main population flows into the country consisted of refugees from the Continent. Some of these became munition workers, such as a large percentage of 240,000 Belgians who made their way to Britain during the First World War, after the German invasion of their country.[15]

During World War Two, two main groups of refugees entered Britain. The first, of 100,000, included Norwegians, Danes, Dutch, Belgians, and French, who had made their way to the country following the fall of their countries to Hitler in the spring of 1940, and approximately 25,000 Austrian and German Jews who had fled to these states previously.[16]

The Poles became one of the largest groups in wartime Britain and grew into an important postwar minority. Their movement originates in the policies of both Germany and the Soviet Union within Polish borders. The first group to enter Britain in June 1940 consisted of the Polish government and forces in exile in France, numbering about 35,500. The Polish Army under British control gradually increased to 249,000 by the summer of 1945. Following the transfer of British allegiance from the Polish government-in-exile to the new Russian sponsored administration, members of the forces eventually received the right to reside in Britain. Consequently, 114,037 entered or remained in Britain and sent for 33,000 dependants. The explanation for the generosity of postwar British government policy simply lies in the need for labour to rebuild the British economy.[17]

Other groups besides refugees also made their way to Britain. The most important, although temporary, consisted of American soldiers, both black and white, who, amongst other things, brought US-style racial segregation to Britain.[18] In addition, there was a limited importation of labour into Britain from the West Indies and Ireland, although this was small compared with the US or German examples mentioned above.[19]

203

Less ambivalent than the effects of World War Two upon immigration into Britain, are its consequences for the growth of racism. Some of the most systematic persecution of racial and ethnic minorities in recent history took place during the two world wars.[20] In Britain during World War Two, there was a rise in hostility towards minorities, especially against those associated with the enemy and this was especially strong during the early stages of the war. Ironically the victims included refugees from Nazism, who were, nevertheless, viewed as Germans, and Italians. More basic racism, of an everyday social and economic variety, also continued, focusing upon both 'enemy' and non-enemy populations. In Britain much of the everyday prejudice was a continuation of the prewar situation. Established Anglo-Jewry continued to face hostility. Many Jewish evacuees faced initial hostility in the areas to which they moved and had to abandon Jewish rituals while they were away from home. Social anti-semitism characteristic of the interwar years continued. 'Clubs such as Les Ambassadeurs in Mayfair refused Jewish members as late as 1943. Many golf clubs followed a similar policy and a *numerus clausus* operated in some private schools.'[21] Black people faced similar hostility. Discrimination in 'hotels and places of public entertainment ... continued unabated' and increased after the arrival of black GIs.[22] Indians faced hostility from both Gentiles and Jews, as is witnessed by their experience in an air raid shelter in Tilbury.[23] 'Enemy' groups also faced discrimination of an everyday variety; for example, the businesses of some Italian shopkeepers folded because local people refused to buy goods provided by 'enemy aliens'.[24]

The most striking example of unofficial wartime racism was the anti-Italian riots of June 1940, which broke out immediately after Mussolini's declaration of war on Britain on 10 June and grew out of an increased sense of insecurity, as the Nazis continued to overrun continental Europe. This insecurity also led to the adoption of a policy of internment and repatriation by the Government. The attacks upon Italians affected several parts of London, as well as Liverpool, the North-East, South Wales, and Scotland.[25]

However, the most dramatic manifestations of hostility towards outgroups during World War Two were directed by the state, through a policy of internment and repatriation. The latter involved sending German and Italian civilian internees to Australia and Canada, a decision reached in early June 1940, under prompting from the new Prime Minister, Winston Churchill. Eventually 8000 aliens went to the Dominions. One of the ships transporting prisoners of war, the *Arandora Star*, was sunk by a German submarine on 2 July, resulting in over seven hundred deaths. This represented a turning point in the history of internment and repatriation in Britain as public opinion turned against these policies.[26] One of the survivors of the *Arandora Star* was Rando Bertoia, who described himself as 'one of the lucky ones'; he could not swim, but with the help of some friends, managed to scramble into a lifeboat.[27]

During the opening months of the war the Government changed its internment policy on several occasions. Discussions in early 1939 had prepared the way for the incarceration of 18,000 prisoners. However, in the early months of the conflict 73,000 enemy aliens were divided into three groups by tribunals. Only those in Category A were regarded as suspect and a security risk and consequently faced internment. Category B consisted of people who could remain at liberty but who faced some restrictions, while those in group C did not face any official interference. 'Of the 73,800 aliens screened, less than 1 per cent were interned and 6,200 were put into category C.'[28]

This remained the situation until the spring of 1940, by which time public opinion and the press had begun to turn against 'enemy aliens' as German armies advanced through the Low Countries and into France. The decision for wholesale internment was reached by the Home Defence Committee of the Cabinet on 11 June, following both Mussolini's declaration of war, and pressure from the military authorities. Police chief constables received instructions to commence immediate internment of class C aliens. In all, approximately 22,000 Germans and Austrians and 4,300 Italians endured a period of internment. However, by the end of July 1940, following the aforementioned change in public reaction towards internment, the Home Office had issued a White Paper which listed eighteen groups of detainees to be released. By April 1941 17,745 internees were free and by the end of August 1941 only 1,300 internees remained in camps, a figure which had fallen to just 25 by April 1944.[29]

The majority of internees found themselves in camps established on the Isle of Man – in Ramsey, Peel, Onchan, Douglas, Castletown, Port Erin and Port St Mary (the last two housed women). At various times there were fifteen camps on the mainland, some of them acting as transit centres from which people were transferred to the Isle of Man. The experience of internment proved difficult for many prisoners and especially traumatic for those who had previously been held in

German concentration camps. Worse still, in some cases, Nazis and Jews were held together. Some of the camps also had poor housing conditions, although they kept within the guidelines of the Geneva Convention. In order to relieve the boredom and depression, internees developed artistic, literary and educational activities, a process helped by the fact that so many of the internees were university graduates. 'Centres of Free German Culture' developed, together with 'People's Universities',[30] but all of this activity did not prevent some suicides.[31] One internee, Anna Spiro, recently recalled that 'it took me a very long time to get over the experience of being interned with some 5,000 women under conditions which, for most of us, despite the country's emergency, were very difficult to accept.'[32]

As far as black American GIs were concerned, official hostility towards them was all-embracing, ranging from the Cabinet and governmental level to local police forces. Indeed, the Cabinet was initially reluctant to allow any black troops to enter Britain and accepted them only under pressure from the US Army. Once in the country, although welcomed to some degree by the British population, the black GIs faced a great deal of official hostility. For instance, some police forces prosecuted white women and black soldiers who associated with each other, a widespread phenomenon in the areas where the black GIs were concentrated. The basis of this official hostility towards mixed relationships lies in more general hostility towards miscegenation, common in all forms of racism, but the extent of the fears and the degree of hostility towards African-Americans suggests that for some people winning the war and making the world safe for 'democracy' was not their first priority. Nevertheless, not only romances but also marriages took place and many brides of black GIs uprooted after the war to live in the USA.[33]

This overview illustrates that British minorities experienced an increase in persecution during World War Two. While not as severe as that in several other European states during the same period, most notably Germany, it undoubtedly occurred. The internment carried out during the war is a typical example of an anti-alien measure of a liberal democracy – as the similar policies of Australia and the USA in both world wars demonstrate.[34] Similarly, the rioting of May 1940 had its equivalent in May 1915, on a larger scale, against the German community.[35] One might pick out positive developments for minorities during the Second World War, notably a loosening of the strict immigration controls which had severely limited entry of immigrants and refugees during the interwar years. However, the new wartime policy was at least partly due to pragmatic reasons in that the British state needed additional labour. Furthermore, it would have been difficult to fight an nati-Nazi war while keeping out the victims of Nazism. Consequently, British wartime treatment of immigrants must be viewed in an objectively negative light, while not ignoring the comparisons with continental Europe.

NOTES

[1] Arthur Marwick's books include *War and Social Change in the Twentieth Century*, Macmillan, London, 1973.

[2] See Panikos Panayi (ed), *Minorities in Wartime: National and Racial Groupings in Europe, North America and Australia During the Two World Wars*, Berg Publishers, Oxford, 1993.

[3] For figures see Panikos Panayi, *Immigration, Ethnicity and Racism in Britain, 1815-1945*, Manchester University Press, Manchester, 1994, pp23-4; and 'Refugees in Twentieth Century Britain: A Brief History', in Vaughan Robinson (ed), *The International Refugees Crisis: British and Canadian Responses*, Macmillan, London, 1993.

[4] *Census of England and Wales 1931: General Tables*, HMSO, London, 1935, p221; *Census of Scotland, 1931: Report of the Fourteenth Census of Scotland*, Volume 2, HMSO, Edinburgh, 1993, p112.

[5] See J.A. Jackson, *The Irish in Britain*, Routledge and Kegan Paul, London, 1963; Frank Neal, *Sectarian Violence: The Liverpool Experience, 1819-1914*, Manchester University Press, Manchester, 1988; and Steven Fielding, *Class and Ethnicity: Irish Catholics in England, 1880-1939*, Open University Press, Buckingham, 1993.

[6] The best general works on Anglo-Jewry are: Geoffrey Alderman, *Modern British Jewry*, Oxford University Press, Oxford, 1993; and David Cesarani (ed), *The Making of Modern Anglo-Jewry*, Basil Blackwell, Oxford, 1990.

[7] See Alison Lockwood, *Passionate Pilgrims: The American Traveller in Great Britain, 1800-1914*, Cornwall Books, London, 1981.

[8] Terri Colpi, *The Italian Factor: The Italian Community in Great Britain*, Mainstream Publishing, Edinburgh, 1991, pp71-97.

[9] James J. Barnes and Patience P. Barnes, 'London's German Community in the Early 1930s', *German Life and Letters*, Volume 46, 1993, pp331-45.

[10] Panayi, *Immigration*, p52.

[11] *Census of England and Wales 1931*, p221; *Census of Scotland, 1931*, p112.

[12] The best work on this subject is Edward Homze, *Foreign Labour in Nazi Germany*, Princeton University Press, Princeton, 1967.

[13] See, for instance, James Grossman, 'Citizenship and Rights on the Home Front during the First World War: The "Great Migration" and the "New Negro" ', in Panayi, *Minorities in Wartime*, pp169-90.

[14] Penny Summerfield, *Women Workers in the Second World War: Production and Patriarchy in Conflict*, Routledge, London, 1984.

[15] Peter Cahalan, *Belgian Refugee Relief in England During the Great War*, Garland, New York, 1984.

[16] M.J. Proudfoot, *European Refugees, 1939-52*, Faber, London, 1957, pp71-2.

[17] J. Zubrzycki, *Polish Immigrants in Britain*, Martinus Nijhoff, The Hague, 1956.

[18] Graham Smith, *When Jim Crow Met John Bull: Black American Soldiers in World War II Britain*, London, I.B. Tauris, 1987.

[19] Holmes, *John Bull's Island: Immigration and British Society, 1871-1971*, Macmillan, London, 1988, pp164-7.

[20] These arguments are examined in Panayi, 'Dominant Societies and Minorities During the Two World Wars', in *Minorities in Wartime*, pp1-23.

[21] Tony Kushner, *The Persistence of Prejudice: Anti-Semitism in British Society During the Second World War*, Manchester University Press, Manchester, pp65-77, 96.

[22] John Flint, 'Scandal at the Bristol Hotel: Some Thoughts on Racial Discrimination in Britain and West Africa and its Relationship to the Planning of Decolonisation, 1939-47', *Journal of Imperial and Commonwealth History*, Volume 12 (1983), pp76-7.

[23] Kushner, *op.cit.*, p55.

[24] Colpi, *op.cit.*, p127.

[25] Lucio Sponza, 'The Anti-Italian Riots, June 1940', in Panikos Panayi (ed), *Racial Violence in Britain, 1840-1950*, Leicester University Press, Leicester, 1993, pp130-48.

[26] Peter and Leni Gillman, *Collar the Lot!: How Britain Interned and Expelled Its Wartime Refugees*, Quartet Books, London, 1980.

[27] See his account in David Cesarani and Tony Kushner (eds), *The Internment of Aliens in Twentieth Century Britain*, Frank Cass, London, 1993, pp230-2.

[28] Gillman, *op.cit.*, pp1-68; Francois Lafitte, *The Internment of Aliens*, Second Edition, Libris, London, 1988, pp62-5.

[29] Gillman, *op.cit.*, pp69-290; Lafitte, *op.cit.*., pp70-91.

[30] Lafitte, *op.cit.*, pp91-123; Michael Seyfert, ' "His Majesty's Most Loyal Internees" ', in Gerhard Hirschfeld (ed), *Exile in Great Britain: Refugees from Hitler's Germany*, Berg, Leamington Spa, 1984, pp163-88.

[31] Kushner, *op.cit.*, p149; Seyfert, *op.cit.*, p187.

[32] Quoted in Cesarani and Kushner, *Internment of Aliens*, p241.

[33] Smith, *When Jim Crow Met John Bull*; C. Thorne, 'Britain and Black GIs: Racial Issues and Anglo-American Relations in 1942', *New Community*, Volume 3, 1974; D. Reynolds, 'The Churchill Government and the Black American Troops in World War II', *Transactions of the Royal Historical Society*, Volume 35, 1985.

[34] See the contributions of Jorg Nagler, Roger Daniels, Gerhard Fischer and Kay Saunders to Panayi, *Minorities in Wartime*.

[35] Panikos Panayi, *The Enemy in Our Midst: Germans in Britain During the First World War*, Berg, Oxford, 1991.

World War Two and the Making of Multiracial Britain

Ian Spencer

Despite its long imperial history, settled black and Asian minorities represented a tiny fraction of the population of Britain in 1939. Officially calculated at the beginning of the war at 7,000, the black and Asian population of Britain was geographically concentrated in London and a number of other ports such as Cardiff, Liverpool and South Shields.[1] Though the history of black and Asian minorities in Britain does not begin with the Second World War, the war was a watershed in the formation of the specific ethnic and cultural character of the multiracial Britain that developed in the last half of the twentieth century. Of the seven major ethnic and cultural groups that comprise the large majority of contemporary black and Asian Britain, three owe their origins and modern development in Britain to the circumstances of the war. Caribbeans, Sylhettis from Bangladesh and Mirpuris from Pakistan now comprise just under a half of the black and Asian population of Britain.[2] The communities developed in Britain despite official hostility. War service or even temporary residence to help with the war effort was acceptable, even welcomed, but permanent residence was another matter. Of course, the officially trumpeted 'open door' of the postwar era was no such thing and as soon as immigrants from the Empire/Commonwealth began to push it open, it was slammed shut.[3]

During the war years the basis was laid for the settlement in Britain of three of the most important minorities that make up a large part of the complex core of non-white Britain. By the beginning of World War Two the foundations of one of the most important South Asian groups had already been laid. The growing presence of Sikh pedlars, even if not a permanent one, had caused the British government to introduce measures designed to limit their movement to the UK.[4] The 'problem' of an influx of immigrants from the sub-continent was apparently first detected in the mid-1930s when the Home Office noted that the police were experiencing increasing difficulty in keeping track of Indian pedlars and seamen. Their response was to 'take steps to restrict, as far as may be possible, the grant of passport facilities.'[5] The Government of India agreed to refer to London for comment all applications for passports to visit the UK that were received from illiterate or unskilled Indian subjects. To be successful, the applicant was required to obtain a sponsor in Britain who could provide guarantees of maintenance and repatriation. The reliability of the sponsor and the availability of reputable and permanent local employment were checked by the police in the UK. The final decision, however, rested with the government of the sub-continent. As a Home Office official put it in the 1950s, the object of these long standing arrangements was: ' ... from our point of view to control the entry into the UK of Indians and Pakistanis who may tend to become pedlars or to resort to undesirable methods of earning their living ...'[6]

The two groups whose roots in Britain were established during World War Two were apparently, as Indian seamen, beyond the reach of passport controls. Recruited mainly from Mirpur and Sylhet, they had been employed for many decades to crew vessels sailing from Bombay and Calcutta. Restrictive employer/union agreements generally prevented their engagement on routes from Britain, such as the busy North Atlantic run, other than those to and from Indian ports. Though there is some evidence of small numbers of Indian sailors settling permanently in Britain before 1939, it was during the Second World War that numbers grew to a level significant enough to begin to cause concern both to local Chief Constables and to the Home Office. The underlying reason for the increase was that during the war far more Lascars were employed on vessels calling at British ports. The Indian sailors were viewed as replacements for the large number of merchant mariners recruited into the greatly enlarged wartime Royal Navy. A significant number of Lascars were subsequently stranded by the loss of their vessels to enemy naval and aircraft actions. Many Indian-crewed vessels were torpedoed off the British coast and others bombed while in harbour. Ample labour opportunities were available during the war years, in munitions and other factories, and many of these stranded sailors elected to take those opportunities to earn money in what must have seemed a safer setting. The Indian population of many industrial towns rose significantly during the war years.

Certain changes in the administration of entry rules may also have inadvertently affected the numbers finding work in Britain during the war. In 1942 the Colonial Office made strong representations to the Home Office about the employment of a 'colour bar' in the application to 'coloured' seamen of the 1925 Special Restriction (Coloured Alien Seamen) Order. Under this regulation of the 1914 Aliens Registration Act, any coloured seaman who could not produce documentary evidence of his national identity could be, and apparently often was, refused entry. Revised instructions were issued to immigration officers to use their discretion in favour of the claimant to British or British protected status, even if they had no documentary proof of identity. Despite this change the Immigration Branch of the Home Office remained hostile to the idea of unrestricted entry for all classes of British subject.[7] Indeed, the major thrust of the discussion about courses of action to be taken in response to the increased numbers of sailors who were settling in the UK was exclusively towards trying to discover ways of limiting the numbers of those who could settle and of reducing the number of those who were already in Britain. Towns in the Midlands, particularly Coventry and Birmingham, appear to have been the most popular areas of settlement; 8-900 were already residing in these two towns by the middle of 1943, a sufficient number for the Chief Constables of the two towns to refer to them as 'a problem'.[8]

A wide range of possible measures to deal with the 'deserters' was examined. Since January 1943 no seaman had been entitled to a National Registration Identity Card. This card enabled the holder to receive coupons for rationed items. In Coventry the local Registration Office had refused to issue identity cards to Indians on the grounds that they were all seamen. An addition to the Defence Regulations that would allow the police to 'collect the deserters in batches and ship them back to India' was briefly contemplated. Scotland Yard had apparently prepared for such an eventuality by keeping a central register of all deserting seamen. A senior policeman argued that despite all the extra work such an action would entail, the police were 'very willing' to take on the task 'since it would relieve them of a burden in the long run.'[9] Recourse to the courts was also considered, but there were major difficulties in proving desertion as it was necessary to produce a copy of the ship's Articles and to bring the sailor to court before the expiry of his agreement.[10]

There is little doubt that the sailors who settled in ports and moved inland during the war provided the basis for the postwar development of the Sylhetti and Mirpuri communities in Britain. Many may have returned to sea at the end of the war, particularly if their employment in war-related industries ceased after the end of hostilities. However, it is likely that a substantial proportion of these men came back to Britain following the partition of the Indian Empire in 1947. The partition had an extremely damaging effect on both communities by locating their place of residence and the port in which they gained employment in different countries. Sylhet became part of East Pakistan while Calcutta became part of India; Mirpur formed part of Pakistani-ruled Azad Kashmir while Bombay was sited securely in India. The income and remittances of the Sylhetti and Mirpuri sailors, upon which their families no doubt depended, were threatened once new employment laws which restricted employment opportunities to nationals of the new states could be made to work. Sailors from both Muslim districts had to seek new sources of earnings. Wartime experience in Britain provided a certain guide.[11]

Whereas Sylhettis and Mirpuris took advantage of wartime opportunities to settle in Britain, Caribbeans were directly recruited in large numbers for wartime work in Britain. It is difficult to estimate with accuracy the number of people of Caribbean origin recruited for service in Britain. The history of particular groups has been researched, but no study has been made of the Caribbean contribution to the war effort in the UK as a whole.[12] One thousand technicians and trainees were recruited for service in war factories on Merseyside and in Lancashire, 1200 British Hondurians as foresters in Scotland and an unspecified but smaller number for the merchant marine. The number recruited for military service, mainly to the RAF, was 10,270 from Jamaica, 800 from Trinidad, 417 from British Guiana with smaller numbers, probably not exceeding 1000 in all from other Caribbean islands.[13] The inter-departmental Overseas Manpower Committee considered the possibility of organising the very large number of unskilled volunteers who were apparently available from the Caribbean for service in Britain but concluded that the costs and risks of trans-Atlantic travel were too high. One vessel carrying Caribbean volunteers had already been sunk off Bermuda and US troops were beginning to embark in large numbers for European service.[14]

There is much evidence to suggest that although most of those who worked in Britain during the war were encouraged to return to the Caribbean, their wartime experience was crucial in forming their determination to settle in Britain after the war. Only a third of the 1000 civilian recruits agreed to accept the government's repatriation terms; most of the rest stayed on in Britain. Just over a half of the Hondurian foresters accepted repatriation with the remainder settling for the most part in Scotland and the north of England. Of the 10,000 or so Jamaican servicemen about two-thirds were demobbed in Jamaica. Many of those who arrived on the first boats bringing immigrants from the Caribbean to the UK after the war were ex-servicemen and volunteers who had worked in Britain during the war. For example, the *S.S. Almanzora* which left Jamaica in late 1947 carried 90 former members of the RAF and ex-munition factory workers, and about two-thirds of the settlers who arrived on the *Empire Windrush* in June 1948 had already seen service in Britain during the war. Griffiths, the Colonial Secretary, suggested in 1950 that of the 2,000 or so immigrant workers who had arrived from the West Indies 'a large number' had served in the RAF during the war and were using their gratuities to pay the cost of the passage to the UK.[15] The returnees formed the core of those coming to Britain in the post war decades. The demobilisation of Caribbean servicemen was half completed when news of the employment of Polish and Italian workers in postwar Britain reached the Caribbean. Ex-servicemen from several territories were active in petitioning their governments to make employment opportunities available for them.[16] The Resettlement Department in Jamaica which had by far the largest task relating to the reintegration of servicemen was operating in an unsatisfactory manner; aspects of its work were described as 'deplorable'. Most returnees faced almost certain unemployment. A senior Colonial Office official, J.L. Keith, was dispatched to the Caribbean in July 1947 to discuss the linked problems of the resettlement of ex-servicemen, unemployment, and what appeared to be an impending flood of immigration to the UK.[17]

Despite their contribution to the war effort black and Asian migrants found a less than enthusiastic official welcome as residents of peacetime Britain. There is evidence, from an examination of the treatment of Caribbean technicians and trainees recruited in Jamaica and Barbados to work in factories in the north-west of England during the war, that officials were keen to prevent their permanent settlement in Britain even though the British economy was desperately short of skilled and semi-skilled labour and shortly began to encourage large numbers of European Volunteer Workers to come to Britain. Officials displayed what can only be described as an unseemly haste in attempting to secure passage back to the Caribbean for these men. Frustrated and delayed by the postwar shortage of shipping, by the reluctance of many of the West Indians to return home to probable unemployment (a number of them had also married English women) and by the workers' insistence that promises about postwar training be kept, the Ministry of Labour nevertheless succeeded in securing the repatriation of the majority by the middle of 1947.[18] No suggestion appears at any stage that such a highly valued group of workers should be encouraged to stay on.

However, the Colonial Office as the proponent of colonial interests in Whitehall took the view that because of the extensive use of European labour in the postwar reconstruction, the Government should look at the possibility of offering employment opportunities to British subjects from the Commonwealth/Empire. At its insistence a committee was established to enquire into this possibility; in 1948 an interdepartmental Working Party on the Employment in the UK of Surplus Colonial Labour was set up, chaired by the Under-Secretary of State at the Colonial Office with representation from the Treasury, the Foreign Office, the Home Office and the Ministries of Agriculture and Fisheries, Fuel and Power, Labour and National Service, Health and National Insurance. Its first task was to determine whether there was a *prima facie* case for the introduction of colonial workers. The committee considered that there was no general shortage of labour in the UK and that, of the sectors of the economy they discussed, only the health services experienced labour demands that could be satisfied from the colonies.[19] The minutes of the meetings contain a record of entirely negative attitudes to colonial labour. Doubts were expressed about the skills and endurance of West Indian Workers, about the availability of 'suitable' accommodation and about the attitudes of workers and unions to the employment of colonial workers. One senior official at the Ministry of Labour expressed the view that the type of labour available from the empire was not suitable for use in Britain and that displaced persons from Europe were preferable because they could be selected for their specific skills and returned to their homes when no longer required. Colonial workers were both difficult to control and likely to be the cause of social problems.[20] A working paper on the possibilities of employing colonial labour produced by the Ministry of Labour for the committee in 1949 did identify areas of labour shortage – for females in the cotton, wool, silk and rayon, hosiery and pottery industries and in hospitals and for males in tin plate and sheet steel, iron foundries, iron ore mines and general engineering.

Considerable problems were anticipated from the unions. The National Union of Agricultural Workers and the National Union of Mineworkers were both sounded out by the Ministry and neither would 'in any circumstances acquiesce in any scheme of organised recruitment.' The Regional Controllers, the key Ministry of Labour officials in the provinces, were unanimous in their view that it would not be feasible to proceed with any version of the proposal to employ colonial workers in Britain.[21] A Ministry of Labour official who had visited the Caribbean in 1947 to investigate the possibility of officially backed schemes of migration had reported negatively. Another compared Polish ex-servicemen settlers who could be 'absorbed' with West Indian migrants who could not. Problems experienced during the war 'even under military discipline' with 10,000 RAF recruits from the Caribbean were noted and the feeling of the department was summed up by C.W. MacMullan: 'My personal view is that these people would be far more trouble than they are worth. If we agree to anything it is out of altruism and not out of self-interest'.[22] In July 1949 the committee recommended that because employment opportunities in British industry were so limited, no organised large scale immigration of colonial workers should be encouraged. Colonial workers would be likely to avoid understaffed industries that were unpopular ones (European Voluntary Workers on the other hand could be directed to them) and the 'inevitable drift to dependence on the National Assistance Board' could not be avoided. Small numbers of females might be encouraged to fill vacancies for domestic servants and hospital orderlies.[23]

Despite these negative attitudes there was a slow growth through the 1940s and 1950s of the Caribbean population of Britain. Efforts at negative publicity in the Caribbean were probably less effective than a shortage of cheap sea passages (before the age of charter flights) in maintaining the slow rate of growth of the black population of Britain. Wartime experiences, predominantly Jamaican ones, provided the foundation for this growth. Comparatively, the Mirpuri and Bangladeshi communities grew even more slowly, perhaps due to the difficulty of obtaining travel documents and the expense of the journey measured by earning power both in Britain and in South Asia. In the early stages of their growth both of these communities were virtually all-male and neither appeared set on permanent settlement. But the wartime pioneers were the basis on which, through the importance of kin and the process of chain migration, the communities were eventually to establish themselves permanently in Britain. Britain's minorities are not a representative cross section of the population of the Empire/ Commonwealth or even of those territories from which movement to Britain occurred. They derive from particular parts of a small number of countries. The explanation for this is to be found partly in the experience of war. The set of the official mind was opposed from the start to the permanent settlement in Britain of these communities even at a time when, just after the war, the demand for labour was at an all-time high. Officially, all subjects of the King were free to enter Britain without let or hindrance. In practice, a major effort was made to restrict settlement from the Indian Empire and official discouragement accompanied Caribbean migration to Britain. During the lengthy and frequent discussions between 1948 and 1961 at Cabinet, ministerial and official level about how (not whether) to limit black and Asian settlement in Britain there was no single echo of the wartime origins of the movement, no recognition that the origins of 'the problem' lay in black and Asian responses to Britain's wartime needs.

NOTES

[1] 'Report of the Working Party on Coloured People Seeking Employment in the United Kingdom', 17 December 1953 in Public Record Office, Cabinet Papers, CAB124/1191 (hereafter CAB).
[2] Sylhettis, Mirpuris, Gujeratis and Sikhs from the Indian sub-continent and Caribbeans, African and Chinese form the basis of Britain's contemporary black and Asian population. R. Ballard and V.S. Kalra, *The Ethnic Dimensions of the 1991 Census: A Preliminary Report*, Census Microdata Unit, University of Manchester, Manchester 1994.
[3] See, I.R.G. Spencer, 'The Open Door, Labour Needs and British Immigration Policy, 1945-55,' *Immigrants and Minorities*, forthcoming, 1995.
[4] See D.S. Tatla, ' "This is our home now": Reminiscences of a Punjabi migrant in Coventry,' *Oral History*, Spring 1993, pp68-74, and Vernon Davis, 'A Sweet Prison,' M.A. dissertation, University of Leicester, 1993, unpublished, pp12-15.
[5] Aliens Department (Home Office) to Chief Constable of South Shields, 20 June 1934, Public Record Office, Home Office Papers, HO 213/242 (hereafter HO).
[6] *Ibid.*

[7] For changes in the treatment of 'coloured seamen' see 'Coloured People from British Colonial Territories' Memorandum by the Secretary of State for the Colonies, 18 May 1950, C.P.(50)113, CAB 129/40 and Memorandum by Howard (Home Office) 15.2.49. in HO 213/869. See also M. Sherwood, 'Race, nationality and employment among Lascar seamen, 1660-1945,' *New Community*, XVII, 2, pp229-44.

[8] This information was revealed in correspondence between the Home Office and the Ministry of War Transport in HO 213/820.

[9] *Ibid.*, Minutes of meeting at the Home Office to discuss the problem of Indian seamen deserters, 4.6.43.

[10] *Ibid.*, Kneale (Ministry of War Transport) to Harrison (Home Office), 10 May 1953.

[11] See M.M. Islam, 'Bengali Migrant Workers in Britain' (unpublished Ph.D. thesis, University of Leeds, 1976) p58. The British Labour Attaché in Pakistan reported that the position of Muslim seamen employed in Bombay and Calcutta was being made very difficult by the introduction by the Government of India of a regulation which insisted that at least 25 per cent of the sailors employed in the two ports were Indian born. Report of Labour Attaché, Pakistan, 1948-9, Public Record Office, Ministry of Labour papers, LAB13/524 (hereafter LAB).

[12] See, for example, M. Sherwood, *Many Struggles: West Indian Workers and Service Personnel in Britain, 1939-45*, Karim Press, London 1985 and A.H. Richmond, *Colour Prejudice in Britain: A Study of West Indian Workers in Liverpool, 1941-1951*, Routledge and Kegan Paul, London 1954.

[13] See 'Civil Manpower: Recruitment of Labour for the UK' 1942, CO 323/1863/2, Note by J.L. Keith on his visit to the West Indies, September 1947, in Public Record Office, Colonial Office papers (hereafter CO), CO 318/476/1, 'Coloured People from British Colonial Territories', Memorandum by the Secretary of State for the Colonies, 18 May 1950, C.P. (50) 113, CAB 129/40 and Richmond, p26.

[14] See P. Noel Baker (Ministry of War Transport) to H. Macmillan (Colonial Office), 17 June 1942, 17 June 1942 in CO 323/1863/2.

[15] Details of the *Almanzora* are in Sir J. Huggins (Governor, Jamaica) to A. Creech Jones (Colonial Office) 24 November 1947 and of the *Empire Windrush* in A.W. Peterson (Home Office) to F. Graham-Harrison (Prime Minister's Office) 5 July 1948 in HO 213/244. See also *Forty Years On*, Lambeth Borough Council, 1988. Numbers of Jamaicans demobbed are given by Keith in his report (see footnote 13) and civilians staying on are estimated by Richmond, p24. Further figures are provided by Griffiths in his 1950 memorandum to the Cabinet, CP (50) 113, CAB 129/40.

[16] See for example, Officer Administering the Government of British Guiana to the Colonial Secretary, A. Creech Jones, 13 April 1947 and Sir H. Blood (Governor of Barbados) to A. Creech Jones, 2 August 1947 in CO 318/476/1.

[17] A. Creech Jones (Colonial Office) to Governor of Jamaica 28 July 1947 and minute by J.L. Keith, 3 October 1947 in CO 318/478/1.

[18] The handling of this question by the Ministry of Labour is dealt with in LAB 26/134.

[19] *Ibid.*

[20] *Ibid.*, see views of Bevin (Ministry of Labour) at the first meeting of the working party, 6 October 1948.

[21] 'The possibilities of employing colonial labour in the UK', Ministry of Labour memorandum, September 1948, CO 1006/2.

[2] Memo by MacMullan, 2 October 1948 LAB 13/42. References to the 'indiscipline' of Jamaicans under military command during the war are frequent in the C.O. and Ministry of Labour papers. See, for example, Minutes of meeting to discuss Keith's Report, 29 September 1947 in CO 318/476/1.

[23] *Ibid.*, report of the working party on the employment in the UK of surplus colonial labour, July 1949.

Women, Internment and World War Two

Rinella Cere

Writing about immigrant women's internment experiences during World War Two has been even more patchy than that about men. This essay aims to redress some of the 'myths' and misrepresentations of women's camps found in the general histories of immigrants' internments, with particular reference to women's experiences and patriarchal notions of woman as psychologically, physiologically and socially inferior and ultimately driven by 'primitive' behaviour. It also examines the ways in which accounts by women internees (and sometimes by the men also) conflict with other accounts of them. Ironically, the most crucial misrepresentation of women's internee experience is *A Bespattered Page? The Internment of 'His Majesty's most Loyal Enemy Aliens'* (1980), by Ronald Stent, himself an internee of Hutchinson camp on the Isle of Man. The pro-alien position of much of the text is transformed once we examine the chapter on women's camps. Two key passages from which I shall quote later illustrate how, after the event, historians can still add insult to injury.

On 21 May 1940, *The Times* ran an article indicating that the 'Re-examination of German and Austrian alien women in category B ... 3500 women ... was begun all over Britain yesterday'. Category B was one of three categories (A, B and C) applied to immigrants and refugees from Germany and Austria – and from Italy after Mussolini's declaration of war on 10 June. These grades were indications of degrees of loyalty towards the predominant political system in 'one's mother country'. Grade 'A', normally given to Nazis and Fascist supporters and sympathisers, meant immediate imprisonment followed by internment and in many cases eventual deportation. To be graded 'B' did not initially entail immediate internment but immigrants and refugees in that category were subject to travelling and location restrictions. With the deterioration of the war and the invasion of France, however, the policy changed and refugees in category 'B' were suddenly perceived as potential spies on British soil. Grade 'C' simply noted origin from an enemy country. Grades were often allocated wrongly, and women were often graded on the basis of their husband's assessed grade.[1] The measurement of loyalty was clearly a very difficult task, one increased by the fact that many 'aliens' were refugees from their own countries. To be loyal to one's country of origin did not automatically mean being loyal to the Nazi and Fascist regimes. Prisoners of war ('A' class Nazis and Fascists) were in many cases better treated than refugees in class 'B' and 'C'.[2]

Women made up a quarter of those interned. The build-up to their internment followed a similar 'ideological route' to that of men, but with the added 'ingredient' of sex. One recent writer has argued that 'female refugee domestics were construed so as to embody simultaneously the peril of sexual subversion, class war and national humiliation'[3]; although the fact that only a quarter of internees were women suggests a gender bias relating to women as 'weaker' beings, the myth of woman as the weaker sex being more prevalent then than it is today.[4]

The 'ideological route' to internment was based on a widespread public anti-alien campaign between 1939 and 1940. Such campaigns were not unknown to British shores, a more drastic anti-alien campaign had taken place during World War One, with tragic consequences for the immigrant communities involved, mainly the German community.[5] Two related factors sparked the 1939-1940 campaign. One was the press hysteria about potential 'spies', the other the arbitrary association of refugees and immigrants (enemy aliens in official language) with fifth column activities (a part of the espionage activities greatly exaggerated in popular mythology and firmly embedded on war national identities). *The Times* article mentioned earlier noted, 'Drastic steps are taken to prevent fifth columnists and German sympathisers from entering Britain in Dutch ships, scores of which have arrived in British ports since the invasion of the Netherlands ...'. These confusions between nationality, 'enemy alien', immigrant, refugee and fifth columnist also contributed to the internment of Fascist with anti-Fascist and Nazi with Jews.

Phrases such as 'we are nicely honeycombed with little cells of potential betrayal',[6] 'the London Italians are an indigestible unit of population',[7] 'the paltriest kitchen maid, with German connections ... is a menace to the safety of the country'[8] and 'nuns from the sky' reflect prejudices against foreigners and 'aliens', sedimented by centuries of assumed superiority, by colonialism and imperialism and by legislation such as the Aliens Act of 1905, aimed at excluding 'undesirable and destitute' immigrants (then largely Russian and Polish Jews).

The internments which followed the political and press scare campaign of 1939 to 1940 and the systematic arbitrary allocation of grades symbolised the xenophobic policies pursued at a particular and crucial moment in the war. The rounding up of women and men was a disorganised and randomised process involving great hardships, for both those interned and for those left at home. This is how an ex-internee, Erna Nelki, remembered her experience of being arrested early in the morning and taken to a special centre to await transportation to an allocated destination: '... we were just asked to pack a few things ... the night was spent huddled on chairs or in dirty cabins; toilet facilities were dirty and insufficient. We were crowded in a special train ... even toilet doors had to be left open during use. Many women cried bitterly ...' The final part of the journey offered no relief because the march through Liverpool towards the harbour was 'accompanied by the boos of the local population'. The ferry journey on which there 'was seating accommodation only for the old and for women with young children' completed the bleak experience.[9] Many women were taken to prison prior to being sent to their final destination, the Rushen Peninsula on the Isle of Man where there were eleven camps – Port Erin and Port St Mary for women. These two small towns, which had been previously holiday resorts, in 1940 hosted internment camps for nearly 3000 women.

The Port St Mary and Port Erin Camps are at the centre of my brief revision of women's internment, as are certain assumptions about the 'nature' of womankind. Stent's descriptions resonate with a reversal of the traditional Christian references: if Eve's downfall had been the presence of a male, in this case male absence was deemed the cause of women's ills. He writes:

> For many women, living together under such unusual conditions in such close proximity created many a problem on a personal level. Nerves often became frayed, ephemeral tiffs were blown up out of all proportions; envy, sloth, all the other deadly sins were bound to

prosper. The absence of male company also did not help to smooth personal relations. It may sound like male chauvinism, but it does appear as if, on the whole, a lot of men in an exclusively male environment can bear each other's company far longer and with less friction, then women can'.[10]

Many themes run through this passage, most of them familiar to the contemporary ear: the first is the way in which the 'female condition' seems to be marked by inherently weak or negative traits; women seem as incapable of relating at a 'personal level' without 'essential' and 'negative' traits getting in the way. Envy, sloth, ephemerality, 'weak' nerves and hysteria have historically been associated with the 'nature' of woman, with a lack of mental and physical strengths. Unless one accepts that the human condition in general is subject to absolute categories of essence and existence[11] however, Stent's analysis neither offers a satisfactory explanation of the problems facing the women nor a convincing account of differences between the responses of women, let alone between those of women and men. Mental, moral and physical strength, Stent seems to believe, may be achieved in 'personal relations' through male company. Without it women are apparently doomed, both at a private and a public level.

Stent's account of the women's 'frustrations' as a result of the lack of male company needs considerable qualification. He cites one woman as saying that the local clergyman 'was mobbed whenever he passed down her street', but does not point out that Jewish refugee women were unlikely to have been amongst those who did so.[12] The notion of unregulated sexuality sits at odds with other accounts, and interestingly in terms of conventional morality, Stent's description applies only to single women, 'The married women whose husbands had also been interned had worries of their own'. Married women, however, were also seen as weak. In relation to meetings between wives and husbands interned on the Isle of Man in different camps, for example, Stent states that: '... the women found it hard to overcome a mood of despondency once the husbands had left again'. Even if this had been the case it seems a fairly justified reaction given the circumstances and one which was partly influential in altering official policy in that one of the women's camps was later transformed into a 'married' camp.

That problems existed in the women's camps is undoubtedly true, as is evident in many of the women's accounts of their experience, but those problems had more to do with the alienating experience of internment and with the random selection of internees than with female 'weakness' and/or sexual frustrations. Jewish refugees and pro-Nazis sympathisers often had to live together at very close quarters, sometimes even sharing rooms. Indeed, the problems associated with the internment of Nazis with anti-Nazis were far more serious for the women than for the men because only a few class 'C' women had been interned. The ratio of pro-Nazi women interned was far higher in the women's camps. There is little documentation available about Italian women's internment and pro or anti-Fascist ratios. Miriam Kochan briefly mentions that some Italian women were interned following the entrance of Italy into the war, but no detail is provided as to how many and under which grade.[13] Terri Colpi's book on the Italian community in Britain suggests that, on the whole, Italian women were not interned in the same proportion as German or Austrian women but were left to fend for themselves in a way alien to traditional Italian family patterns. However, Colpi refers only to the business community, by no means the largest Italian grouping, and does not tell us very much about the Italian women, except that they had to rely on 'charity from the Italian Community' as well as the population at large.[14] What is important here is that Italian women, given their subordinate position within their culture, were believed by the British State to constitute less of a threat than women from other communities. The general non-internment of Italian women was another example of the gender-biased policies of internment during World War Two; paradoxically, in this case their gender served to help avoid internment.

To return to the women's camps and to Stent's writing, 'heavy' with irony at the expense of women. His description of the organisation of women's camps is interspersed with comments which undermine his attempt to recover a 'piece' of history buried under the layers of supposed shame and 'official discourses': 'Little workshops were established for sewing, dressmaking and shoe-repairing; a hair-dressing salon and a laundry were set up; squads were formed for wood-chopping and gardening.' This contrasts with the description of one of the men's camps (Hutchinson, where the author himself was interned) where '... internees were chosen to be in charge of welfare, of educational facilities such as the university and the technical college; of the camp news-sheet; of concerts and art exhibitions; of other leisure activities and of the canteen.'[15] All activities described in relation to the women's camps are considered primarily in terms of their domestic 'ambience', from cleaning to raising children, whilst in the men's camps the atmosphere is rarefied even when concerning the same domestic chores. Men in the camps seem to be mostly concerned with the activities of the intellect, of art, the academy and science and, although there were more university professors interned in the men's camps than in the women's one, this difference only reflected the gender differences in European academia as a whole. Stent emphasised the fact that 'The first lectures took place within three days of the opening of the camp, and eventually covered most of the subjects normally taught at a university'. At the same time, Stent made light of, if not ignored, other experiences of these male intellectuals. Professor P. Jacobsthal who, like Stent, was interned in the Hutchinson camp, wrote of the conditions found in the camp in his memoirs. He dwelt in particular on the regimentation implemented, he believed, because of 'lack of precedent' by the authorities who simply applied the regulations in force for prisoners of war. Jacobsthal described himself and his fellow internees as 'embittered'.[16]

Stent endowed men's involvement with domestic tasks with 'higher' purposes; 'Each boarding house catered for itself, with one of the resident internees volunteering as *chef de cuisine* ... The Isle of Man government in due course published a booklet, "Three Hundred Recipes Based on the Dietary for the Isle of Man Internment Camps" '.[17] For men, foodstuffs became tools for 'artistic creativity'. One does not want to detract from the importance of murals 'made with jam, porridge, ink, herring skins and olive oil', but Stent is constantly less generous to women in terms of the status he affords their activities.[18] Everything established in the women's camps is depicted as of a lesser stature than those related to the men's camps. When Stent describes the socioeconomic system implemented in the women's camps, the judgment is unrepentantly negative: 'Tokens were issued in this "Services Exchange" as payment for work done ... Community economics had reverted to a primitive barter stage'.[19] The paragraph continues to describe the organisation of the women's camps in the same vein, even when it acknowledges the development from 'primitive barter' to a more 'sophisticated system', which extended beyond primary utility goods to 'tickets for library, for concerts, for coffee and pastries in the "Konditorei"'.[20]

There are, however, two texts, at present in typescript form and lodged at the Imperial War Museum, which describe rather differently the experience of women in the camps, just as they do the various aspects of the camps' organisation. These originate from two very different sources, and are valuable in different ways to the reassessment of women's experience in internment camps. One, by ex-internee Erna Nelki, was written in 1940 and translated in 1981; the second, a more 'official' document, consists of notes by Dame M. Corbett-Ashby on her visit to the Isle of Man internment camps in February 1941.[21] The first (by far the most important in terms of the women's experience of the camps) gives an account of the internment of 1940 to 1941. In the section on 'The shock of internment', Nelki discusses the indiscriminate internment of Jews and other refugees from Germany together with pro-Nazi women, and the organisation of the camp – describing the varied activities therein. Nelki's account is not only hers but also that of other women internees (Hilde Blank, Lotte Cromwell, Emma Loewenthal, Ira Rischowski, Ilse Rolfe) whom she interviewed with the express purpose of writing their collective experience. She writes of their arrival: 'When we arrived at camp it seemed to lack all planning and organisation. The authorities had housed us, told us our duties with regard to housework, but all activities which were gradually undertaken only developed through pressure exerted by the internees themselves'.[22] This suggests a considerable degree of organisation on the part of the women, to formulate demands as well as to present and lobby for them. The camps, at first under the command of Dame Joanna Cruikshank who had little sympathy for Jewish women ('As far as she was concerned we were all Germans'),[23] was run along egalitarian lines. The 'Service Exchange' and 'Tokens' system, so derided by Stent and described as a form of 'primitive barter', had been instituted at the instigation of Dr Borchard, a woman with experience of unemployed people in Hamburg who 'started to organise an independent camp economy based on services rendered and paid for by camp money, or Tokens as we called them'.[24] This system enabled all the women, not only those who had brought money, to benefit from the different services set up within the camp.

Women were indeed preoccupied with domestic tasks, but it should be remembered that many of them had their children with them. They also directed their attention to other activities, including education: 'Various activities sprang up to occupy our leisure-time. There were a number of gifted and talented women who tried to make our life in forced seclusion more interesting and valuable'.[25] Intellectual and educational activities were organised and the only difference from those in the male camps was that they were called adult education rather than universities: 'There were courses in the English language and literature, history, biology, crafts including carpentry; and even in manicure. Theatre and music groups got under way including various choirs'.[26] Social activities focused around the establishment of a café which became 'a cultural centre'. The tokens systems allowed the women to order coffee and cakes and buy and sell 'handiwork items' exhibited in it: 'It was a very good system and helped to create a sense of meaning and purpose in the lives of many internees'.[27] Although not all of Nelki's writing suggests such a positive outlook amongst the women, it is clear that the camp she describes was very different from that described by Stent. Women's 'sloth' when living together is certainly not in evidence. What is in evidence is the traumatic situation caused by continuous uprooting (85 per cent of the women interned were Jewish refugees, who already had had to flee from Nazi persecution). The 'absence of male company' noted by Stent is portrayed here as a deep sense of loss and in some cases the actual loss of companions/husbands either in concentration camps or en route to Australia, as for example with the sinking of the *Arandora Star*.[28] Unlike Stent, and without patronising tones, Nelki also describes without 'contempt' or 'mirth', the life of single heterosexuals and lesbians in the camps.

The report written following the visit of Mrs Corbett-Ashby to the Isle of Man, also suggests a 'homely' and social atmosphere, not present in the regimented and hierarchical structures in place in men's camps. She wrote that, 'The women's camps are wonderful in comparison [with the men's], women within curfew hours can wander at large, drink coffee and gaze at shops, though shopping beyond 5s a week can only be done by permission of the Commandant'.[29] She also goes on to describe the hive of educational and manual activities taking place: 'The women's representatives presented a detailed scheme for new industries and are most anxious for a similar test to the Pioneer Corps for the younger women. They are holding a survey of qualified women. They were much disappointed at Sir Herbert Stevenson's remark "Women can't be trained".'

There is still much to be researched and written about a piece of history blighted by wrongdoings, but I hope that future historians will bear in mind Erna Nelki's words: '... it remains to be said that internment was not only cruel but wrong'. To date, unfortunately, that applies to some of the writing of its history.

NOTES

[1] M. Kochan, 'Women's Experience of Internment', in D. Cesarani and T. Kushner (eds), *Immigrants & Minorities: The Internment of Aliens in Twentieth Century Britain*, Volume 11, Number 3, Frank Cass, London, 1992, p148; M. Kochan, *Britain's Internees in the Second World War*, Macmillan, London, 1983.

[2] I. Rischowski, *Correspondence Relating to Internment, 1940-41*, Imperial War Museum Library; F. Lafitte, *The Internment of Aliens*, Penguin, Harmondsworth, 1940, p91; 'Re-examination of German and Austrian Alien Women in Category "B"', *The Times*, May 1940.

[3] T. Kushner and D. Cesarani, 'Alien Internment in Britain During the Twentieth Century: An Introduction', in Cesarani & Kushner, *op.cit.*, p14.

[4] Kochan, *op.cit.*, p147.

[5] P. Panayi, 'An intolerable Act by an Intolerable Society: The Internment of Germans in Britain during the First World War', in Cesarani and Kushner, *op.cit.*, pp53-78; A.W. Simpson, *In the Highest Degree Odious: Detention Without Trial in Wartime Britain*, Oxford University Press, Oxford, 1992.

[6] *Daily Mirror*, 27 April 1939, cited in P. and L. Gillman, *Collar the Lot: How Britain Interned and Expelled its Wartime Refugees*, Quartet, London, 1980, p150; 'Isle of Aliens', *The Times*, I June 1940.

[7] Gillman, *op.cit.*, p149.

[8] Kochan, *op.cit.*, p149.

[9] E. Nelki, *The Internment of Women in England 1940*, typescript, Imperial War Museum Library, 1981, p2.

[10] R. Stent, *A Bespattered Page? The Internment of 'His Majesty's most Loyal Enemy Aliens*, Andre Deutsch, London, p197.

[11] H. Arendt, *The Human Condition*, University of Chicago Press, Chicago, 1958.

[12] Stent, *op.cit.*, p197.

[13] Kochan, *op.cit.*, p150.

[14] T. Colpi, *The Italian Factor: The Italian Community in Great Britain*, Mainstream Publishing, Edinburgh, 1991, p126: T. Colpi, 'The Impact of the Second World War on the British Italian Community', in Cesarani and Kushner, *op.cit.*; L. Sponza, 'The British Government and the Internment of Italians', in Cesarani and Kushner, *op.cit.*

[15] Stent, *op.cit.*, p162.

[16] P. Jacobsthal, *Memoirs*, typescript, Imperial War Museum Library, 1940, p30.

[17] Stent, *op.cit.*, p159.

[18] *Ibid.*, p171.

[19] *Ibid.*, p195.

[20] *Ibid.*, p195.

[21] Mrs Corbett-Ashby, Notes on her Visit to the Isle of Man Internment Camps, 3-10 February, 1941, typescript, Imperial War Museum Library. She was Co-Honorary Secretary for the National Council of Women of Great Britain and Ireland, also Liberal candidate for the Borough of Richmond Parliamentary elections, 1922.

[22] Nelki, *op.cit.*, p5.
[23] *Ibid.*, p3.
[24] *Ibid.*, p8.
[25] *Ibid.*, p7.
[26] *Ibid.*, p7.
[27] *Ibid.*, p8.
[28] *Ibid.*, p4.
[29] Corbett-Ashby, *op.cit.*, p1.

Section 6: Personal Testimonies

Fragments of Shrapnel

Peter Davison

> *What wond'rous life is this I lead!*
> Andrew Marvell, *The Garden*

I tú? que has fet per la victòria? demanded a Republican poster in the Spanish Civil War. As Orwell put it, 'What have *you* done for democracy?' All he felt he could reply was, 'I have drawn my rations'. There was no victory for the Republic, of course, but that did less than justice to his contribution to democracy; however, it adequately sums up my contribution to the war of 1939-45.

Much of my summer holiday of 1939 I spent swimming lengths at Finchley Road baths. Back and forth, back and forth. Always the breaststroke. Someone had told my mother I might be 'a prospect'. The Olympic Games were mentioned – 1944, perhaps. 'Could I train him?' 'Oh yes, of course,' said my mother. So: to and fro, to and fro. Towards the end of August we went north, to Northumberland. My mother was to earn a little money putting on a pageant at Linden Hall. She had been a stage manager at the Ambassadors and Garrick Theatres, for the Farjeons – the first woman stage manager, they said. Linden Hall is a classy hotel now, but was then a private home and estate owned by two maiden ladies, Muriel and Eve Adamson. They also ran Richmond Theatre where my mother read scripts whilst waiting for something better to turn up. Part of the deal was that my younger brother and I should have the run of the estate for two weeks. In memory, it was idyllic. In fact it was also idyllic. The head gamekeeper taught me how to catch rabbits bare-handed. 'Thrwabbits', he called them, in the Northumbrian country manner. Was that how Shakespeare heard Percy Hotspur speaking thick? We rambled and fished; we were completely free. And there was always a home-grown peach in our bedroom before we went to sleep.

It was at Longhorsely Parish Church that we heard that we were at war. Seven days later I was thirteen. My brother stayed for six long,

long years, shifted from pillar to post, an evacuee. I went back to London, first to our lodgings, which my mother helped run – but the baths were closed because of the glass roof – and then to my 'Institution'. The pageant and the idyll were over; the baths vanished, though whether by bomb or through demolition I do not know. They've built a Sainsbury's instead. So much for dreams of Olympics, however empty.

'Institution?' you ask (perhaps). Technically, yes, so it was entitled. A rather fine orphanage might be more accurate. We lived near Lord's Cricket Ground and at the Lisson Grove Corner there was then another, less fancy, institution. Around its brickwork was emblazoned: 'FOR ORPHANS WHO HAVE LOST BOTH PARENTS'. As we swung round the corner on a 53 bus (it was the 53 in those days and turned the corner past the Grace Gates), my eye once caught this entablature. 'But I thought orphans *had* lost both parents!', I said. My mother had a penetrating voice. She had briefly trained as an opera singer and had worked as a chorus mistress for West End shows. 'Don't be silly. *You're* an orphan' – my father had died in 1933 as an indirect result of exposure at sea. The whole bus looked at me. Not just the top deck. At the bottom of the stairway, as we got off, I felt every eye turn on me: 'Orphan', they seemed to say.

I still see that building, though now the site is filled by a block of council flats – sold off, I expect. The orphans were evacuated and it was used during the incessant raids on London to house firemen from Sheffield. They had come to London to relieve their fellows, then near exhaustion. Something had to replace it and council flats must have seemed appropriate, for a bomb landed on it, square if not fair. They said forty firemen were killed. I suppose there must be a plaque to their memory, but I've only seen those commemorating the builders: St Marylebone Borough Council.

At school, for safety, we slept two to a bed in the corridors under the cloisters. (Would they dare now? Years before my wife was my wife, she shared a bed with a stranger for three months whilst on a course at Cambridge. 'Keep y'r feet still, Geordie hinny!') The school looked like a barracks by moonlight so it was not unreasonable that we were showered with incendiaries one night and that on another night, bright as day, a parachute mine should be dropped on us. It missed the clock tower by a few feet and exploded harmlessly in the next field, leaving a huge crater. On my bed in the dormitory where we no longer slept lay a huge and jagged sheet of glass. I've long lost my two treasures from those events: an incendiary fin (which I painted black and gold) and a short length of the main parachute cord. I still feel that loss, like the half cup of tea that's thrown out by mistake after the pot's been emptied. It is curious how one actually *feels* such an absence.

During the 1939 Christmas holiday I took round warnings for the local ARP post to those showing lights from their windows, breaking the blackout. I remember vividly taking notices round Langford Court in the Abbey Road, where Orwell and his wife were to live a couple of years later. The odd thing was, the occupants were nearly all refugees. It seemed so strange to me that they should do anything so careless, even unwittingly, as to attract the attention of those from whom they were, with good reason, fleeing.

Masters disappeared into the services and boys who had lately been prefects would return to sport their uniforms before us. The school had provided the setting for the film, *Goodbye Mr Chips*, in which a long-serving deputy takes over from the head in World War One. Ironically, precisely the same happened to us. Replacement teachers could find the going tough. We cruelly barricaded-in our kindly but ineffective French replacement. When the biology master joined the Navy we had – wonder of wonders – a *woman* to replace him. She proved a splendid teacher and suffered no such fate. Once we did see her in tears, when the boy who sat next to me (his name, by a twist of fate, was Peace) died suddenly of meningitis. I can still see his face. And there was the reading out of names of those who had fallen, just as in *Goodbye Mr Chips*.

I remember, as if it were yesterday, three deaths. The head of school for a time was a boy – a man – called Good. We didn't use first names in those days. He had amongst us the reputation for being a communist, though heaven knows we'd no idea what a communist was. (About 1941 I read *Crime and Punishment*: it might have been contemporary Russia to me. I could recite the stations on the Trans-Siberian Railway, at speed, but I'd not then even heard of the Revolution of 1917.) We admired Good, even wondered at him. He seemed to us, as his name implied, 'Good'. He went down when the destroyer on which he served sank. Strange, Peace and Good, both dead. My housemaster in our junior school, G.V.C. Carlin, was not very well liked, yet he was kind to me. I was always embarrassed by his kindness. One Christmas he sent me a book token for five shillings. I bought an atlas, stuck in the counterfoil on the inside cover, 'To Peter Davison. From G.V.C.' in his small, neat handwriting, then hastily pasted it over with a blank sheet of paper so that no one should see the source of my gift. Why should we be so ashamed of kindness shown us? Is it characteristic of a child's life? Nearly sixty years on, I still have that atlas and it has been round the world with me. I remember, with two other boys, helping him pack up his books to store in the roof space in the summer term of 1939. 'Why?' we asked – perhaps with hope that he was leaving. *En cas de guerre*, he replied. He was a Paymaster Lieutenant Commander on HMS *Hood*. *Hood* was struck at long range in the chase for the *Bismarck* on 24 May 1941. She sank in four minutes. Of the crew of 1,416, three survived – as I recall, a rating, a petty officer, and an officer: that's egalitarian selection for you! When the news came of Carlin's death I was making a model warship. 'Good riddance', said one boy. I could have wept, but didn't dare. I still cannot understand it. Mind you, *he* modelled aeroplanes.

Stephens was one of our prefects. Perhaps the kindest, jolliest, of all those set in authority over me in that little world. Back he came in his RAF uniform, excited about flying. That was the first time. He returned a second time, far less assured, even apprehensive. He'd flown a Hurricane or a Spitfire for the first time and its speed appalled him. We never saw him again. They said he went down on his first mission, but they always say that, don't they? Perhaps it was his second.

Our house usually accommodated music and drama students from the various London academics. The business was owned by a former actress, Daisy Tresahar – she had once performed before Edward VII at Sandringham with the great music-hall comic, Dan Leno – and had been founded by her mother, one of the first women journalists in London. My mother assisted in a variety of ways, initially to help her pay her rent, but eventually took over. During the war our large garden was converted by her into what was virtually a smallholding. Whether it was her skill or the bees that she also kept, or both, it was not only remarkably productive, but she won prizes for the best garden of its class in North London. She certainly provided a great deal of food. Christmas Humphreys, later a judge, lived in our street and when he went off to prosecute at the Japanese War Crimes Trials after the war my mother looked after his bees.

We not only had students, but also refugees. Daisy had taken in German and Austrian Jewish refugees from 1933. The register she was required to keep – which I still have – is full of German names from then until the early 1940s. Several of these served Britain and the Allied cause with distinction. Erich and Margarete Esslinger came to us from

Mannheim on 3 September 1936 and stayed for four years. He worked undercover ahead of troops advancing into Germany – for a Jew, a particularly dangerous job. Erich taught me to play chess. Dr Kurt Lewkonja arrived from Göttingen on 3 January 1940 but was interned on the Isle of Man six months later. My mother waged a battle with the authorities on his behalf, and that of several others, eventually having him released into her charge on 30 January 1941. In no time it was realised that what my mother had argued was, in fact, true, that he was a brilliant engineer and he was shipped off to Birmingham to organise the production of ball bearings, of which we had far too few. He would come to see us whenever he had a spare weekend. His brother was also an engineer and he was employed on the making of Bailey Bridges. After Dunkirk we had a group of Polish airmen – Squadron Leader Mieczyslaw Sühs and his colleagues, Popek, Mucha, Becko, Bucior, and Michniewicz. They stayed with us for a couple of months and then went off to join Polish Air Force units.

Perhaps the most unusual of our guests in the 1930s, and one who had a very unusual connection with the war, was Ichiro Kawasaki, who worked at the Japanese Embassy and came to us from Tokyo on 8 August 1935. He was very fond of England and he and I (though when he arrived I was not quite nine) became quite close friends. We spent many an afternoon at Lord's Cricket Ground. We must have looked an odd pair! When Pearl Harbor was attacked, he returned to Tokyo but before doing so came to see Daisy and my mother to offer his profound apologies. We heard, but how I have no idea, and it may well be apocryphal, that on his return home, in shame, he committed suicide.

In the early raids on London, when a single bomber would drone overhead, occasionally letting fall a bomb, my mother would admonish me: 'You may be frightened but don't you ever let me see it'. She had served in the First World War, one of the first recruits to the WAACS (I still have her badge), and nursed through the Spanish flu epidemic that killed more than did the war itself. She never showed fear. But those first few nights of bombing *were* nerve-wracking. For the first few, we stayed up, waiting. No anti-aircraft defences were to be heard, only that continuous drone and an occasional thump. Then, to celebrate my fourteenth birthday, Churchill organised that the A.A. guns should all open up at once. The racket was starkly comforting. We never went to a shelter. 'You're quite as safe in your own bed. If a bomb has your name on it ... etc, etc.' In any case, simply entering a shelter could be fatally dangerous. At Bethnal Green tube station, on 3 March 1943, a woman with a small child tripped at the foot of the first twenty-step flight of stairs. Those following-on tumbled down after her. Although the sirens had sounded, Jerry had not arrived on the scene and no guns had opened up. The baby was killed with 177 others. The mother survived. My wife-to-be managed to be bombed out three times in 24 hours, which was, frankly, careless, but my life seemed (as it has since) to be charmed. Only once, when I was leaving the Swiss Cottage Odeon one night, did I have anything like a close shave. It must have been about the time when rocket guns were first used. Shrapnel hailed down and, in far more danger than the German pilots, I sheltered in a doorway, just as one would in a heavy rainstorm, until calm was restored.

The theatres having closed, my mother worked in a rest centre in Camden Town, 24 hours on, 24 off. She spent her time comforting the bereaved and bombed-out, finding somewhere for them to live, and somehow getting hold of the bare necessities – clothes, pots and pans, bedding, basic (very basic) furniture. In her spare time she photographed families of servicemen (at their request) who had been separated for months, even years. Cameras were not then as common as they are now and film was in short supply, but the YMCA organised a scheme to enable those serving abroad to 'see' their families. She made up an album of those she photographed, with letters of thanks, and, in just one instance, a letter from a commanding officer telling her that the photograph had arrived after the soldier had been killed. Some families would not be photographed, fearing that might cast the spell of death over a husband or son. Her album is now in the Imperial War Museum, the only one of its kind.

In June 1942, having, to everyone's amazement, not least my own, matriculated, I left school, aged 15¾, and joined the Crown Film Unit as an assistant cutter. It proved to be a very happy time. The normal working week was then of 48 hours but I always did a half-hour's overtime each day, six days a week, to prepare the day's film for my editor. The number of hours worked could rise sharply (though, being too young, we were not paid for more than something like 55 hours) to as much as eighty when we dubbed *Close Quarters*, a film about the submarine service. The actors were genuine submariners and went back to 'The Trade' after shooting the film had finished. From time to time we would hear that this man or that had been lost. It gives that film, which occasionally still pops up on television, a particular

poignancy. I worked with people who have since become legendary –
Humphrey Jennings and Stewart McAllister – and there was a
wonderful camaraderie. And National Dried-Milk Cocoa, served to
those of us under eighteen (a Ministry of Food product designed to
keep us healthy), was also pretty good.

It was a time when there were frequent calls for a Second Front to
relieve pressure on the Russians. Those of us in the cutting rooms in
line for call-up became more and more irked as union meeting after
union meeting would be called, in lunch break after lunch break (a
ploy resorted to when the intention was to tire all but the most
determined activists), to pass motions, always proposed and spoken to
by those in reserved occupations, demanding 'A Second Front Now!'
A final vote would always be deferred until the organisers were sure
that they could manipulate a majority. We hit upon the counter-ploy
of challenging the chair. There would be a vote – which took ages – and
we would all ostentatiously vote *for* the current chairman. Once
re-elected, he (a very nice fellow) would feel so hurt he would resign.
But no, we would not have that either and proposed him and voted for
him again, and again. It put paid to the lunch-time meetings and the
calls from Pinewood Studios for a Second Front. 'What did you do in
the war, daddy?' 'I voted against a Second Front.'

On 28 July 1943, I joined the No. 5 (Pinewood) Platoon of the 10th
Battalion of the Buckinghamshire Home Guard. I was still sixteen. We
only trained and it became increasingly obvious that although the
Spigot Mortar was fun we should never use it in action. Six months
later I transferred to (of all Orwellian numbers), the 101st 'Z'
Anti-Aircraft Battery at Slough. We had sixty-four launchers, each
capable of firing two six-foot rockets which, when they burst, filled a
huge area with shrapnel. The rockets were so heavy I could scarcely
manhandle them and so was entrusted (unwisely) with taking orders
over the intercom. Our only 'success', as I recall, was at Southsea, on a
training exercise, when we opened fire by mistake and hailed shrapnel
on a destroyer out at sea. Unfortunately, it was one of our own and
our efforts were not appreciated. We laughed though. But we did
shoot down a plane. That, too, was one of ours. His own fault, of
course. Sent out the wrong recognition signals. Happily the crew all
baled out safely. And, remarkably, the rear gunner lived in the same
lodgings as I did and he was less than pleased.

My most exciting experience in uniform was when I attended a
meeting of the Association of Cine Technicians (Membership Number

5323) standing in for our shop steward, the Chief Sound Recordist, Ken Cameron. I was the last to arrive and the meeting had started. Encumbered with gas mask, tin hat, and rifle, I made my way into the tiny, ill-lit committee room; there was a sudden scramble and *I swear* that at least one member of the committee dived under the table. Ivor Montagu (translator of Pudovkin's *Film Technique* – the assistant cutter's bible in those days: I still have my copy) was there, and, of course, the General Secretary, Elvin. 'Never come in uniform again!', I was sternly admonished, 'we thought it was the military'. It's always good to know which side you are on.

When Hitler's 'Revenge Weapon', the V-1, was first launched against England in the summer of 1944, my task at Pinewood Studios was to climb 60 feet up a vertical ladder to the roof of one of the film stages and spot for any coming in our direction. That saved everyone having to take shelter unless absolutely necessary. Most fell well short of us. As the V-1 had a 1¼ ton warhead, that was handy. My association with the buzz-bomb, or doodle-bug, still at long range, took a more fruitful form in that I made the initial cutting copy of the film about the V-1, *The Eighty Days*. The *Evening Standard* for 20 November carried an illustration of a piece of sound track that I cobbled together showing the buzz, the silence, and then the explosion. Or rather, as it was printed in reverse, the explosion, the silence, and then the oncoming buzz. *That* souvenir I still have.

One delight of my time with Crown Film Unit was the screening of historic films and those not available on general release. One I particularly remember was Orson Welles', *The Magnificent Ambersons*, shown one Saturday afternoon after work. Another occasional delight was the concerts arranged at lunch-times: Myra Hess (having featured in Humphrey Jennings's *Listen to Britain*) came to give us a live performance in just the manner of her National Gallery concerts. Little did I think that, nearly twenty-five years later, the second horn of the RAF Orchestra, briefly glimpsed in that film sitting next to Dennis Brain, would teach me the french horn. Solomon also came. He played not only his formal concert (my introduction to the *Waldstein* sonata) but carried on for an hour or so afterwards for those whose who could escape from their work.

By the time I was seventeen, those called up tended to be directed to the Army or the mines. I preferred the Navy and so tried to avoid direction by volunteering. Thrice I made the trek to the Drill Hall at Edgware, each time to be rejected. These occasions involved a personal agony: peeing to order. I had never realised how much of our war effort depended upon filling small bottles with urine at the right moment, in the right quantity. It was not, it seemed, a case of the battle being lost for want of a screw. Why did the defeat of Hitler (and we said 'Hitler', rarely 'the Nazis', still less often 'the Germans' – yet we spoke of defeating 'the Japs') depend on being able to micturate to order? When I was called up, the recruiting Petty Officer at Edgware recognised me and I did join the Navy on 27 December 1944 as P/JX 737303. First to Skegness, renamed *Royal Arthur*, where I learned to lash a hammock in which I was never to sleep, strung between the uprights of the porch of a Butlin's Holiday Camp hut in the snow, hands bleeding with cold. Then to Malvern for six weeks basic training during which I distinguished myself at rifle practice by missing a large target at fifty paces and had to be searched in case I was concealing live ammunition. There I enjoyed one of those ever-to-be-remembered, glorious days when, because one of the regular staff fell out, I was drafted into the ship's hockey team for a game against, I think, Felsted School, evacuated from Essex. It was followed by the sort of tea normally denied 'men dressed as seamen' (that most perfect of naval descriptions) who had less seatime than a crossing on the Gosport ferry. Then to Manchester to what was then the College of Technology but is now UMIST, to be trained as a radar mechanic. There were several such instruction centres and the Navy, with its facility for names, if nothing else, called them collectively HMS *Shrapnel*. There we were inducted into the mysteries of soldering and the Puckle time-base. We did PT each morning in a hall surrounded by reproductions of classical statues, useful props for our clothes, watched by the girls of the chemical inspectorate. So, on 30 May 1945 I was accosted on the back stairs by one of that troupe (who all knew our timetables better than we did and by which staircases we got from one classroom to another) and four years later we married, and are still married. By then the war was long over and I had spent much of the intervening time on the port radar base and Suara radio transmission station at Singapore.

It was, for me, a very easy war. I gained far more than I lost. I should never have been good enough for the Olympics, and the Crown Film Unit was for me the university which I was never to attend. And Manchester – the laboratory girls, between their testing airstrip tarmac, sea-soap, parachute fabric, and all the *matériel* of war; the wonderful Catholic Women's Association which devotedly ran an all-night canteen for servicemen; the cinema usherettes inveigled into holding down Jack's collar as he struggled into his overcoat; even the Church Army Hostel in which we lived at Chrolton-on-Medlock and learning to sleep on the luggage racks of trains – not to mention a wife: but that is another story.

But ... but ... on Remembrance Sundays, and in Westminster Abbey this year on the seventy-fifth Anniversary of the first Armistice Day, I hear Binyon's familiar lines with throat constricting and eyes pricking. I have grown old, but age has not wearied Good, Stephens, and Carlin ... I see their faces as I saw them then; and, for those Sheffield firemen, I still see that institutional building for 'orphans who have lost both parents', whose destruction orphaned so many more.

End and Beginning: 1945

Alan Sillitoe

On the first day of 1945, aged sixteen, I got willingly and automatically out of bed at half past six and dressed in the dark. My father, already down in the living room, with a fire burning and a kettle on the gas, called up the stairs of the two-up-and-two-down terrace house that it was time for work. My two younger brothers slept on in the bed and, being already in my shirt, I put on trousers, overalls, boots, and jersey, and went down the steep narrow stairway for a breakfast of tea and bread-and-jam.

I centre these recollections on 1945, rather than on the opening of the war, because that year stands out as the one in which the world came of age as, it seems to me, did I. Life has not been the same since, for which Fate was more responsible than circumstances.

Little was said as we warmed ourselves at the kitchen fire. Then, at a quarter past seven, we put on our jackets, went through the small scullery, and stepped out of the back door. At the end of the yard, my father on foot and me pushing a bicycle, I rode up the street, while he walked down, to turn left at the bottom and go into the neighbouring Raleigh Bicycle Factory which, since 1940, had been on full war production.

As we parted he called out: 'Happy New Year!' My only response was to wave goodbye, knowing we would both be back in the house by evening. Maybe he realised how much more important the new year would be to me than it could be to him. Only the beginning of the day seemed important when, getting myself into consciousness from the oblivion of sleep, I mulled on what I would be doing after coming out of the factory at half past five in the evening. Work was an eight-hour stint in which to earn the requisite amount of money that would make up my wages by the weekend. Playing the capstan lathe was like

241

pressing the buttons of a cash register, for I was on piece work.

I peddled up the incline of cobbles on my bike. Everyone was going to work. The top decks of trolley buses on the main road were so covered with breath and cigarette smoke that faces could hardly be seen within. Feet, hands and face were frozen as I sped by the castle, going around the city centre rather than through the middle, so as to avoid a steep hill.

The small factory made parts of aero engines for the Rolls Royce plant at Derby. I clocked in twenty minutes before the machinery was set going because of an arrangement with the owner to clean the place before the rest of the people got there at eight o'clock. Sweeping the empty and silent gangways clear of steel, aluminium and brass droppings, earned me an extra tax-free ten shillings a week.

That's how 1945 must have begun.

Before leaving the house my father and I listened to the news, in which we took an extraordinary interest, while my mother and four other children slept on an extra half hour upstairs. The voice from the wireless overshadowed our lives: 'Here is the news, and this is Alvar Lidell reading it.' Each advance towards the heart of Nazi Germany, exciting though it was to hear about, made the future more mysterious and unknown. The end of the war would mark a new beginning in everyone's lives, though none of us could imagine the kind of world it would be. The news also provided entertainment in that it created a species of horse race in which the winners had always been foretold. All through the war it never occurred to us that anything we heard was a lie, or even in any way inaccurate. Equally unrealistically, there was never the slightest doubt that we would *win*.

Only my father didn't see it entirely that way. He hated Churchill. I thought my father was misguided, and think so still, and sometimes wondered at the time whether he much cared if the Allies won or lost, though he was carried away by euphoria when the end seemed certain. All I'm sure about was that he despised Hitler even more than he distrusted Churchill.

A state of war seemed to have been on since birth. Dreadful expectations had hovered around the words Manchuria, Abyssinia, and Spain, as well as Austria and Czechoslovakia, and then Poland. Through childhood every adult said that war with Germany was inevitable, while all looked on the prospect with fear and dread.

I realised quite early on in the war that sooner or later it would be necessary to take part in the common effort. As soon as I was fourteen, in 1942, I went to the headquarters of the local Home Guard company and asked to be enrolled, but the captain told me with a smile to come back in a year, on the assumption that I would then be an inch or so taller. I was already on the ration strength, at work in a factory, and issued with an identity card, so it was impossible to lie about my age.

But at fourteen the Air Training Corps took me on, and from then on my ambition was to get into the Royal Air Force and become a navigator. Perhaps navigation, both an art and a science, appealed more to me than piloting an aerial vehicle through the sky. I was given a uniform, and three or four times a week went on the parade ground to have my physical reactions smartened up by becoming adept, along with other cadets, at split-second drill. In the classroom we were instructed in elementary navigation, mathematics, meteorology, aero engines, and all matters connected with aviation. For several weeks a year it was agreeable to live under canvas or in nissen huts at aerodromes. I learned to fire a rifle, practised street fighting, and acquired the basics of wireless and morse. Because I studied hard the exams were easy, and I couldn't wait to join up for aircrew training, galled that the minimum age for volunteering was eighteen.

Taking the occasional day or week off work I would go on training flights at an aerodrome, one time in a troop-carrying glider doing 'circuits and bumps' towed by a Halifax bomber. I would stand behind the pilot's seat and, when the tow rope was jettisoned silence but for the sibilant rush of air would fill the empty glider stretching behind like a long wooden shed as we drifted around the circuit. At the turn-in for landing the glider appeared to stand on the edge of an invisible cliff, the runway as if vertically below, and I gripped the handles in wonder and excitement, and then the glider tilted at a sharp angle and went down, wheels under the fragile fuselage suddenly trundling and bouncing along the earth. Each time as we hung at eight hundred feet above the end of the runway I knew I preferred to fly in a powered aeroplane, but could not resist staying in the glider when it was again hooked to the tail of the bomber, the line tautening as we lifted level with the towing plane and joined the circuit once more.

The years as a cadet seemed to go on forever. Even the war had already lasted a lifetime, and though the Allies were at the frontiers of Germany by autumn 1944 it still appeared to me, looking at one of the many maps in my cupboard in the bedroom, that with so much land yet to be conquered, and fighting on interior lines, Germany could go on resisting for years.

The surprising German counter-offensive in the Ardennes, in December 1944, certainly suggested the possibility. My map of the area was scored with pencil lines. The wireless announcer had given news of the fighting before my father and I set out for our respective factories, he to help in the making of shellcaps, and me to turn out more items on my capstan lathe for Lancaster and Spitfire engines, many of which would no doubt end up half-buried beside dead aircrew members in some German field or wood.

During January of the year in question the RAF dropped thirty thousand tons of bombs on Germany, while the United States Air Force unloaded the same amount. As a cadet I heard of a new bomber to replace the Lancaster, called the Lincoln, which would carry a larger bomb load and need a bigger crew. Five hundred were being made ready for 1946, no one yet sure that the war would end in 1945. It was better not to believe in the future until some kind of future was assured. Many people on the mainland of Europe had more reason to hope for a quick end to the conflict, and until the last days of April we did not know in what vast numbers these victims were.

Victory seemed a long way off in January. Maximum effort could be kept up only if everyone believed that the war might never end. It was a peculiar time. Some people did sense victory, manifested by a headier atmosphere. Yet a weariness was also apparent, and people could only respond to it by taking the war-to-last-forever in a more relaxed way.

Certainly the war had meant full employment for working people, after the difficulties of the 1930s, both for men and women. Unemployment had been ended by the call up of millions, and everyone was needed. In the small factory I worked at twenty were women, half a dozen were youths like myself, and the other few were either toolsetters in a reserved occupation, men unfit for military service, or men beyond the age of call up. The owner also worked there, a big man of about fifty with grey swept back hair and a florid face. Before the war his workshop had turned out slot machines – one-armed bandits – but his industrial capacity, small as it was, had been commandeered for war production like every other workshop. I was offered the possibility of escaping military service by being trained as a toolsetter. Though I did not dislike my job, and though the work was as good a way as any of earning a living, and for which I was paid well enough, I only wanted to join up.

My few possessions were stored in a bedroom cupboard, except for the cadet uniform hanging behind the door, and a bicycle leaning against the palings in the backyard. The dozen books were mostly by Alexandre Dumas and Victor Hugo, except for a prize Bible from school whose main use was to conceal my saved pound notes between its thin leaves. I little knew that my mother borrowed from my stock whenever she was short, replacing the notes carefully on Friday night from the three wage packets that came into the house.

On another shelf were maps and navigation charts, the latter well-worn with dead-reckoning plotting exercises which invariably led by cunning and diverse legs to the heart of Nazi Germany. There was a tin of drawing instruments, a morse practice buzzer, pens and inks. I had everything I wanted, except a watch, for which I had to wait until my cousin in the army came on leave from Germany after VE Day, and sold me one of the many he had either looted or bartered.

It was impossible to get into the RAF before the age of eighteen, but it was put about that you could volunteer for the Fleet Air Arm at seventeen. Shortly after my birthday I went to the school downtown which served as a recruiting centre and enlisted, much to the disgust of my father who, too young to fight in the First World War, did everything possible to avoid call up – or any kind of duty – in the second war.

On 2 May I was ordered to go before an aircrew selection board at Crewe. Only the best candidates could hope to pass, and even grammar school boys had been known to fail. My education, such as it had been, had stopped at fourteen, so I was a mixture of overconfidence and pessimism. Failure would be devastating, because I had been training for three years, and had learned all that had been on the syllabus.

I got up at six, washed thoroughly, and after breakfast took a bus to the railway station. On such a warm clear day there was no sign of the war, unless I had become so used to it that they were no longer noticeable. After Derby the line for Crewe ran through the Potteries, an area of grimy back-to-backs among the smoking kilns which made the place look scruffier even than Nottingham.

The Navy had its aircrew testing facilities in a large Victorian house. After the medical, and a series of aptitude tests in a class room with half a dozen others, I stood to attention in front of four elderly naval officers, who fired simple questions at me such as: 'If a triangle has an angle of fifty six degrees, and another of sixty four, how many would the third angle need to have?' I was somewhat flustered, but the right answer came. On being asked my favourite sports, they seemed satisfied with my feigned enthusiasm for cricket and football, and my keenness for swimming and cycling.

After a meal in the mess there were more aptitude tests, reminiscent of the eleven-plus scholarship exam at the age of eleven, which I had failed twice. I didn't expect the present result for some weeks, but at the end of the afternoon a naval rating told me that I had passed. A clerk gave me three shillings for my first day's pay, and a small red naval identity card which referred to the holder as a Naval Airman Second Class with the number: FX643714.

Such luck was hardly believable. Were they kidding me? Hadn't some mistake been made? Everything had been so informal. I floated to the station rather than walked. Looking back, it seems a low hurdle to have crossed, yet I thought of it as the first real success of my life. All I had to do now was go home and wait to be called for training on *HMS Daedalus*. The fact that I had wanted to be a navigator, and had been accepted for training only as a pilot, was hardly a disappointment.

Newsagency messages in morse could be picked up by me from short wave on the radio in the kitchen, and I remember taking down something about Hitler's demise, amazed at what was written on the paper. I turned to my father. 'Hitler's snuffed it.'

'About bloody time,' he said coolly.

Berlin was crumbling street by street before the Red Army. The German armies in Italy capitulated. The surrender signed on Luneburg Heath became effective by eight o'clock on 5 May. Did this mean the end? It was hard to believe. Battles were being fought in Prague. There was street fighting in Copenhagen. The Russians captured Swinemunde and Peenemunde on the 5th. General Blaskowitz gave in in Holland. On the 7th Breslau fell after an 82 day siege. But how much longer could resistance be kept up in the so-called Mountain Fortresses of Bavaria and Austria?

By the morning of 8 May it was over, without any doubt, and turned into a day of flags, bonfires and boozing. If Delacroix had painted 'Liberty' on that day she would have been a big blousy bespectacled woman of fifty in the crowded White Horse pub doing a can-can on one of the tables, showing her Union Jack bloomers with each high kick of her shapely legs, to the cheers of all the drinkers – of whom I, with my girlfriend and parents, was one.

Slightly less inebriated, I was able to get them safely home and tucked up in bed. My father went to the lavatory to throw up, and came out minus his false teeth – top and bottom – whose loss he didn't realise till the following morning. The toilet had been well used after him, and they had gone forever down the gutterspout. In order to mollify him for his vital loss, I gave him nine pound notes out of my Bible so that he could buy some more.

Life would never be the same again, for more reasons than one was able to enumerate at the time. In April or May (I forget the exact date), a doublepage spread of the *Daily Mirror* had shown us the ultimate barbarity. I came home from the factory, and my mother passed the newspaper, saying: 'Open that, and see what *they* have done to people.' She implied that if the Germans had got to England they would have done the same to us.

Photographs of the dead and dying of Belsen were spread over the pages. My lack of proper understanding prevented a full assessment. These people were civilians, not soldiers. The fact that they were Jews was not apparent. Perhaps the text had not made it clear, or else my eyes had uncomprehendingly slewed over the words because of the startling and horrifying pictures.

Why had the Germans done this? Or some of them, anyway? No reason would or could ever come, therefore the pictures seemed unreal. One knew about the lunatic philosophy of those Germans who followed Hitler – and we assumed that all of them had, and did – but to have connected it to this kind of indisputable reality needed a jump of the imagination that I, in my complete preoccupation with self, and a desire to get into the war, had been incapable of making. I had seen the documentation of German atrocities against the Soviet people, produced by the Russians, and printed in Russia, and sold ouside the Raleigh factory in magazines when I had worked there, but death on such a scale, and against the Jews only, I had not been prepared for. Perhaps if I had read *The Times* every day, and listened to the BBC European Service instead of only bulletins put out for home consumption, more would have been surmised.

I was numbed. One needed time for the fact of such barbarism to sink in. Yet it did go in, as indeed it had to. The anti-Nazi propaganda had not been strong enough, apparently. We had listened to Lord Haw-Haw on the Deutschlandsender from Hamburg, for a laugh now and again, and had heard in 1940 that Goering had declared to his aircrews: 'Bomb the cities! Bomb the poor!' which later made us look with callous satisfaction at the hundreds of four-engined Lancasters streaming out night after night to bomb the German poor. Thus was morality and human feeling defenestrated, but deliberate killing on the scale of the extermination camps we hadn't thought about. We were presumably born with defective imaginations. Belsen was one of dozens of such places, and what I thought had been done at one place by a handful of fanatics and sadists had been part of a plan which had killed six million entirely innocent men, women and children.

The Million Skulls of Merv, the ashes of the Inquisition, the bodies of the Armenians, had been multiplied, and it had happened while I was at school, or working in the factory, or studying to be a navigator (which would have led me to drop bombs on civilians if the war had lasted long enough); in other words, while I had been safe due only to an accident of birth. The emotional and intellectual ramifications of those photographs of Belsen, and then of other places, were to be endless, hardly ever absent from the mind after that time, in that they also cast a spell of guilt upon the whole world and on myself no matter where I was or what I thought, or what I had been doing. I was now part of the world and responsible for everything.

Not being the masters of Time, we are unable to turn back history. On how many occasions since 1945 have I not wished it had been possible to turn back the sprocket of the calendar so that certain dreadful events would not have happened, to put my foot onto that God-like clockface and stop it at 1914, or 1933, or even at 1939, and say: 'No more!' to all the vile historical events that have killed and maimed so many. Alas! Where is progress?

After the San Francisco Conference a general election was held in Great Britain, on 5 July. For five years the country had consented to the necessary dictatorship of Mr Churchill and his Cabinet, and everyone assumed that he would be allowed to stay and lead the country at least until the end of the war with Japan. A 'Young Turks' group of us fixed Labour posters on the walls of the factory, to see them immediately taken down by the boss. Only when the results came did I realise how interesting the time could be. A socialist government had been voted in, and there would be no mass unemployment as in the 1930s, a government which would be friendly with Soviet Russia (we didn't yet know what barbarisms had been perpetrated in that country against its own peoples) which would nationalise the mines and the railways, and create a health service. It also seemed to promise an egalitarian society, though as far as I was concerned, I felt equal to anyone, and didn't need to be told that from now on I was equal. To have someone tell me that I was equal was as impertinent as being told that I was not.

I lived from day to day, and life was the same no matter who ruled, or who thought they ruled. The unimaginable had already happened in that Hitler was dead, and all his works exposed. I knew nothing at the time, yet thought I knew everything. Not knowing that I knew nothing led me to think I knew more than everything. All I needed was to go on living, and slowly dissolve the block of what I thought I knew so as to discover what I truly knew.

Such was history, and life went on, but with the thought that nothing was unthinkable anymore. All the same, it was a time of political immaturity, since I was hardly of the age to make much of a connection with anyone except my girlfriend. Parents are there, and if they are not, they would hardly be missed. The circuits and bumps of life had commenced, the tow-rope detached, and I was at last going under my own power, sometimes hitting the runway a bit too hard on landing, but not thinking of the next minute because the present was so powered with meaning and possibility, and fuelled by those instinctive actions which the young devise in order to survive.

On Wednesday 9 May, I was back at work, sore-headed but going flat out at my lathe. War production went on, because Japan had not yet been defeated. In some ways I had a dread of total peace because I thought that the unemployment of prewar days would come back. The statement that everybody would be busy on reconstruction did not entirely convince. Even my aircrew training would be in jeopardy if the Japanese War ended, though it seemed likely that it might go on for two or three years, in which case I would be flying from aircraft carriers, which had a higher accident rate, apart from battle casualties. The possibility that I might get killed was a block against imagining the future, though there was no trouble disregarding such a fear.

At work, orders from Rolls Royce were falling off, and we wondered whether Bert Firman, our boss, would go back to the construction of gambling machines. If so, he would not want so many hands, and in any case, I wouldn't care to do such work if I could get any other.

Young men were wanted to work in air traffic control, and those who had spent time in the Air Training Corps and had acquired a grounding in aviation were given priority, so I applied for the job, while continuing to work at the factory. At the beginning of August I went on a two-week navigation course at RAF Halton in Buckinghamshire, and the following week a friend waved a newspaper at me saying that a bomb dropped on Japan had wiped out a whole city. The war, even in the Far East, would be over any minute, he added. Another such bomb was lobbed on Nagasaki, and on 15 August came news of the Japanese surrender.

We fled from classes and went to London, thirty miles away, paying nothing on public transport because we were in uniform, to mingle with the crowds and witness the King and Mr Churchill waving from the balcony of Buckingham Palace. It was my first trip to London, and I was surprised at how, on the underground trains, a mere second or so in time seemed to elapse between the appearance of one station and the next, an indication perhaps as to how little was in my mind. On the other hand, maybe the time between stations seemed so short because my reflections were so intense!

I got the job as an air traffic control assistant, and after a two-week course at an RAF airfield was posted to Langar aerodrome in Nottinghamshire. At six in the morning I got up and took a bus into the town centre. The *Daily Herald*, a Labour paper, went into my pocket, to be read on the twelve-mile bus ride to Langar with the rest of the aircraft workers, getting me to duty before eight. In the evening the airfield was closed, and I went home.

York airliners were produced at the nearby A.V. Roe factory, and my work was to signal take-offs and landings from the control tower when they were tested. I was employed by the Ministry of Aircraft Production as a temporary civil servant, and my wages were half of what I had earned in a factory, but it was a far more congenial job. Never again would my hands get soiled and cut in order to earn a living. Even my Nottingham accent changed to a more neutral English, due to using the telephone, and speaking over the radio to in-flying aircraft.

At the control tower an officer was in charge of us two assistants. Little flying was done, so most of the time was spent reading, or gazing out of the window, or playing darts, or doing interception exercises on the sort of exotic plotting charts that would be used by pilots in the Navy.

In winter there was even less work to do, and at the end of 1945 I had good reason to be pleased with what changes had come about in the world and in myself. Life is a long road for the lucky, and the war was over.

Notes on Contributors

Kathleen Bell is a lecturer in English at De Montfort University. Her chief research and teaching interests are in interwar literature, poetry and popular culture.

Alan Burton is Junior Research Fellow in Media Studies at De Montfort University and is currently writing a doctoral thesis on the Co-operative Movement's use of film. He is author of *The People's Cinema: Film and the Co-operative Movement* (1994).

Deborah Cartmell is a lecturer in English at De Montfort University and her research interests are in Renaissance poetry, Shakespeare and film, and black writing in English.

Rinella Cere lectures in Media and Cultural Studies at De Montfort University. She is currently researching on European and national identities in the Italian and British media. She has written on women and gender issues, on female genital mutilation, *Silent Tears* (1989), and on pornography and computers.

Steve Chibnall teaches Media and Cultural Studies at De Montfort University, Leicester, and writes about postwar cultural history. He is Chair of the British Association of Paperback Collectors and curator of one of the largest archives of paperbacks and pulp fiction.

Peter Davison, Visiting Professor and Acting Head of English, Media and Cultural Studies, De Montfort University, was formerly a Fellow of the Shakespeare Institute, Professor of English, St David's, Lampeter, and of English and American Literature, University of Kent. He is editor of the twenty-volume edition of Orwell's works, to be published in 1996.

Pat Kirkham is Professor of Design History and Cultural Studies at De Montfort University. She has written widely on design, gender and film. Her recent publications include *You Tarzan: Masculinity, Movies and Men* and *Me Jane: Masculinity, Movies and Women* (edited with

Janet Thumim) (1993 and 1995 respectively) and *Charles and Ray Eames: Designers of the Twentieth Century* (1995).

Stephen Knight is Professor of English at University of Wales Cardiff and was formerly Professor of English at De Montfort University. He is the author of books and essays on literature and its social context, such as *Form and Ideology in Crime Fiction* (1980) and, most recently, *Robin Hood* (1995).

Pierre Lanfranchi is Research Professor in History at De Montfort University. He previously taught at the University of Florence and writes on football and society. His work includes *il calcio e il suo pubblico* (1992), and *Les footballeurs professionnels* (with Alfred Wahl) (1995). He previously directed the research project on sports culture in Europe at the European University Institute.

Adrian Lewis has research interests in recent British art and mid-nineteenth century French art. He teaches in the School of Arts at De Montfort University and is also a practising painter.

John Newsinger is Senior Lecturer in History at Bath College of Higher Education and previously taught at De Montfort University. He has published numerous articles on aspects of Irish and British history as well as cultural studies and contemporary politics. He is the author of *Feminism in Mid-Victorian Britain* (1994) and is currently completing a book on Orwell's politics.

Michael O'Shaughnessy lectures in Film and Media Studies at Edith Cowan University, Western Australia, and formerly taught at De Montfort University. He has written on British cinema, affectivity and film and masculinity.

Tim O'Sullivan is Principal Lecturer and Subject Leader for Media Studies at De Montfort University. His recent publications include *Studying the Media: An Introduction* (1994). He has particular research interests in the domestic history of radio and television in Britain.

Panikos Panayi is a Senior Lecturer in History at De Montfort University. He has published very widely in the area of immigration, race and minorities in the nineteenth and twentieth century.

WAR CULTURE

One of the most traumatic periods of British history was also a time of exciting social upheaval. **War Culture** seeks to understand the social and cultural changes that were wrought during this time by charting the experiences of the adults and children, men and women, and different ethnic groups who lived the hard life on the home front.

The book covers a wide range of issues ranging from wartime experiences of race and racism to women's dress of the period, from professional football to morale in the blitz, compellingly written by academics from many different areas of social and cultural study. **War Culture** also includes an autobiographical section with original essays by Alan Sillitoe and Peter Davison providing an informed personal slant to this impressive archaeology of Britain's past.

Pat Kirkham is Professor of Design History and Cultural Studies at De Montfort University.
David Thoms is Professor of Economic and Social History, also at De Montfort University.

Contributors Kathleen Bell, Alan Burton, Deborah Cartmell, Rinella Cere, Steve Chibnall, Peter Davison, Pat Kirkham, Stephen Knight, Pierre Lanfranchi, Adrian Lewis, John Newsinger, Michael O'Shaughnessy, Tim O'Sullivan, Panikos Panayi, Robert Richardson, John Rimmer, Alan Sillitoe, Ian Spencer, Matthew Taylor, David Thoms, Paul Wells, Imelda Whelehan.

Cover design Jan Brown Designs
Cover photograph *Woman*, 1941. Courtesy *Woman*, IPC

ISBN 0-85315-824-X

Lawrence & Wishart
144a Old South Lambeth Road
London SW8 1XX

9 780853 158240 >